Library of Congress Cataloging-in-Publication Data

Bertram, Anne.
  NTC's dictionary of euphemisms : the most practical guide to
unraveling euphemisms / Anne Bertram.
      p.   cm.
  Includes index.
  ISBN 0-8442-0842-6
    1. English language—Euphemism—Dictionaries.   I. Title.
PE1449.B46   1998
423'.1—dc21   97-49341
                                                        CIP

Ref.
PE
1449
.B46
1998

Interior design by Terry Stone

Published by NTC Publishing Group
An imprint of NTC/Contemporary Publishing Company
4255 West Touhy Avenue, Lincolnwood (Chicago), Illinois 60646-1975 U.S.A.
Copyright © 1998 by NTC/Contemporary Publishing Company
Manufactured in the United States of America
International Standard Book Number: 0-8442-0842-6
18   17   16   15   14   13   12   11   10   9   8   7   6   5   4   3   2   1

Contents

Introduction

Euphemisms are entertaining because they show the weaknesses of people who design words and expressions in order to avoid being direct, obvious, or literal. Not only are euphemistic expressions entertaining, but they are alleged to reveal what people *really* think and to show to the outside world bits of deep-seated modesty lurking in the remote corners of the subconsciousness. Euphemisms, though, represent all sorts of verbal avoidances and sincere efforts to avoid producing negative reactions to one's words—a big order these days.

In this pluralistic society, there are probably as many interpretations of the cultural significance of euphemisms as there are euphemisms. Euphemisms and their uses mean different things to different people; you are free to make your own interpretation.

This collection includes examples of the most widespread and widely celebrated categories of euphemism, such as death, drunkenness, and pregnancy, as well as a few terms for the downstairs body parts and noisier body processes. It focuses not only on tabooed words and expressions, but on mundane verbal pussyfooting, politically correct words and phrases, and innocent expressions that really *do* have some cultural significance.

Whereas this book does not take a position for or against specific euphemisms or the use of euphemisms in general, it will probably irk some people by labeling as euphemistic some of the more frequently heard shibboleths of political correctness. So be it. *Server* (waiter and waitress) and *pass away* (die) are both classic expressions of verbal avoidance that are meant to be substituted for less desirable terms or concepts. It is important to note that most euphemisms have a literal meaning; however, only the euphemistic meaning is included in these pages.

This collection is brand new, up-to-date, and unique in that it covers more than just the lewd or attention-getting euphemisms. Each concise definition is followed by at least two example sentences that illustrate the use of the euphemism in everyday language. A thematic index at the back of the book lists entries under 32 broad themes that allow the reader to get a good idea of the use of euphemism in various categories.

This book is especially useful for the learner of English and for writers, as well as anyone interested in words or the English language in general.

abbatoir a slaughterhouse. (French.) □ *The crime scene looked like an abbatoir.* □ *The beef is shipped directly from the abbatoir in refrigerated trucks.*

abdomen the belly; the visible stomach. □ *The doctor felt the patient's abdomen.* □ *I had terrible cramps in my abdomen.*

abdominal protector a cup worn to protect the penis and testicles. (See also **(athletic) supporter, cache-sexe, cup.**) □ *All the boys on the Little League team had to wear abdominal protectors.* □ *Joe forgot his abdominal protector, so the coach wouldn't let him in the game, fearing that he would get hurt.*

aberration sexual intercourse with a person of the same sex. (Offensive to homosexual people.) □ *Despite his youthful aberrations, Jim married and became the father of a happy family.* □ *The gossip hinted at some aberration in Jane's private life.*

ableism a prejudice against people who cannot walk or move easily. (See also **handicappism.**) □ *Debbie uses a wheelchair. When she was looking for a job recently, she was upset* *by the ableism of many of the job interviewers.* □ *Bill thought that his coworkers' insensitive jokes revealed their ableism.*

above critical [of a nuclear reactor] melting down. □ *One second more, and the reactor would have been above critical.* □ *If the power plant is above critical, it won't do any good to evacuate the personnel.*

abstinence the practice of refraining from sexual intercourse. □ *The counselor recommended abstinence as a very effective birth control method.* □ *The book encouraged young people to practice abstinence.*

abuse someone to rape someone. (Note: **abuse** does not always mean *rape*. Judge from the context.) □ *That awful man had been abusing his stepdaughter since she was six years old.* □ *The invading soldiers killed all the men in the village and abused the women.*

AC/DC bisexual. (Slang.) □ Lɪɴᴅᴀ: *I thought Jim was gay.* Jᴏᴇ: *No. He's AC/DC.* □ *I heard that Angela was AC/DC, and I didn't want her flirting with my girlfriend.*

acceptable damage ᴀɴᴅ **acceptable losses** wartime damage that would not destroy the armed forces. □ *At present, the enemy's first strike capability would produce acceptable damage.* □ *The general indicated that the fifty thousand casualties were within the range of acceptable losses.*

acceptable losses See acceptable damage.

accident 1. an unplanned pregnancy. □ *Their fourth child was an accident.* □ *Did they intend to have a baby so soon after getting married, or was it an accident?* **2.** urination or defecation in an inappropriate place. □ *Billy had an accident in the middle of the night.* □ *The dog has had an accident right next to the front door.*

accost someone [for a prostitute] to ask someone for business. □ *Three different women accosted me as I walked down 42nd Street.* □ *The sex worker regularly worked Linden Park, accosting likely customers.*

accouchement the act of giving birth. (French. Old-fashioned.) □ *The time was drawing near for her accouchement.* □ *Her mother came to stay with her and to help with her accouchement.*

account for someone to kill someone. □ *The soldier accounted for six of the enemy.* □ *One of our sharpshooters accounted for the sniper.*

a certain number of years young a certain number of years old. (Cute.) □ *This lovely lady is eighty-three years young today.* □ *My father, God bless him, is seventy-eight years young.*

acquire something to steal something. (Note: **acquire** does not always mean *steal*. Judge from the context.) □ *I, uh, acquired this software from the computer at work.* □ *Jill acquired a Cadillac convertible from somewhere, even though she couldn't possibly have afforded it.*

acquisitiveness greed. □ *Joe's acquisitiveness got him into trouble when he tried to take business away from the powerful company.* □ *Not even the purchase of her third home could satisfy Jane's acquisitiveness.*

action 1. violence. □ *Jill likes movies with action. I prefer love stories.* □ *That TV show always has lots of action, like gunfights and car chases.* **2.** battle. □ *Our unit last saw action in February.* □ *The soldier was killed in enemy action.*

action figure a doll, especially one intended for boys. □ *The Soldier Joe toy helicopter comes with everything you see* *here. Action figures sold separately.* □ *Jimmy wants a Space Patrol action figure for his birthday.*

active 1. engaging in sexual intercourse. □ *Jim has been active since he was fourteen.* □ *The nurse asked me if I was active, and if I needed birth control.* **2.** [of an old person] doing many things. □ *Grandma is still spry and active, bless her heart. Just this spring, she went on a Pacific cruise.* □ *Mr. Simmons is eighty-two, but alert and active.*

active euthanasia the giving of pain-killing drugs in increasing doses, in order to kill the person who is taking them. (Compare with **passive euthanasia**.) □ *The doctor considered active euthanasia to be immoral.* □ *The patient, who was in great pain, requested active euthanasia.*

activist a person who fights for a political cause, and may be willing to break the law in order to do so. □ *Anti-abortion activists were suspected of vandalizing the abortion clinic.* □ *Environmental activists prevented the loggers from cutting down the trees.*

act of love an act of sexual intercourse. (Similarly: act of shame, bit of fun, coition, conjugal rites, conversation, fun and games, horizontal exercise, nooky, roll in the hay. See also **catch someone in the act, (sexual) act**.) □ *The young man was inexperienced in the act of love.* □ *The newlyweds were too exhausted by the wedding festivities to perform the act of love.*

actor a man or woman who acts in plays or movies. (Replaces *actor* for men and *actress* for women.) □ *Jane is an actor with training in Shakespeare and the classical theater.* □ *The director needed five actors, two men and three women.*

4

act out to behave badly. (Usually used to describe young people.) □ *Your son has been acting out in the classroom, and we feel that professional intervention is desirable.* □ *After their mother died, the kids acted out in a number of ways. Mary started smoking, and Billy was caught shoplifting.*

adipose fat; heavy. □ *Bill has a medical condition which makes him adipose.* □ *After Ellen stopped exercising and started eating all those sweets, she became downright adipose.*

adjourn to take a break in order to urinate or defecate. (Jocular. Note: adjourn does not always have this meaning. Judge from the context.) □ *Excuse me while I adjourn. I'll be back in a minute.* □ *May we adjourn? I need to use the ladies' room.*

adjustment a decrease. (See technical adjustment, workforce adjustment, currency adjustment, inventory leakage.) □ *The memo stated that an adjustment in the number of personnel would be taking place in the next six months.* □ *Owing to the stock market adjustment, your account shows negative growth for the month of October.*

adjust one's dress to fasten up the zipper on one's pants. (British.) □ *Please adjust your dress before leaving the lavatory.* □ *"You may want to adjust your dress," Nigel warned me when I came out of the W.C.*

administrative assistant a secretary. □ *My administrative assistant will set up the appointment.* □ *The budget spreadsheets were prepared by Jill's administrative assistant.*

adult pornographic. (See also (adult) novelty.) □ *That theater shows adult movies.* □ *You must be 21 years old to purchase adult magazines.*

adultism a bias against children. □ *Wayne's adultism kept him from realizing that children are intelligent and capable.* □ JANE: *Kids shouldn't be able to decide what parent they want to live with after a divorce. They don't know what's good for them.* CHARLES: *That remark smacks of adultism.*

(adult) novelty a sex toy. (See also **adult**.) □ *This catalog carries enticing lingerie, erotic videos, and a variety of novelties.* □ *At Susan's wedding shower, her friends surprised her with funny gifts, including a few adult novelties.*

advanced in years old. □ *Mrs. Sanders is considerably advanced in years, but she is well able to take care of herself.* □ *The librarian was a kind gentleman, quite advanced in years.*

adversary, the Satan. □ *Some days, I tell you, I feel that computers were sent into this world by the adversary himself.* □ *If the adversary tempts you, resist him.*

adviser a soldier. (Note: **adviser** does not always mean *soldier*. Judge from the context.) □ *The United States sent five thousand advisers into the disputed territory.* □ *The Marine Corps is sending advisers at the request of the prime minister.*

aesthetically advantaged good looking. (Usually jocular.) □ *He was tall, dark, and aesthetically advantaged.* □ *When she was a teenager, Linda learned that being aesthetically advantaged could be a problem when it came to making true friends. Everyone seemed to like her for her looks alone.*

aesthetic procedure cosmetic surgery. (See also **cosmetic surgery, plastic surgery, procedure**.) □ *Have you considered an aesthetic procedure to reduce the size of your chin?* □ *Dr. Jones specializes in aesthetic procedures.*

affair sexual relations outside of marriage. □ *He discovered that his wife was having an affair.* □ *The two co-workers tried to conceal the fact that they were having an affair.*

affirmative action a policy that favors women and minorities. □ *There was a rumor that Jane was hired because of affirmative action, and not on her own merits.* □ *The school follows affirmative action in its admissions policies.*

affordable cheap. □ *The car has many luxury features, but is surprisingly affordable.* □ *A number of units in this building have been set aside as affordable housing for people on welfare.*

afterlife AND **afterworld** the life after death. □ *Many mourners accompanied the deceased on his journey to the afterlife.* □ *The dying man hoped to see his parents and his brother in the afterworld.*

afterthought an unplanned baby. □ *They had three children one right after the other. Then, ten years later, Andy came along, an afterthought.* □ *My next oldest brother is almost fifteen years older than me. I was an afterthought.*

afterworld See afterlife.

ageism a bias against old people. □ *You shouldn't treat old people as if they're stupid. That's ageism!* □ *Again and again, the company refused to give promotions to employees over the age of 50. This ageism was the basis of a lawsuit brought by the employees who had been discriminated against.*

agent 1. a deadly poison. □ *The nerve agent could cause death in fifteen seconds.* □ *As a result of the accident, a chemical agent was released into the atmosphere.* **2.** a spy. □ *A number of agents were assigned to monitor radio broadcasts* *from the capital.* □ *The ambassador's secretary was, in reality, an enemy agent.*

aging old. □ *The aging residents of the neighborhood were concerned about crime in the area.* □ *Bill is aging. He isn't as active as he was when he was younger.*

aid money given from one country to another. □ *The parliament voted to send aid to Mexico.* □ *We are sending humanitarian aid. None of it may be used to purchase weapons.*

air support the dropping of bombs from airplanes. □ *The Air Force unit will provide air support.* □ *After we have weakened the city's defenses with air support, the ground troops can move in.*

all there alert, aware, and mentally sound. (Usually in the phrase *not all there*, not mentally sound.) □ *After talking with Larry today, I get the feeling that he's not quite all there.* □ *You do such foolish things sometimes! I wonder if you're all there.*

almighty "damned." □ *If you're so almighty smart, you figure it out!* □ *He's almighty heartless when it comes to business dealings.*

Almighty, the God. □ *Trust in the Almighty.* □ *They got down on their knees and prayed to the Almighty.*

alter to remove the testicles or uterus of an animal so that it cannot reproduce. □ *Fluffy can't have kittens. We had her altered.* □ *The animal lovers' organization debated whether or not it was cruel to alter house pets.*

alternative controversial. □ *The health insurance policy does not pay for alternative medicine, such as massage or* *homeopathy.* □ *Jane lives with her boyfriend and their baby. She calls it "an alternative living arrangement." Her grandmother calls it "living in sin."*

alternative container a plain box or bag used for burying a person. □ *If you choose cremation without a viewing, you may wish to save on the expense of a casket and purchase an alternative container instead.* □ *She did not want a fancy or expensive funeral. Her will stated that she wanted to be buried in an alternative container.*

alternative energy source a fuel other than oil, gas, or coal. □ *If your home is heated using an alternative energy source, you may be entitled to a special tax credit.* □ *The utility company is exploring a number of alternative energy sources, such as wind and solar power.*

Alzheimer's (disease) a disease that destroys the memory. (Replaces *senile dementia.*) □ *I'm in shock. My mother has been diagnosed with Alzheimer's disease.* □ *Mr. Lawrence suffers from Alzheimer's. He may wander off on his own and get lost if someone doesn't look after him.*

ambidextrous bisexual. (A play on words. Ambidextrous usually means *able to write with either hand.* See also **ambivalent.**) □ *Jim: Is Bill interested in men? Jane: Let's just say he's ambidextrous.* □ *The rock singer was widely supposed to be ambidextrous. There were many rumors about her affairs with both women and men.*

ambivalent bisexual. (See also **ambidextrous.**) □ *Until he was seventeen, Jason was sure that he was straight. Then he got a crush on one of his soccer teammates, and decided he was ambivalent.* □ *Although Lydia is married, she is ambivalent in her sexual preferences.*

amenities a toilet. □ *We soon discovered why the hotel room was so cheap. It lacked the amenities.* □ *Does the cabin have amenities?*

amour a sexual relationship outside of marriage. (French.) □ *Don Juan was famous for his amours.* □ *I gather that Aunt Sarah had numerous amours in her youth.*

amour propre self-centeredness; selfishness. (French. Literally *self love.*) □ *Mary tells wonderful stories about herself and her adventures, but after a while, one tires of her boundless amour propre.* □ *Larry thought that nothing but the best was good enough for him. This amour propre led him almost to bankruptcy.*

ample fat; large. □ *He eased his ample bottom into the chair.* □ *The women in Rubens' paintings are generally of ample proportions.*

anatomical gift a gift of one's dead body or organs to a hospital or medical school. □ *His will stated that he wished to make an anatomical gift.* □ *You may sign the back of your driver's license to indicate that you are willing to make an anatomical gift.*

anatomically correct [of a picture or figure] showing the genitals. □ *The therapist used anatomically correct dolls to talk to the children about sexual abuse.* □ *These baby dolls are anatomically correct.*

anatomy the genitals, especially the penis. □ *"I didn't care for the nude beach," said Nancy. "I didn't like having to see everyone's anatomy just hanging out."* □ *We were impressed by the size of the horse's anatomy.*

angler a person who fishes. (Replaces *fisherman*, which does not include women.) □ *Dozens of anglers were out on* *the lake.* □ *The anglers gathered at the bar to discuss the day's catch.*

Anglo-Saxon swear words. (Many swear words in English come from the Anglo-Saxon language.) □ *When I told him I wouldn't pay for such shoddy work, he treated me to a burst of Anglo-Saxon.* □ *I was surprised that such a young girl would have such a fine command of Anglo-Saxon.*

animal control the catching and killing of unwanted animals. □ *The Department of Animal Control publishes a pamphlet on how to get rid of rats.* □ *There is hardly any animal control in the city. Starving stray cats and dogs live in all the alleys.*

anomaly something wrong. □ *The reporter found some anomalies in the police file on the suspect.* □ *A radar anomaly made it appear as if a plane were approaching, when in reality, there was nothing there.*

answer the call to die. (Folksy. See also **call, the**.) □ *Grandma answered the call and went home.* □ *Our dear brother has answered the call and gone to his eternal rest.*

anticipating pregnant. □ *It's easy to get worried about many things when you're anticipating.* □ BILL: *Do you know when Mary's baby is due?* JILL: *I didn't even know she was anticipating!*

anticipatory attack an attack. (See also **preventive strike**.) □ *We staged an anticipatory attack to prevent the enemy from attacking first.* □ *The anticipatory attack caught the enemy forces completely by surprise.*

antipersonnel designed to kill people. □ *At what point should the antipersonnel weapons be deployed?* □ *This antipersonnel device is designed to leave buildings unharmed.*

antiperspirant a preparation that reduces sweat. (See also **deodorant**.) □ *To control underarm odor, use an antiperspirant.* □ *This antiperspirant will help keep your clothes from getting stained.*

anti-Semitic anti-Jewish. □ *Her anti-Semitic remarks were deeply offensive to her Jewish co-workers.* □ *The politician was accused of being anti-Semitic.*

antisocial 1. criminal or almost criminal. □ *Chris' antisocial behavior, such as threatening or hitting other students, is of great concern to his teachers.* **2.** avoiding other people. □ *I invited Nancy to my party, but I doubt she'll come. She's very antisocial.* □ *Gifted children are sometimes antisocial.*

apartheid a policy of keeping black and white people separate. □ *Under apartheid, living conditions for blacks were much worse than for whites.* □ *The speaker compared housing discrimination to apartheid.*

appeasement a policy of giving the opposing side what they want, in hopes of avoiding war. □ *Giving up that territory would be appeasement. That is unacceptable.* □ *The government's attempt at appeasement did not work. The enemy forces invaded.*

appetite suppressant a drug that reduces your appetite; a diet pill. □ *This appetite suppressant really works! I lost 35 pounds and kept the weight off!* □ *The appetite suppressant contained a powerful, dangerous drug.*

applesauce nonsense. □ *She claimed to have a degree from Oxford, but that's pure applesauce.* □ BILL: *I didn't know you were saving those plums for your breakfast.* MARY: *Applesauce! I told you as much!*

appliance 1. a wig. □ *Our custom-made appliances are so natural-looking, everyone will think it's your hair.* □ *Is Fred wearing an appliance? It looks like it's a different color from his own hair.* **2.** an artificial limb. □ *He has a hernia, so he has to wear an appliance.* □ *She lost the lower half of her arm in an accident, but she is able to use her appliance to open doors and grasp things.*

apprehend someone to arrest someone. □ *The officer apprehended the suspect outside a nearby gas station.* □ *Can you give us any more details about the man who robbed you? Every piece of information will help us apprehend him.*

appropriate correct or polite. □ *Louis felt that the joke you told was not appropriate.* □ *Such informal behavior is not appropriate to the office environment.*

appropriate (something) to steal. (See also **misappropriate (something)**.) □ *Jim somehow appropriated a car and left town.* □ *She appropriated company software for her own use.*

Arch Enemy, the Satan. □ *These temptations come to us from the Arch Enemy.* □ *The Arch Enemy set many snares in her way, but she kept her eyes on God.*

area bombing the practice of bombing cities. □ *Their air strategy was to employ area bombing on major enemy targets.* □ *Area bombing wiped out the entire western quarter of the city.*

armed reconnaissance the act of dropping bombs while flying over an area. □ *The planes were on a mission of armed reconnaissance.* □ *The enemy has not yet responded to our armed reconnaissance.*

arouse someone to excite someone sexually. □ *Her suggestive talk aroused him.* □ *The love scenes in the movie aroused her.*

artisan a person who makes things. (Replaces *craftsman*, which does not include women.) □ *The craft show will feature potters, weavers, woodworkers, and other artisans.* □ *The cabinetmaker is an artisan, and I respect her skill.*

artiste a stripper. (**Artiste** does not always mean *stripper*. Judge from the context.) □ *Tracy is an exotic dancer, a real artiste.* □ *Would you care to meet the artistes after the show, sir?*

ask someone to step down to fire someone. □ *The board of directors asked Jane to step down.* □ *The governor has asked the state parks commissioner to step down.*

asleep (in Jesus) AND **asleep in the Lord** dead. (See also **fall asleep.** Similarly: cold, done for, gone the way of all flesh, gone to glory, gone to Kingdom Come, gone to the last muster, gone to the last sleep, in the sweet by and by, lights out, pushing up daisies, ran the good race.) □ *Our baby is asleep, not lost to us but gone on before.* □ *Our beloved brother is asleep in Jesus.* □ *The grave marker said, "Asleep in the Lord."*

assassinate someone to murder someone. □ *The writer of the anonymous note threatened to assassinate the prime minister.* □ *The terrorists plotted to assassinate the president.*

assault someone to rape someone. □ *The police are searching for the man who assaulted a woman in the park yesterday morning.* □ *He had beaten and assaulted at least three other women.*

assertive very forceful; rude. □ *JANE: You always say you agree with everybody, even when you don't. You should be more assertive. JILL: OK.* □ *She's very assertive, and she knows what she wants.*

asset a spy. (Note: **asset** does not always mean *spy*. Judge from the context.) □ *The intelligence office has a number of assets in the capital.* □ *Bill is one of our best assets. We can't risk blowing his cover.*

assignation a meeting with one's lover. □ *They arranged an assignation in a hotel just outside of town.* □ *He discovered, quite by accident, that his boss was using the conference room for her extramarital assignations.*

assistance money, especially money from the government. (See also **relief, financial aid.**) □ *My family has been on assistance ever since I got sick and had to quit working.* □ *Some people felt that too much tax money was spent on public assistance.*

assisted dying the practice of helping people kill themselves. (See also **physician assisted suicide, planned termination, self-termination.**) □ *She was in so much pain that she wanted to end her life, so she sought information about assisted dying.* □ *Dr. Andrews, what is your opinion about assisted dying?*

associate 1. having low status. □ *She was promoted from associate professor to assistant professor.* □ *The associate attorneys hoped they would one day be partners of the firm.* **2.** an employee with low status. □ *One of our banking associates can help you with that transaction.* □ *Here at Jones and Associates, we believe that every one of our associates makes a valuable contribution.*

association a sexual relationship outside of marriage. (Compare with **attachment**.) □ *The senator was rumored to have an association with an old college friend.* □ *Jane has ended her association with Bill. Her husband threatened to divorce her if she did not.*

asylum a mental hospital. (Somewhat old-fashioned.) □ *The poor soul was raving mad, and had to be sent to an asylum.* □ *Sometimes this office seems like an asylum!*

(athletic) supporter a cup worn to protect the penis and testicles while playing sports. (See also **abdominal protector, cache-sexe, cup**.) □ *All members of the football team must wear athletic supporters during practice.* □ *Jim bought a supporter at the sporting goods store.*

at liberty without a job. □ INTERVIEWER: *What position do you currently hold?* CANDIDATE: *I am currently at liberty.* □ *You may consider yourself at liberty to seek other employment.*

at-need AND **immediate need** [of a funeral] not paid for in advance. (Compare with **pre-need**.) □ *Perkins and Sons provides both at-need and pre-need funeral services.* □ *We have a number of payment plans for our immediate need clients.*

at peace dead. (See also **at rest**.) □ *After struggling with cancer for many long months, Steven is finally at peace.* □ JIM: *I'm sorry to hear about your grandmother.* JANE: *At least now she's at peace.*

at rest dead. (See also **at peace, lay someone to rest**.) □ *After a long, weary life, Emily is at rest.* □ *There he is, at rest in his coffin.*

attaché a spy. (French. **Attaché** does not always mean *spy*. Judge from the context.) □ *We have just received some interesting information from one of our attachés in Washington.* □ *The attaché tried to start a conversation with the junior diplomat in hopes of learning where the ambassador had gone.*

attachment love, or a sexual relationship. (Compare with **association**.) □ *His attachment for the young lady is unfortunately deep.* □ *Mary and Bill seem to have some kind of attachment.*

attendant a person who stands with the bride or groom during the wedding. (Replaces *bridesmaid* and *groomsman*, which are specific to women and men, respectively.) □ *The bride had four attendants.* □ *Could I have the attendants with the bride and groom in this picture, please?*

attendant AND **bellhop** a person who carries luggage for hotel guests. (Replaces *bellboy*, which does not include women.) □ *How much should I tip the attendant?* □ *I'll call the bellhop to take care of your luggage.*

attentions sex or sexual behavior. □ *Several women were competing for his attentions.* □ *I hinted that her attentions were unwelcome.*

attorney a lawyer. □ *You'll be hearing from my attorney.* □ *Ellen is an attorney, and her husband is a physician.*

au naturel naked. (French.) □ *He answered the door completely au naturel.* □ *She likes to sunbathe au naturel.*

(authentic) reproduction a copy of something old and valuable. □ *This sideboard is an authentic reproduction of an English antique.* □ *Is that a genuine Stickley chair, or a reproduction?*

authoritarian totalitarian; run by a dictator. □ *The country's government could be said to be authoritarian.* □ *Under the general's authoritarian regime, all newspapers were subject to state censorship.*

autoeroticism masturbation. □ *It is common for young people to indulge in autoeroticism.* □ *Her sexual fantasies increased the pleasure of autoeroticism.*

auto-euthanasia AND **voluntary euthanasia** suicide; killing oneself. (See also **euthanasia**.) □ *She sought a means of auto-euthanasia that would be painless and quick.* □ *Bill does not think that voluntary euthanasia should be a crime.*

available 1. unmarried. □ *The new woman in our office is cute. I sure hope she's available.* □ *I didn't see a wedding ring on his hand, so I assumed he was available.* **2.** interested in sex. □ *His seductive looks made me think he was available.* □ *She was beautiful and available.*

avail oneself of someone AND **avail oneself of someone's services** to have casual sexual intercourse with someone. □ *When her husband is not available, she avails herself of the gardener.* □ *He availed himself of the prostitute's services.*

aversion therapy hurting or threatening someone until that person changes his or her behavior. (See also **behavior modification**.) □ *Every time the patient demonstrated sexual arousal at pictures of children, he was given an electric shock. It is hoped that this aversion therapy will prove effective.* □ *I lost weight through aversion therapy. Every time I ate one of my favorite foods, I had to take a drug that made me throw up.*

aviator a person who can fly a plane. (Replaces *airman*, which does not include women, and *aviatrix*, which does not include men.) □ *Jane is an aviator. She has had her pilot's license for many years.* □ *The meeting concerns all aviators who fly in and out of this airport.*

avocation a hobby. (See also **vocation**.) □ *Julie is a stockbroker. Art is only her avocation.* □ *Photography is such an interesting avocation.*

awkward dangerous or embarassing. □ *It could be awkward if the boss finds out I've been borrowing money from the cash register.* □ *The governor was put in an awkward position when her secret memo was made public.*

bacchanal(ia) a party at which people get very drunk. □ *Did you go to the party at Jim's house last weekend? It was quite a bacchanalia!* □ *It started as a few people from work going out for drinks, and turned into a bacchanal that lasted till two in the morning.*

bachelor's wife a prostitute. (Old-fashioned.) □ *Julia isn't exactly married. She's a bachelor's wife, if you know what I mean.* □ *The only women he knew were the bachelor's wives who walked the downtown streets.*

backfire to expel gas from the anus. (Slang.) □ *Excuse me! I backfired.* □ *Green peppers always make me backfire.*

backside the buttocks. (Similarly: anatomy, back way, backdoor, balcony, booty, bum, buns, can, cheeks, duster, heinie, hinterland, keester, rumpus, tail, tochus.) □ *My mama would always whack me on the backside if I was fresh to her.* □ *He had a great big bruise on his backside from when he fell down.*

backward 1. not smart. □ *Jane's not a very good learner. She's a bit backward, you know.* □ *His teachers thought he was backward because he misbehaved all the time.* **2.** [of a place] poor or primitive. □ *In the cities, you can count on* *all the modern conveniences, but in the country, things are still very backward.* □ *The aid was intended to help backward countries set up education programs.*

bad language swearing. □ *There's no need for bad language. Be civil.* □ *I heard a stream of bad language coming from the next room.*

bad man, the Satan. (Often capitalized.) □ *If you don't behave, the bad man will come and get you.* □ *The wizard had sold his soul to the Bad Man.*

bad place, the Hell. (Often capitalized.) □ *If you're not good, you'll go to the bad place when you die.* □ *Jake was such a scoundrel, there's no doubt he went to the Bad Place.*

balderdash nonsense. □ CHARLIE: *I saw a flying hippopotamus yesterday.* JIM: *Balderdash!* □ *I got a letter from Jane. It was full of balderdash about how I've always been her favorite aunt.*

ball attendant See court attendant.

baloney nonsense. (Slang. Replaces *bullshit*.) □ *That car salesperson is full of baloney if she told you the car won't need maintenance.* □ *Don't give me any of that baloney.*

bar assistant AND **bar attendant** a person who serves liquor at a bar. (Replaces *barmaid*, which is specific to women.) □ *He left a generous tip for the bar assistant.* □ *The bar attendant will bring you your drinks.*

barnyard epithet the word *bullshit*. □ *He dropped the hammer on his toe and uttered a barnyard epithet.* □ *The politician was famous for her free use of the barnyard epithet.*

base player a person who plays one of the base positions in baseball. (Replaces *baseman,* which does not include women.) □ *Mary is the third base player on our baseball team.* □ *You're good at catching. You can be a base player.*

basically definitely. □ *He's basically a difficult boss to work for.* □ *It was basically a very unpleasant situation.*

basket a bastard; an unpleasant person. (Cute.) □ *If I get one more nasty phone call from that basket, I'm going to quit.* □ *The little basket didn't show up for work again today.*

bat attendant a person who takes care of the bats for a baseball team. (Replaces *batboy,* which does not include adults or girls.) □ *I got a summer job as a bat attendant.* □ *Mary was bat attendant for her college baseball team.*

bathhouse a place to meet people for casual sex. □ *The two of them met in a gay bathhouse.* □ *He picked up a woman at the bathhouse.*

bathroom a toilet; a room containing a toilet. (Similarly: altar room, biffy, excuse-me, head, jane, john, library, private office.) □ *Where can I find the bathroom?* □ *I need to use the bathroom.*

bathroom tissue AND **toilet tissue** toilet paper. □ *This brand of toilet tissue is the softest.* □ *The ladies' room is out of bathroom tissue.*

battle fatigue AND **combat fatigue** depression caused by fighting in a war. (Replaces *shell shock.* See also **post-traumatic stress syndrome**.) □ *The soldier was diagnosed with battle fatigue.* □ *His combat fatigue was so severe that he was sent home for a prolonged rest.*

bawdy house a house of prostitution. (Folksy. See also house of ill repute, bordello.) □ *He frequented a bawdy house on the wrong side of the tracks.* □ *She ran a bawdy house with half a dozen girls.*

bay window a fat belly. □ *Jim has a hard time getting suit coats to fit him, because of his bay window.* □ *You wouldn't have that bay window if you didn't eat so many sweets.*

B.C.E. See Before the Common Era.

beautician a hairdresser. □ *I called the beautician and asked for an appointment.* □ *Mel is a licensed beautician.*

beauty parlor AND **beauty salon** a place where hairdressers work. □ *She's saving money to start her own beauty parlor.* □ *Do they do manicures at that beauty salon?*

bedpan a container in which a bedridden person can defecate or urinate. □ *The nurse brought the patient a bedpan.* □ *He was so weak that he couldn't get out of bed. He had to use a bedpan.*

bedroom having to do with sexual intimacy. □ *The star's autobiography gave intimate details of his bedroom exploits.* □ *The play was a bedroom farce, filled with innuendoes and double entendres.*

before need [of funeral plans] paid for before death. (See also pre-need, pre-planning.) □ *We offer several before need payment plans.* □ *One of our funeral specialists would be happy to discuss before need arrangements with you.*

Before the Common Era AND **B.C.E.** before the year 1 of the Western calendar. (Replaces *Before Christ* or *B.C.*, which have a Christian bias. Compare with **in the common era**.) □ *The ancient city of Ur was founded somewhere in the* *fourth millennium Before the Common Era.* □ *The Qin Dynasty in China begin in 221 B.C.E.*

be gathered to one's fathers to die. □ *He was gathered to his fathers in his eighty-seventh year.* □ *When my time comes, and I am gathered to my fathers, I will rest in the knowledge that my children and grandchildren will carry on.*

beggar a worthless person. □ *That rotten beggar couldn't tell the truth to save his soul.* □ *If I ever see that little beggar again, I'll slap him.*

behavior disorder a condition that causes a person to behave in a rude or uncontrollable way. (See also **learning disorder**.) □ *Timmy is taking medication for a behavior disorder.* □ *Jane was acting out in class. Her teacher suspected that she must have a behavior disorder.*

behavior modification the practice of making someone do something they are afraid of or dislike, until they are able to do it easily. (See also **aversion therapy**.) □ *My psychiatrist felt that a course of behavior modification would help me overcome my fear of airplanes.* □ *Through behavior modification, the child was able to learn to sit still and concentrate on her homework.*

behind the buttocks. □ *The father swatted the child on the behind.* □ *She has a birthmark on her behind.*

be in Abraham's bosom AND **rest in Abraham's bosom** to be dead. (Folksy.) □ *He is in Abraham's bosom.* □ *Our dear grandmother has gone to rest in Abraham's bosom.*

be intimate with someone to have sexual intercourse with someone. □ *He had never been intimate with a woman* *before.* □ *They were intimate with each other for the first time that night.*

belief system a religion. □ *Our church welcomes people of all belief systems.* □ *Whether you belong to a mainstream religion, or whether you favor an alternative belief system, this workshop will help you reach your spiritual goals.*

bellhop See attendant.

bend sinister a birth out of wedlock. (Literary. A noble person born out of wedlock would have a diagonal line called a "bend sinister" on his coat of arms.) □ *He is rumored to have a bend sinister in his ancestry.* □ *She felt the bend sinister in her family's history to be a terrible and shameful thing.*

bend the rules to cheat. (Slang.) □ *Even as a child, he would bend the rules in order to win.* □ *It became apparent that the senator had bent the rules when filing her taxes.*

bereavement counselor an undertaker. □ *The bereavement counselor is here to help you with all the arrangements.* □ *I am so sorry to hear of your loss. I will schedule an appointment with one of our bereavement counselors right away.*

bestiality the practice of a person having sex with animals. □ *The pornographic movie showed acts of bestiality.* □ *He was accused of committing bestiality.*

best woman a female friend who accompanies the bride in a wedding ceremony. (Replaces *maid of honor,* which does not include married women, and *matron of honor,* which does not include unmarried women.) □ *I want Laura to be my best woman.* □ *Jim is the best man, and Julie will be the best woman.*

be taken home See go home.

betray someone to have sexual intercourse with someone else while married to someone. (See also **cheat on someone, deceive one's spouse.**) □ *She betrayed her husband, and he divorced her.* □ *I can't believe he would betray me.*

between jobs unemployed. □ INTERVIEWER: *Tell me about your current position.* JOB CANDIDATE: *I'm between jobs right now.* □ *When Jill was between jobs, she took a computer class at the community college.*

between the sheets in bed. □ *What goes on between the sheets is nobody's business but theirs.* □ *Jane was horrified to see her husband and her best friend between the sheets.*

be with someone to have sexual intercourse with someone. (To **be with someone** does not always have this meaning. Judge from the context.) □ *She could tell that he wanted to be with her.* □ *"I want to be with you," he breathed, looking deeply into her eyes.*

B-girl a prostitute who works in a bar. (Slang.) □ *The bar was full of B-girls and derelicts.* □ *All I wanted was a drink, but this B-girl kept trying to pick me up.*

bi bisexual; interested in having sex with either men or women. (Slang.) □ *I'm not gay. I'm bi.* □ *Having an affair with another man convinced Bill that he was bi.*

bibulous fond of drinking alcohol. (Literary.) □ *Cathy is a trifle bibulous, but I wouldn't say she's an alcoholic.* □ *He shunned the bibulous companions of his youth.*

big-boned large; fat. □ *Honestly, honey, you're not fat. You're just big-boned.* □ *He was a big-boned youth.*

big C, the cancer. (Slang.) □ *The doctor tells me it's the big C. Well, I'm going to fight it all the way.* □ *My dad died of the big C, you know, so it's definitely in the family.*

big house, the a prison. (Slang.) □ *He got five years in the big house for larceny.* □ *When I got out of the big house, I had a hard time getting a job.*

bikini having to do with pubic hair; referring to the area that shows when someone wears a bikini, a very brief swimsuit. (Most often used in the expressions *bikini line* and *bikini wax. Bikini line* is the line at the edge of a bikini swimsuit. *Bikini wax* is the practice of applying wax in order to remove pubic hair.) □ *The salon offers a bikini wax.* □ *She shaved her legs up to the bikini line.*

biological father AND **birth father** a father; the man whose sperm joined with a woman's egg to form a child. (See also **biological mother.**) □ *Jim is my adoptive father. I never knew my biological father.* □ *We will be the baby's parents, but we want her birth father and birth mother to be involved in her upbringing as well.*

biological mother AND **birth mother** a mother; the woman whose egg joined with a man's sperm to form a child. (See also **biological father.**) □ *The adopted child wanted to learn her biological mother's identity.* □ *Michael's birth mother was of Italian descent.*

birds and the bees, the the facts about sex. (See also **facts of life, the.**) □ *Jane is growing up. It's about time we talked to her about the birds and the bees.* □ *His parents gave him a book about the birds and the bees.*

birth control devices or drugs that prevent pregnancy. □ *The clinic offers birth control at low cost.* □ *The doctor discussed condoms, diaphragms, and other forms of birth control.*

birthday suit nakedness. (Cute.) □ *He used to sit in his backyard and sunbathe in his birthday suit.* □ *I like to lounge around the house in my birthday suit.*

birth father See biological father.

birth mother See biological mother.

birth name the family name that a person received at birth. (Replaces *maiden name,* which is specific to women and assumes that women change their names when they marry.) □ *Write your last name on line 5. If your birth name is different, write it on line 6.* □ *I am Mary Evans-White. Evans is my birth name. White is my husband's name.*

blankety-blank damned. (Blank in this expression refers to a blank line, which the listener is supposed to fill in with the swear word of his or her choice.) □ *CHARLIE: Why are you yelling? JANE: I dropped the blankety-blank hammer on my foot!* □ *I'm sick and tired of your blankety-blank laziness!*

blarney lying nonsense. (Irish.) □ *Helen told you she likes classical music? That's a load of blarney!* □ *Don't you believe all the blarney you hear on the news.*

blasted damned. □ *Darn it! I spilled the blasted soup all over the tablecloth!* □ *Where did I put my blasted wallet?*

blazes Hell. □ *Go to blazes!* □ *What the blazes is he talking about?*

bleep a replacement for a swear word. (On radio and television programs, a bleeping sound was used to cover swear words.) □ *Who is responsible for this bleeping mess?* □ *He kicked him right in the bleep.*

blemish a pimple. □ *This blemish cream heals while it conceals.* □ *Many teenagers get blemishes on their skin.*

blessed damned. □ *Must you slam the door every blessed time you come in?* □ *What a terrible day. I can't do a single blessed thing right.*

blessed event a birth. □ *My sister is expecting a blessed event sometime in May.* □ *The young couple anxiously awaited the blessed event.*

blighter a worthless person. (British.) □ *Don't lend that blighter money.* □ *His wife left him soon after their house burned down. Poor blighter.*

blinking AND **blinkered** damned. (British.) □ *The blinking neighbors kept me awake all night with their noise.* □ *I can't get this blinkered computer to work.*

blip a nuclear explosion. □ *It is unclear at this time whether the blip at the power plant was caused by electronic malfunction or by human error.* □ *The alarms went off. The equipment had detected a blip.*

blood disease syphilis. (Old-fashioned.) □ *The composer died of a blood disease.* □ *She suffered from a blood disease brought on by youthful excess.*

blood money a payment for killing or betraying someone. □ *Pretty Boy demanded blood money for betraying the Boss to the cops.* □ *The hit man refused to accept blood money for killing Jones. "I'm happy to do it for free," he said.*

bloomers women's or girls' underpants; specifically, underpants with long, full legs. (Old-fashioned.) □ *She was wearing a skirt without any bloomers.* □ *She scrubbed out her bloomers and hung them up to dry.*

blooming damned. (British.) □ *I have to go back to the flat. I forgot to shut off the blooming cooker.* □ *Shut your blooming mouth!*

blue collar lower class; of a job or a worker, having to do with manual labor. (Contrasts with *white collar*. A blue shirt does not show dirt and sweat as a white shirt would.) □ *His parents were both blue collar workers. He was the first person in his family to go to college.* □ *They bought a house in a nice, settled, blue-collar neighborhood.*

blue language swearing. □ *Blue language is not appropriate in the workplace.* □ *She uttered a stream of blue language.*

blue movie a pornographic movie. □ *That theater shows blue movies.* □ *For Bill's bachelor party, his friends rented a bunch of blue movies and bought a bunch of liquor.*

B.M. a bowel movement; an act of defecation. □ *I'm afraid something might be wrong with the baby. She hasn't had a B.M. for two days.* □ *Drinking coffee helps me get my B.M., you know.*

B.O. body odor; the smell of sweat. □ *Someone should tell Harry he has a B.O. problem.* □ *I've tried all kinds of deodorants, but I can't get rid of this B.O.*

bodice ripper a historical novel that includes dramatic sex scenes. (A *bodice* is the top part of a woman's dress, and is frequently ripped open in this kind of book.) □ *I know these bodice rippers are trashy fiction, but I enjoy reading them.* □ *This novel pretends to be serious historical fiction, but it is really nothing more than a bodice ripper.*

bodily functions anything the body does automatically, especially urinating and defecating. (See also **private func-**

tion, natural functions.) □ *The dog needed to go outside and perform her bodily functions.* □ *It is not polite to discuss bodily functions at the dinner table.*

body a dead body. □ *The relatives came to the funeral home to view the body.* □ *The police officer discovered a body in the alleyway.*

body shaper a corset; a garment that squeezes the stomach and waist. □ *For our full-figured customers, we offer a full line of body shapers.* □ *I can fit into that dress if I wear a body shaper underneath.*

body worker a prostitute. (See also **(commercial) sex worker**.) □ *The clinic held a workshop to train body workers on the use of condoms.* □ *A number of body workers inhabit that neighborhood.*

bold nearly pornographic; showing sex. □ *Some critics were shocked by the book's bold depictions of unusual sexual practices.* □ *The movie is fairly bold. I would not recommend it for young people.*

Bomb, the the nuclear or atomic bomb. □ *He built a fallout shelter in his backyard to protect his family from the Bomb.* □ *The face of warfare has changed since we invented the Bomb.*

bonded stone AND **bonded bronze** plastic containing particles of stone or bronze. □ *This authentic reproduction of the Venus de Milo is crafted in bonded stone.* □ *This elegant sculpture is molded from bonded bronze.*

bon vivant a person who greatly enjoys drinking and eating. (French.) □ *Ned knows all the best restaurants in town. He's a real bon vivant.* □ *This wine shop caters to bon vivants.*

boom boom defecation. (Baby talk.) □ *Did baby make boom boom in her diapers?* □ *Mommy, I have to go boom boom!*

bordello a house of prostitution. (See also **bawdy house, house of ill repute.**) □ *"That velvet wallpaper makes the restaurant look like a bordello," Jill said.* □ *The madam ran a very exclusive bordello.*

born on the wrong side of the blanket born out of wedlock. □ *Paula's first baby was born on the wrong side of the blanket.* □ *Sam's classmates teased him because he was born on the wrong side of the blanket.*

borrow something to steal something. □ *The bank robber borrowed a car to drive out of state.* □ *I discovered that my office mate had been borrowing money out of my wallet when I wasn't looking.*

borscht nonsense. (A mild replacement for *bullshit*.) □ *Oh, borscht! That isn't true!* □ *What borscht! Don't take it seriously.*

bosom the breasts. (Similarly: appurtenances, bazooms, boobs, boulders, gazongas, globes, hooters, jugs, knockers, melons, pair.) □ *She has a big bosom.* □ *That dress shows too much of your bosom.*

bother someone to make unwanted sexual advances to someone. □ *My boss keeps bothering me. I don't know what to do.* □ *Quit bothering my sister!*

bottle, the alcohol. □ *His friends thought he was a bit too fond of the bottle.* □ *She tried to stay away from the bottle, but she never could manage it for long.*

bottom the buttocks. □ *Quit that, or I'll spank your bottom!* □ *That swimsuit barely covers her bottom.*

boudoir photo a photograph of a woman wearing very little and looking sexy. (See also **glamour photograph**.) □ *For Bill's birthday, his girlfriend gave him a boudoir photo of herself.* □ *She bought some black lace underwear to wear in the boudoir photo.*

bovine excrescence nonsense; bullshit. (Jocular.) □ *The Republican candidate hinted that the Democrat's promises were just so much bovine excrescence.* □ *This research paper is not acceptable. Bovine excrescence is no substitute for thoughtful argument.*

bracelets handcuffs. (Slang.) □ *The officer put the bracelets on the suspect.* □ *The prisoner wore bracelets and leg irons.*

brave attempt, a a failure. □ *This interesting first novel is a brave attempt.* □ *My boss made a brave attempt at explaining the new sick leave policy.*

break wind to expel gas from the anus. □ *Someone in the bus broke wind. It smelled terrible.* □ *He broke wind with an embarrassing noise.*

breathe one's last to die. □ *She breathed her last at about two o'clock that afternoon.* □ *Cradled in his wife's arms, he breathed his last.*

breath freshener a perfume used to cover bad breath. □ *He used a breath freshener before every date.* □ *That sales clerk could use a breath freshener.*

briefs underpants. □ *Our men's briefs come in sizes from regular to extra large.* □ *Three pairs of cotton briefs are $12.00 on sale.*

bring someone to justice to punish someone for a crime. □ *The police officer swore she would not rest until she had brought the killer to justice.* □ *Years later, the rapist was finally brought to justice.*

Britisher a person from Great Britain. (Replaces *Englishman*, which does not include women, and *Englishwoman*, which does not include men.) □ *Emma is a Britisher.* □ *Many Britishers have gone on the dole at some point in their lives.*

broad-beamed AND **broad in the beam** having wide buttocks. □ *She was broad-shouldered and broad-beamed.* □ *He had a thin torso, but he was broad in the beam.*

broad in the beam See broad-beamed.

brothel a house of prostitution. □ *The police officers raided the brothel.* □ *The celebrity was seen leaving a notorious brothel.*

B.S. bullshit. □ *My boss promised me a raise, but that's just a bunch of B.S.* □ *Don't let Jim fool you with his B.S. about how important he is.*

budget cheap. □ *We stayed in a budget hotel. It wasn't fancy, but it was clean.* □ *The travel agency offers budget airfares to Mexico.*

budget constraint a lack of money. □ *Due to budget constraints, we are forced to downsize.* □ *Budget constraints do not permit us to upgrade the computer system.*

bull nonsense; bullshit. □ *That's a bunch of bull.* □ *All her stories about her great business career are a load of bull.*

bullpeep nonsense; bullshit. (Folksy.) □ *Don't you believe any of that bullpeep.* □ JILL: *I can lift three hundred pounds.* JANE: *Bullpeep. The other day, you couldn't even lift that twenty-five-pound bag of dog food.*

bunk(um) nonsense. □ CHILD: *My teacher says I'll always be a C student.* FATHER: *Bunk. You can do anything you set your mind to.* □ *The mayor's speech included all the usual bunkum about the great progress the city is making.*

burial vault a concrete lining for a grave. □ *We sell monuments and burial vaults.* □ *The pre-need plan includes funds for a burial vault.*

burly fat; heavy. □ *Jim is a burly guy.* □ *The heavyweight wrestler was big and burly.*

burp to belch. □ *Soda pop makes me burp.* □ *Brenda burped, and then said, "Excuse me."*

bushwa nonsense; bullshit. (Folksy.) □ JIM: *Just because they're laying us off doesn't mean they're definitely going to fire us.* MARY: *Bushwa. We'd better look for new jobs.* □ *Jane gave me a load of bushwa about how sorry she was to miss my party.*

business class [of airplane travel] first class. □ *Would you like to upgrade your reservation to business class?* □ *I always travel business class. I like the extra legroom and the bigger seats.*

businessperson a person who works in or owns a business. (Replaces *businessman* and *businesswoman*.) □ *My mom is a businessperson. She owns several investment prop-*

erties. □ *The airline magazine is written for businesspeople on the go.*

busperson See busser.

busser AND **busperson** a person who clears the dishes from tables in a restaurant. (Replaces *busboy*, which does not include adults or girls.) □ *Leave an extra tip for the busser.* □ *I asked the busperson to send our server over to our table.*

bust the breasts. □ *Her bust began to develop when she was only twelve years old.* □ *Measure around the fullest part of the bust.*

buxom having large breasts and hips. □ *She was a skinny child, but a buxom woman.* □ *She had a hard time finding clothes that looked good on her buxom figure.*

buyer a person who buys stolen goods. (See also **receiver**.) □ *The thief needed a buyer for the electronics she stole.* □ *The pawnshop owner is known to be a buyer.*

by gad! See by George!

by George! AND **by Godfrey!** AND **by gum!** AND **by gad!** "by God." □ *By George! You startled me.* □ *By Godfrey, that's a big dog!* □ *He said he'd win the race, and by gum, he won it!* □ *I won't let her get the best of me, by gad!*

by Godfrey! See by George!

by gum! See by George!

by Jove "by God." (British. Somewhat old-fashioned.) □ *By Jove, it's good to see you!* □ *By Jove! I never would have guessed it!*

caboose the buttocks. (Slang.) □ *Park your caboose in that chair.* □ *She's got a cute little caboose on her.*

cache-sexe a cup worn to protect the penis and testicles. (French. See also **abdominal protector, (athletic) supporter, cup**.) □ *Each of the male ballet dancers wore a cache-sexe.* □ *You can get a cache-sexe at the sporting goods store.*

call girl a prostitute. □ *She worked as a call girl for five years.* □ *He walked through the downtown, hoping to find a call girl.*

calling card AND **visiting card** the feces of a small animal, especially a pet. (Jocular.) □ *Someone's dog has been leaving his calling card on our lawn every morning.* □ *There's been a raccoon in my basement. I find its visiting cards every time I go down there.*

calling on behalf of someone or something calling to ask for money for someone or something. □ *My name is Joanne, and I'm calling on behalf of the Alliance for Better Living.* □ *I'm calling on behalf of Senator Johnson.*

call of nature a need to urinate or defecate. (Sometimes used in the expression "Nature calls," meaning *I need to use* *the toilet. See also* **needs of nature**.) □ *The camp counselor told us to squat behind a bush if we needed to answer a call of nature.* □ *In the middle of the meeting, I felt a call of nature.*

call, the death. (Folksy. See also **answer the call**.) □ *"I hear the call, and I'm coming," Aunt Martha cried, then fell back in the bed.* □ *The call came very soon in Daniel's young life.*

camp follower a prostitute who gets customers from an army. □ *The general had a rule against camp followers.* □ *When the army moved, the camp followers and their children moved with them.*

capacity a job. □ *In my capacity as Mail Room Specialist, I was responsible for handling several thousand pieces of mail every day.* □ *Have you ever worked in a similar capacity to the position we are offering here?*

capital involving the death penalty. □ *He has committed a capital offense. The death penalty is the only option.* □ *This organization lobbies against capital punishment.*

cardiac arrest a heart attack. (See also **coronary**.) □ *The patient has gone into cardiac arrest.* □ *She died of a sudden cardiac arrest.*

career politician a person who has worked in politics for many years. (Replaces **elder statesman**, which does not include women.) □ *Senator Helen Baum is a respected career politician.* □ *The president's cabinet included several career politicians whose opinions he respected.*

careful (with one's money) stingy; hating to spend money. (See also **close with one's money**.) □ *Jim is very careful. He doesn't spend a lot on himself.* □ *Kathy could afford a better car. She's just careful with her money.*

caregiver a person who takes care of others. (Replaces *caretaker*, which can also be used for a person who takes care of a piece of property.) □ *Nurses, social workers, and other professional caregivers are encouraged to attend this class.* □ *He is the primary caregiver for his two children, and also for his elderly father.*

carry to be pregnant. (Folksy.) □ *Is she carrying, or has she just gained a lot of weight?* □ *I can't wait to tell my parents that I'm carrying. They'll be so excited to have a grandchild.*

carry on with someone to be having sexual intercourse regularly with someone outside of marriage. □ *She's been carrying on with her secretary. It's a scandal.* □ *He drinks, he takes drugs, and he carries on with half a dozen women at a time.*

cash advance a cash loan on a credit card. □ *Use your WonderCard for a convenient cash advance!* □ *I had to pay eighteen percent interest on that cash advance.*

cash flow problem a lack of money. □ *My real estate business has a temporary cash flow problem.* □ *Due to his cash flow problem, he was unable to pay his employees that month.*

casket a coffin. □ *He looks so peaceful, lying there in his casket.* □ *We have several premium caskets appropriate for earth burial.*

casualty a dead or injured person. □ *The bombing caused thousands of casualties.* □ *She was one of the casualties when the building burned down.*

catch someone in the act to catch someone having sexual intercourse. (See also **act of love, (sexual) act.**) □ *She caught her boss in the act with one of the sales representatives.* □ *The hotel maid practically caught them in the act.*

categorical inaccuracy a lie. □ *The president's earlier statement was a categorical inaccuracy.* □ *I wish to correct the impression that may have been made by the categorical inaccuracies in my speech last week.*

categorically needy, the people who will always need help. □ *The welfare-to-workfare program is not appropriate for the categorically needy.* □ *The blind, the elderly, and the categorically needy are the focus of our advocacy.*

Caucasian a person of European ancestry. □ *The suspect is a female Caucasian, five foot four inches tall.* □ *The neighborhood was inhabited mostly by Caucasians.*

C.E. See in the Common Era.

cease fire an agreement not to fight. □ *Both sides have violated the cease fire since it was declared two weeks ago.* □ *There have been several incidents of shelling since the cease fire took effect.*

cellulite fat. □ *This new cream makes cellulite vanish!* □ *I hate the way all that cellulite looks on my thighs.*

cemetery a graveyard. □ *For Memorial Day, the cemetery was beautifully decorated with American flags.* □ *Mr. and Mrs. West bought themselves a space in the cemetery.*

certifiable insane. □ *I always knew Ray was eccentric, but the way he's been behaving lately makes me think he's certifiable.* □ *If the boss thinks this policy is going to be popular, she's definitely certifiable.*

chair(person) the person in charge of a group, especially a committee. (Replaces *chairman* and *chairwoman*.) □ *Dr. Hampton is the chair of the Math Department.* □ *We are* *accepting nominations for the position of chairperson of the operations committee.*

challenge a serious difficulty. □ *Finding new funding sources will certainly be a challenge.* □ *Many of our young recruits find boot camp to be a challenge.*

challenged lacking the ability to do something. (See **developmentally challenged, quantitatively challenged**.) □ *The doctor can prescribe appropriate medication for your behaviorally challenged child.* □ *Jim may be physically challenged, but he is perfectly capable of living independently.*

chamber of commerce a house of prostitution. (Jocular. **Chamber of commerce** only rarely has this meaning. Use with caution.) □ *Well, it's almost midnight, and I should be on my way. Can any of you gentlemen tell me where I might find the local chamber of commerce?* □ *She works in the chamber of commerce, if you know what I mean.*

chamber pot a container in which to defecate or urinate. □ *The cabin doesn't have indoor plumbing, but you'll find a chamber pot under the bed.* □ *I had to use a chamber pot when I was sick in bed.*

change (of life) menopause. □ *The change of life affects each woman differently.* □ *Jill started the change when she was forty-seven.*

char AND **charworker** a person who cleans a house or other building. (British. Replaces *charwoman*, which does not include men.) □ *I can't hold down a job, raise the kids, and clean the house all by myself. I'm thinking of hiring a char.* □ *The charworkers have keys to all the offices.*

character line a wrinkle in the skin. ☐ *She's old enough to have character lines around her eyes.* ☐ *The character lines in his forehead gave him a worried look.*

charms a woman's breasts or buttocks. ☐ *Jill's charms were abundant, Jim thought.* ☐ *She developed her obvious charms when she was a teenager.*

charworker See char.

chassis a person's body. (Slang. **Chassis** is usually used to refer to the body of a car or truck.) ☐ *That young man has a very fine chassis.* ☐ *I don't know about her mind, but I like that chassis.*

cheat on someone to have sex with someone other than one's spouse. (See also **betray someone, deceive one's spouse**.) ☐ *I heard a rumor that Bill is cheating on his wife.* ☐ *She cheated on him, so he divorced her.*

checker a worker who totals the cost of each customer's purchase in a store. (Replaces *checkout girl*, which does not include adults or boys.) ☐ *The checker ran my purchases through his scanner and told me what the total would be.* ☐ *The checker in that line is really slow.*

chemical health services a program to help people end their addiction to drugs. ☐ *The company health plan provides for chemical health services.* ☐ *We recognize that addiction is an illness, and our chemical health services department exists to help you manage that illness.*

chemise a slip; a woman's undergarment shaped like a dress. ☐ *This lovely Victorian-style chemise is one hundred percent cotton.* ☐ *She answered the door wearing only her chemise.*

chess piece one of the set of figures used to play chess. (Replaces *chessman*.) □ *He got out the board and set up the chess pieces.* □ *She concentrated on the current positions of the chess pieces.*

chest the breasts. (**Chest** does not always mean *breasts*. Judge from the context.) □ *She had a flat chest.* □ *All the women in that crime show have big chests.*

children's ranch a prison for children. □ *After she was convicted of shoplifting, she was sent to a children's ranch for three years.* □ *When I was in the children's ranch, my aunt and uncle came to visit me every Saturday.*

choice words AND **choice language** swear words. □ *When the mechanic told me how much he was charging for labor, I gave him a few choice words.* □ *The customer used some choice language when he made his complaint.*

choir director a person who leads a choir. (Replaces *choirmaster*.) □ *Linda is the choir director at our church.* □ *The choir director wore a handsome robe.*

chronologically advantaged AND **chronologically gifted** old. (Often jocular.) □ *This company values its chronologically advantaged employees. We benefit from their experience.* □ *I'm not old and fat. I'm chronologically gifted and quantitatively enhanced.*

chubby fat; heavy. □ *She's kind of a chubby kid, but she has a cute face.* □ *He had chubby cheeks and a round chin.*

chunky fat; heavy. □ *Bill's the chunky guy wearing the brown jacket.* □ *She was chunky when she was a teenager, but she slimmed down as she got older.*

churchyard a graveyard. □ *He's buried in the north corner of the churchyard.* □ *I brought some flowers to the churchyard, to put on my parents' grave.*

cinerarium a place for keeping urns containing the ashes of dead people. (See also **columbarium**.) □ *The inurnment will take place in the cinerarium.* □ *Mary's name was engraved on a brass plaque in the cinerarium.*

civilian impacting the killing of civilians. (See also **collateral damage**.) □ *The civilian impacting of the bombing sorties was judged to be negligible.* □ *There was some civilian impacting in the urban areas. That is all I am authorized to say at this time.*

claim responsibility for something to say that one did something, usually an act of terrorism. □ *No group has yet come forward to claim responsibility for placing the bomb on the airliner.* □ *A fringe group claimed responsibility for blowing up the bus.*

claim the lives of some number of people AND **claim some number of lives** to kill some number of people. □ *To date, the record high temperatures have claimed the lives of thirty-three people.* □ *A gas explosion has claimed at least fifty lives.*

clandestine secret and illegal or immoral. □ *She had a clandestine affair with a man she met in a bar.* □ *The administration gathered clandestine reports on members of the opposition party.* □ *The unit was sent to perform clandestine operations in the southeast.*

claptrap nonsense. (Replaces *crap*.) □ *I can't stand to listen to that TV commentator and all his claptrap.* □ *The sales brochure for the ocean cruise was full of claptrap about romance and escape.*

classism snobbery; the belief that some social classes are better than others. □ *Whenever I talk about good taste and bad taste, I am accused of classism.* □ *Because Jim did not speak standard English, middle-class people often assumed he was stupid. This classism made him angry.*

clean bomb a nuclear bomb with a limited range. □ *The generals discussed the tactical possibilities of the newly developed clean bomb.* □ *Protesters surrounded the lab that was working on the clean bomb.*

cleaning lady a woman who cleans a house or other building. (Replaces *cleaning woman.*) □ *I have a cleaning lady come in twice a week.* □ *He left a tip for the cleaning lady.*

cleavage the space between a woman's breasts. □ *The gown showed a lot of cleavage.* □ *This bra flatters your shape and enhances your cleavage.*

client 1. a customer. □ *The attorney sent a bill to her client.* □ *The hair salon caters to the most discriminating clients.* **2.** a prisoner. □ *The social worker escorted his client to the detention facility.* □ *How many clients are in residence at this facility?*

clinical death the death of the brain. □ *Clinical death occurred at 0223 hours.* □ *If clinical death has occurred, then the family may decide to withdraw life support.*

cloakroom a toilet. (British.) □ *Which way to the cloak-room?* □ *She stopped at the cloakroom in the train station.*

close its doors [for a business] to fail. □ *The restaurant closed its doors after only five months in business.* □ *If we can't attract regular customers, we will have to close our doors.*

closet AND **closeted** [of a homosexual person] not acknowledging his or her homosexuality in public. □ *Jim is a closet homosexual.* □ *Mark wants to be my boyfriend, but he wants to stay closeted, so he doesn't want me to say anything about it.*

close with one's money stingy; hating to spend money. (See also **careful (with one's money)**.) □ *Don't even ask Jane for a contribution. She's extremely close with her money.* □ *Jim's children complained that he was too close with his money.*

clothing optional [of a place] allowing people to appear in the nude; nudist. (See also **free beach**.) □ *This is a clothing optional beach.* □ *She spent her vacation at a clothing optional resort.*

coat room attendant a person who runs a coat room. (Replaces *coat check girl*, which does not include adults or boys.) □ *He collected his coat and tipped the coat room attendant.* □ *The theater is now hiring coat room attendants.*

codependent willing to help someone else continue a bad habit. □ *Helen would probably be able to stop drinking if her husband weren't so codependent.* □ *I realized that our relationship was bad not just because Jim was addicted to gambling, but because I was codependent.*

cohabit [for sexual partners] to live together outside of marriage. (See also **live in sin, live together, roommate**.) □ *She is cohabiting with her boyfriend.* □ *They cohabited for several years before they got married.*

coitus AND **coition** sexual intercourse. □ *They were interrupted before coitus had taken place.* □ *He had engaged in coition with a large number of partners.*

collaborator AND **collaborationist** a traitor. □ *After the war, he was accused of being a Nazi collaborator.* □ *The collaborationists conspired to hand over the city to the enemy.*

collateral damage the killing of civilians and destruction of their property. (See also **civilian impacting**.) □ *Collateral damage was considerable.* □ *Our strategy aims to limit collateral damage.*

collection agency a business that collects money that people owe. □ *When Dan failed to make the payments on his car, the collection agency sent someone to his apartment.* □ *I haven't been able to pay my bills for months. Now I'm getting angry letters from collection agencies.*

color correct something to dye something, especially hair. □ *Your stylist can color correct the gray in your hair.* □ *Can you color correct my beard and mustache?*

colorful [of language] profane. □ *The language in that movie was rather colorful.* □ *She used several colorful expressions in scolding me for my poor performance.*

colors colors that represent a gang. □ *The principal was alarmed when some of her students began wearing their colors to school.* □ *Black and yellow are our colors.*

columbarium a place for storing the ashes of dead people. (See also **cinerarium**.) □ *The urn will be placed in the columbarium.* □ *A marble columbarium stood in the middle of the cemetery.*

combat fatigue See **battle fatigue**.

combat ineffective dead or wounded. □ *The exchange of fire left most of the unit combat ineffective.* □ *Your aim is to render them combat ineffective.*

come out (to someone) to announce one's homosexuality (to someone). □ *Kathy came out when she was sixteen.* □ *When I went home for the holidays, I came out to my parents.*

comfort station a toilet. □ *Comfort stations are provided in the transit center.* □ *The amusement park had numerous comfort stations, all with changing tables for babies.*

commerce sexual intercourse. (Literary or old-fashioned.) □ *The king was required to have commerce with each of his concubines.* □ *Although they were married, they did not have commerce with each other.*

(commercial) sex worker a prostitute. (See also **body worker**.) □ *Many of the patients we see at this clinic are commercial sex workers.* □ *This study addresses the spread of sexually transmitted diseases among sex workers and their customers.*

commission a bribe. (**Commission** does not always mean *bribe.* Judge from the context.) □ *The customs agent will want a commission when we bring this stuff across the border.* □ *The price includes commissions for the usual officials.*

commit someone to send someone to a mental hospital. (See also **institutionalize someone**.) □ *After Mary took all those sleeping pills, her parents committed her.* □ *Jim's family decided to commit him.*

committal the burial of a dead person. □ *After the funeral service, we drove to the cemetery for the committal.* □ *The dead man's children each spoke briefly at the committal.*

committeeperson a person who works for a political party in a city ward. (Replaces *committeeman* and *committeewoman*.) □ *I called the committeeperson to complain* *about the potholes on our street.* □ *The committeeperson came by to remind me that Tuesday was election day.*

commit to someone to have sexual relations with only one specific person. □ *Jane says she loves me, but she's not ready to commit to any one person.* □ *If you can't commit to me, then this relationship is over.*

commode a toilet. (Usually used to describe the toilet as a piece of furniture.) □ *This walnut commode is an authentic reproduction of an original in the Tuileries palace.* □ *The basin and commode are in matching ivory porcelain.*

common law husband a man with whom a woman has been living for many years without marriage. □ *Fred is Mary's common law husband.* □ *She left no will, and so her common law husband was not able to inherit her property.*

common law marriage a form of marriage, legal in some places, that occurs when a couple has been living together as spouses for many years, although they have not participated in a marriage ceremony. □ *Bill's parents had a common law marriage.* □ *Does the state of Ohio recognize common law marriage?*

common law wife a woman with whom a man has been living for many years without marriage. □ *Mary is Fred's common law wife.* □ *As his common law wife, she has certain rights.*

communication arts See language arts.

community 1. a minority group. (See also **defense community, intelligence community, faith community.**) □ *We must join with other members of the community and make our voice heard. We must let others know that this kind of discrimination is unacceptable.* □ *The black community* protested the dismissal of the African-American teacher. **2.** a city. □ *This is a thriving community of seventy-five thousand people.* □ *Our community has many thriving arts organizations.* **3.** a subdivision; a group of streets and houses designed and built at the same time. □ *The real estate developer specializes in planned communities.* □ *I live in a gated community with private security.*

community treatment center a place where people can live who have recently left prison or the hospital. (See also **halfway house**.) □ *My social worker got me a bed in a community treatment center.* □ *The community treatment center is located in a residential neighborhood. Our residents are encouraged to become a part of the community.*

compact (car) a small car. □ *Mary drives a compact.* □ *I'm planning to buy a compact car. They get good gas mileage.*

companion a lover. □ *The movie star and her companion flew to Hawaii.* □ *Jim has been Bill's companion for many years.*

companion animal a pet animal. □ *The veterinarian specializes in companion animals.* □ *Our organization educates people in giving the best possible care to their companion animals.*

compensation payment. □ *Compensation for this position includes a stock option.* □ *We will discuss compensation at your annual review.*

competency a skill; something that a person or organization does well. □ *We will focus on our core competencies and eliminate unnecessary programs.* □ *The consultant identified the firm's competencies.*

complication a problem, usually a medical or legal one. □ *Complications occurred during the surgery.* □ *If you sell the property, you will create complications for your divorce settlement.*

complimentary free; included in the price of something. □ *Today's flight includes complimentary beverages and a snack.* □ *This hotel provides complimentary morning newspapers.*

compromising bad for one's reputation. □ *The documents were extremely compromising for the mayor.* □ *Bill's wife learned some compromising information from his administrative assistant.*

concentration camp a death camp. □ *The evacuees were taken to a concentration camp.* □ *Reports state that beatings, rape, and other forms of torture are common within the concentration camp.*

concern a fear or complaint. □ *As for your business proposal, I have a few concerns I'd like to share with you.* □ *Your professors have expressed some concerns about your schoolwork.*

concert leader AND **concert director** the person who plays first violin in an orchestra. (Replaces *concertmaster.*) □ *Ms. Jones is the concert leader of the symphony orchestra.* □ *Competition for the position of concert director was fierce.*

condition 1. pregnancy. □ *Liz should know better than to smoke in her condition.* □ *A woman in her condition should take better care of herself.* **2.** an illness. □ *I have a heart condition.* □ *He has to take medication for his liver condition.*

confirmed bachelor a homosexual man. (Cute. Use with caution.) □ *SALLY: I'd like to introduce Bill to my cousin*

Mary. I think they'd make a great couple. JANE: *Not likely. Bill is a confirmed bachelor.* □ *Mrs. Johnson's older boy is a confirmed bachelor.*

confiscate something to steal something. □ *The soldiers confiscated a truck.* □ *The rancher confiscated several dozen sheep from her neighbor.*

conflict a war. □ *The conflict in the Middle East escalated today.* □ *The House debated whether the country should become involved in the conflict overseas.*

confounded damned. □ *I wish the baby next door would quit her confounded crying.* □ *I can't find the confounded screwdriver!*

confrontation an armed fight. □ *There was a confrontation between the rival gangs.* □ *A confrontation with enemy troops left eleven dead.*

confused 1. drunk. □ *My friend is a little confused. I'll call a cab for him.* □ *She was quite confused by the time she left the bar.* **2.** senile. □ *Aunt Louisa is eighty-nine, and she gets confused from time to time.* □ *I'm not confused, young man. I know exactly what I'm talking about.*

conjugal relations sexual intercourse within marriage. (See also **marital relations**.) □ *The husband alleged that his wife had refused conjugal relations.* □ *Their conjugal relations were unsatisfactory, so they went to a marriage counselor.*

connections acquaintances who can help with something, especially something secret or illegal. □ *She has connections in Panama.* □ *Most people couldn't have gotten past the border, but Jim had connections.*

connubial pleasures sexual intercourse within marriage. □ *The bride and groom enjoyed their connubial pleasures to the fullest.* □ *They had been married twenty-five years and their connubial pleasures had not diminished one bit.*

consenting adult an adult who consents to engage in sex. □ *The law should not be concerned with anything that happens between consenting adults.* □ *State law prohibits several behaviors, even between consenting adults.*

consideration a fee or bribe. □ *For a consideration, the doorman will show you the movie star's apartment.* □ *The taxi driver agreed to be our guide, for a small consideration.*

console someone to have sex with someone. (*Console* does not always have this meaning. Judge from the context.) □ *After Jim's divorce, his best friend started consoling his wife.* □ *Many women were eager to console the rich young widower.*

consort with someone to have sex with someone. □ *The celebrity consorted with numerous young men.* □ *Everyone in the office knew that Ron was consorting with Helen.*

consultant a businessperson who works independently, often because he or she has been fired from a longtime job. (See also **independent contractor**.) □ *James is no longer with the company, but we are bringing him in as a consultant from time to time.* □ *Since leaving Wondatronics, I have been working as an independent consultant.*

consummate (a relationship) for the people in a relationship to have sexual relations with each other. □ *Fred and Mary had been seeing each other for two years before they consummated their relationship.* □ *The young couple* *consummated their marriage on the first night of the honeymoon.*

contain something 1. to hide the truth about something. □ *The president's staff worked to contain the reports of wrongdoing.* □ *The mayor wanted to contain any leaks about the city's annual financial report.* **2.** to limit something by force. □ *The military attempted to contain the conflict in the south.* □ *They were able to contain the rebels in an area just outside the city.*

contingent worker a temporary worker. □ *Our agency provides highly trained contingent workers who understand the needs of today's workplace.* □ *The company brought in a dozen contingent workers after firing several permanent employees.*

contribution a bribe to a politician. (Note: **contribution** does not always have this meaning. Judge from the context.) □ *The factory owner made a contribution to the Democratic candidate.* □ *The reporter investigated contributions made to the senator's re-election campaign.*

controlled substance an illegal drug. □ *The report claimed that eighty percent of high school students had experimented with controlled substances.* □ *The arresting officer found a controlled substance in the glove box of the suspect's car.*

convenience a toilet. □ *Where can I find the convenience?* □ *The rest stop is fully equipped with conveniences.*

conventional [of weapons] not nuclear. □ *The conflict was carried out with conventional weapons.* □ *The strategies used in conventional warfare no longer apply.*

convince someone to do something See persuade someone to do something.

convivial often drunk. □ *He was a convivial man, and always invited his friends in for a drink after work.* □ *Our convivial hostess kept everyone's glass full.*

cooperate with someone to be forced to help someone. □ *He is cooperating with the police in their investigations.* □ *She agreed to cooperate with the authorities.*

copulate to have sex. □ *Two cats were copulating in my backyard last night.* □ *They copulated in cheap hotel rooms and in apartments borrowed from friends.*

(cordless) massager a battery-operated, vibrating massager designed to stimulate sexually. (See also **vibrator**.) □ *We carry cordless massagers in the pharmacy section of the store.* □ *Have you ever tried using a massager?*

coronary a heart attack. (See also **cardiac arrest**.) □ *Joe had a massive coronary right in the middle of a meeting.* □ *The doctor says that Grandmother won't survive another coronary.*

corpulent fat; large. □ *His corpulent body looked as though it was going to burst from his clothes.* □ *The corpulent woman went on a diet.*

correctional institution AND **correctional facility** a prison. □ *I work as a guard in a correctional institution.* □ *He was sentenced to ten years in a medium-security correctional facility.*

corrections having to do with prison. □ *Bill is a corrections officer in a low-security facility.* □ *I majored in corrections studies in community college.*

cosmetician AND **cosmetologist** a person who cuts and styles hair and applies makeup. □ *All of our stylists are licensed cosmetologists.* □ *One of our cosmeticians can help you with that pedicure.*

cosmetic preparation AND **cosmetic restoration** the grooming of a dead body for a funeral. □ *Our funeral service practitioners are experts at cosmetic preparation.* □ *Mr. Harvey, the victim of a car accident, was in need of cosmetic restoration.*

cosmetic surgery surgery to remove fat or wrinkles. (See also **aesthetic procedure, plastic surgery, procedure.**) □ *Paula has had cosmetic surgery several times.* □ *I am interested in having cosmetic surgery to correct the wrinkles around my eyes.*

costume jewelry jewelry with fake metal and stones. □ *They have some lovely costume jewelry in the department store.* □ *These aren't real pearls. They're just costume jewelry.*

council member AND **councilperson** a member of a city council. (Replaces *alderman, alderwoman.*) □ *I complained to my councilperson about the lack of police patrol in the neighborhood.* □ *Ms. Andrews was elected council member from our ward.*

counsel a lawyer. □ *Eric Millbank is counsel for the prosecution.* □ *"Counsel may confer with her client," said the judge.*

counterinsurgency an armed rebellion. □ *Troops were sent north to deal with the counterinsurgency.* □ *Rival warlords formed a counterinsurgency.*

counterintelligence spying. (See also **intelligence.**) □ *We have several agents gathering counterintelligence.* □ *He ana-*

lyzed the counterintelligence emerging from behind the enemy lines.

counterproductive not helpful; destructive. □ *Discussing side issues at this time would be counterproductive. Let's stick to the topic.* □ *These objections of yours are, I feel, counterproductive.*

court attendant AND **ball attendant** a person who gathers balls during a tennis game. (Replaces *ball boy*, which does not include adults or girls.) □ *She worked as a court attendant during the summers.* □ *The ball attendant collected the ball.*

courtesan a high-class prostitute. □ *The business travelers were entertained by courtesans.* □ *Madame du Barry was a famous courtesan.*

courtesy free; included in the price of something. □ *The hotel provides a courtesy airport van.* □ *We offer courtesy laundry services.*

covert action AND **covert operation** spying. □ *The agent engaged in several covert actions in Paris before returning to Moscow.* □ *The covert operation involves electronic surveillance.*

cover up something to hide the truth about something. □ *The representative tried to cover up her involvement in the scandal.* □ *The memo was a clear attempt to cover up the executive's criminal activities.*

cow-brute a bull. (Folksy.) □ *I keep six cows and one cow-brute.* □ *The farmer sold the cow-brutes out of the herd.*

cowhand a person who herds cows. (Replaces *cowboy, cowgirl.*) □ *The ranch employs sixteen cowhands.* □ *The cowhand branded the calf.*

cow pie AND **cow pat** the feces of a cow. □ *I almost stepped in that cow pie.* □ *The dirt road was covered with cow pats.*

creamery butter butter. □ *We serve whole wheat toast with creamery butter.* □ *The pastry is made with the finest creamery butter.*

creative dishonest. □ *The investigation showed that the mayor had done some creative bookkeeping.* □ *Her methods of financing the new building were creative, to say the least.*

credibility gap a reputation for lying. (See also **revenue gap**.) □ *The management at our company is concerned about a perceived credibility gap.* □ *The discovery of the mayor's illegal activities caused an immense credibility gap with the townspeople.*

cremains the ashes of a dead person. □ *The inurnment of the cremains will take place at 1:30 P.M.* □ *And what plans do you have for the final disposition of the cremains?*

crematorium a place where dead bodies are burned. □ *The committal service will take place at the crematorium.* □ *The mourners gathered at the crematorium to bid their loved one goodbye.*

crewed space flight a space flight with people on it. (Replaces *manned space flight.*) □ *This will be a crewed space flight for the purpose of repairing a major weather satellite.* □ *The first crewed space flights took place in the 1960s.*

crime against nature a homosexual act. (Old-fashioned. Offensive to homosexual people. Use with caution.) □ *He was accused of crimes against nature.* □ *The two young men were proven to have committed crimes against nature and were accordingly dismissed from the college.*

cripes! AND **crumbs!** "damn!" □ *Cripes! I broke it!* □ *Crumbs! I didn't bring a map with me!*

critical care facility a hospital for very ill or dying people. □ *We have moved your husband to a critical care facility.* □ *The staff at the critical care facility are specially trained in the needs of the critically ill and their families.*

cross-cultural communications conversation between people from different countries. □ *Youth organizations like this promote cross-cultural communications between their members all over the world.* □ *These arms negotiations mark a new era in cross-cultural communications.*

cross over to die. (Folksy.) □ *We all have to cross over someday.* □ *My wife crossed over last year.*

crotch the genitals. □ *The ball hit him right in the crotch.* □ *He got athlete's foot fungus in his crotch.*

crown jewels See (family) jewels.

crumbs! See cripes!

cuddly fat. (Cute.) □ *What a cuddly baby!* □ *I don't think you're fat. I think you're nice and cuddly.*

cull something to remove and destroy members of something, usually a group of animals. □ *The wildlife manager is responsible for culling the deer herds in the park.* □ *The* *goldfish farmer culled the newly hatched fish, keeping those that had the best shape and color.*

culturally advantaged rich; upper-class. (See also (culturally) deprived.) □ *I can't deny I had a culturally advantaged upbringing.* □ *The charity appealed to the culturally advantaged to give their time, money, and expertise to those less fortunate.*

(culturally) deprived poor; lower-class. (See also **culturally advantaged**.) □ *Joe is working at a summer camp for culturally deprived children.* □ *Jane grew up in a deprived area. She learned her street-smarts at an early age.*

culturally disadvantaged poor and lower-class. (See also **disadvantaged, economically disadvantaged**.) □ *I work with culturally disadvantaged youth in the inner city.* □ *The nature camp reaches out to culturally disadvantaged children and helps them appreciate the outdoors.*

cup a cup worn to protect the penis and testicles. (See also **abdominal protector, (athletic) supporter, cache-sexe**.) □ *The coach requires every player to wear a cup during games.* □ *Wash that cup thoroughly at least three times a week.*

currency adjustment a reduction in value of a country's money. □ *The currency adjustment caused a certain amount of unrest in the capital.* □ *The new administration's first move was to implement a currency adjustment.*

curse, the a menstrual period. (Similarly: bloody Mary, curse of Eve, feeling poorly, flowers, having a friend to stay, having a little visitor, monthlies, observing holy week, on the rag, red flag is up, riding the cotton bicycle, roses.) □ *I'm a little under the weather today. It's the curse.* □ *Mary says she has no pain at all when she gets the curse.*

curvaceous [of a woman] big-breasted. □ *Just look at that curvaceous girl.* □ *The skater was muscular, yet curvaceous.*

cuspidor a spittoon; a container for spitting tobacco into. □ *He used the wastebasket for a cuspidor.* □ *The bar has a brass cuspidor for those who chew tobacco.*

custodian a janitor; a person who cleans a building and fixes things in it. □ *The school custodian waxed the floors in the afternoons after the students had gone home.* □ *I called the custodian and asked her to fix the hot water heater.*

customer a person who uses a prostitute. (Note: **customer** does not always have this meaning. Judge from the context.) □ *The prostitute had an average of five customers a night.* □ *The call girls walked up and down the street looking for customers.*

customer service representative a salesperson. □ *If you would like to place an order, please dial 7 to speak to a customer service representative.* □ *The customer service representative for the western region is Ms. Andrews.*

CYA to protect oneself. (The letters stand for "Cover Your Ass.") □ *Get all work orders in writing, so you can CYA.* □ *He tried to CYA by asking us to lie for him.*

czar a person in charge of a large government program. (American.) □ *Johnson is rumored to be the president's top choice for drug czar.* □ *As energy czar, he sought to use the press to educate the public about saving energy.*

damage control an attempt to lessen the harm done by a harmful act or statement. □ *After word got out that the mayor often made racist jokes, his staff immediately started working on damage control.* □ *The management committee discussed strategies for damage control after the disappointing financial report was released.*

dang See darn.

dark meat the leg meat of a bird. (Compare with white meat.) □ *Do you prefer white or dark meat?* □ *Most of the leftovers from the turkey are dark meat.*

darn AND **dang** damned. □ *I can't get the darn door open.* □ *What time is that dang show on, anyway?*

Davy Jones' locker the bottom of the sea; death at sea. □ *The pirate sent the ship's crew to Davy Jones' locker.* □ *The ship exploded. Every last sailor went to Davy Jones' locker.*

D&C See dilation and curettage.

deal with someone to kill someone. □ *"Spike, you deal with that cop," said the crime boss.* □ *The agent planned how best to deal with the rebel leader without getting caught.*

death benefit insurance money paid on someone's death. □ *This policy has a death benefit of $10,000.* □ *If you should be killed as a direct consequence of something that happens on the job, your family will receive a death benefit.*

deceased, the a dead person. □ *The name of the deceased is James Morton.* □ *The deceased was taken to the nearest hospital.*

decedent a dead person. (A legal term.) □ *Ms. Randall is the decedent's next of kin.* □ *"What was your relationship to the decedent?" the lawyer asked the witness.*

deceive one's spouse to have sexual relations with someone other than one's spouse. (See also **cheat on someone, betray someone**.) □ *He had deceived his wife with three different women.* □ *She did her best to hide the fact that she was deceiving her husband.*

decent clothed. □ *Are you decent? Can I come in?* □ *Wait a sec. I'm not decent.*

decollete [of a woman's garment that has] a low neckline that shows the tops of the breasts. (French.) □ *Her decollete displayed her beautiful skin and shapely bosom.* □ *The decollete on that gown gives a dramatic effect.*

defecate to produce feces. □ *The dog defecated on the sidewalk.* □ *Someone has been defecating in our alley. It's disgusting.*

defense having to do with warfare. □ *The new head of the Defense Department gave a press conference today.* □ *Over thirty percent of the country's budget is used for defense spending.*

defense community, the the army, navy, air force, and those that build and research weapons. □ *The defense community felt some stress as a result of the budget cutbacks.* □ *Respected members of the defense community testified before Congress about the proposed bomber.*

deficit a lack. □ *I wear glasses because I have a vision deficit.* □ *Children with learning deficits are included in normal activities as much as possible.*

defund something to stop giving money to something. □ *The arts program in this school district has been defunded.* □ *The legislature is threatening to defund the building of the new sports stadium.*

delinquent 1. a young criminal. (See also **juvenile**.) □ *This facility houses delinquents and attempts to train them in basic life skills.* □ *When Jim's mother caught him smoking marijuana, she called him a delinquent and kicked him out of the house.* **2.** late. □ *Please remit your delinquent payment upon receipt of this notice.* □ *You are delinquent in your car payment.*

delivery having to do with dropping or launching bombs. □ *The contractor is developing a more efficient delivery system for the stealth bomber.* □ *The delivery vehicle can be moved by truck or train.*

deliveryperson a person who delivers things. (Replaces *deliveryman*.) □ *The deliverypeople carried the sofa up the front steps.* □ *I left a note for the deliveryperson to leave the flowers on the back porch.*

deluxe expensive; fancy. □ *Our deluxe hotel suites include complimentary breakfast.* □ *This deluxe sedan has an all-leather interior.*

dementia senility. □ *Uncle Lenny was diagnosed with dementia.* □ *The dementia has progressed to the point where he is no longer able to take care of himself.*

demerit a bad quality. □ *The hotel is at least reasonably priced, whatever its demerits may be.* □ *Ed's boss considers his outspokenness to be a demerit.*

demimondaine a prostitute. (French.) □ *The neighborhood was inhabited mostly by transients and demimondaines.* □ *His favorite companions were drug dealers and demimondaines.*

demise the death of a person or organization. □ *You will inherit the property upon your father's demise.* □ *Since the demise of the city's only morning newspaper, I haven't had anything to read in the mornings.*

demographic strain overpopulation. □ *Demographic strain in the area has resulted in grave environmental damage.* □ *Birth control can reduce demographic strain.*

dentures false teeth. □ *This toothpaste gets dentures really clean.* □ *I went to the dentist to be fitted with a set of dentures.*

deodorant a substance that reduces the smell of sweat. (See also **antiperspirant**.) □ *He showered and put on his deodorant.* □ *This deodorant works even when I'm playing football.*

departed dead. □ *He yearned to see his departed wife.* □ *My dear departed mother gave me good advice that still helps me.*

depart (this life) to die. □ *He departed this life on April 20, 1973.* □ *She departed peacefully, in her sleep.*

dependency an addiction. □ *His friends were afraid that he had a chemical dependency.* □ *Her dependency on alcohol was growing dangerous.*

depilation the removal of hair. □ *The beauty salon also does cosmetic depilation.* □ *There are many methods for depilation of the legs, underarms, and face.*

derriere the buttocks. (French.) □ *She slapped him on his derriere.* □ *She fell on her derriere.*

destabilize something to overthrow something. □ *The agents worked to destabilize the government.* □ *It was feared that rebel elements would destabilize the regime.*

destroy something have something, usually a pet, put to death. □ *The animal control division is responsible for destroying unwanted animals.* □ *The cat has rabies. We will have to destroy it, I'm afraid.*

detainee a prisoner. □ *The detainees were kept in a holding cell.* □ *The detainee repeatedly requested medical attention.*

detain someone to arrest someone. □ *Police are detaining two suspects in connection with the robbery.* □ *He was detained without being told the charges against him.*

detente an agreement not to fight. (French.) □ *The two sides in the conflict have reached a detente.* □ *It was feared that the arms buildup would disrupt the detente.*

detention prison. □ *The authorities kept the activists in detention for three months before bringing charges against them.* □ *He was placed in detention and not allowed to communicate with his attorney.*

deterrent weapons, usually nuclear ones. □ *The new government's powerful deterrent alarmed its foreign neighbors.* □ *The nation's nuclear deterrent will preserve global peace.*

detox a program that helps people stop drinking alcohol or taking drugs. □ *She checked into detox, determined to beat her addiction.* □ *The judge ordered the drunk driver to undergo detox.*

deuce devil. (British or old-fashioned.) □ *What the deuce is going on here?* □ *Deuce take it! I've lost my wallet!*

develop to grow breasts. (See also **round out, fill out.**) □ *She began to develop when she was thirteen years old.* □ *She developed later than other girls in her class.*

developer a person who obtains money to construct buildings. (See also **develop something.**) □ *Jane is a real estate developer.* □ *The developer was offering limited partnerships in a new subdivision.*

developing [of a country] poor; without industries. (See also **emerging, underdeveloped.**) □ *The charity sent aid to developing countries.* □ *It is a developing country rich in natural resources.*

developmentally challenged AND **developmentally delayed** AND **developmentally disabled** slow to learn. (Replaces *mentally retarded.*) □ *Their oldest child is severely developmentally challenged. He will never be able to live independently.* □ *The school helps developmentally disabled individuals to learn basic skills.* □ *Mike is somewhat developmentally delayed, but he is able to do just fine in a regular classroom.*

develop something to construct buildings on something. (See also **developer.**) □ *I want to develop that acreage*

I own outside of town. □ *The environmentalists protested the city's plans to develop the wilderness area.*

device a bomb, especially a nuclear bomb. □ *The country maintained a stockpile of nuclear devices.* □ *The device was detonated on a testing range in the Pacific.*

dialogue a conversation. □ *I invite dialogue from all participants in this process.* □ *We have been able to enter into an informative dialogue with the union representatives.*

dialogue with someone to talk with someone. □ *I would like to dialogue with each one of you about this matter.* □ *The mediator will help the two opposing sides to dialogue with one another.*

dickens, the the Devil. (Folksy.) □ *What the dickens are you doing in there?* □ *She was yelling like the dickens.*

die after a brief illness to commit suicide. (Compare with die after a long illness.) □ *The newspaper obituary says that Jim died after a brief illness.* □ *Mary died after a brief illness. She is survived by her parents and one sister.*

die after a long illness to die of cancer. (Compare with die after a brief illness.) □ *Ms. Smith died after a long illness. She is survived by her husband and two children.* □ *I am sorry to have to inform you that Uncle Ted died after a long illness, early last spring.*

die by one's own hand to commit suicide. □ JANE: *I just heard that Bill died. I didn't know he was sick.* DAN: *He wasn't sick. He died by his own hand.* □ *She died at the age of fifty, by her own hand.*

differential a profit. □ *The differential for our information services division was twelve percent in the first quarter* *of this year.* □ *The differential has shown a steady increase since Sue took charge of the company.*

differently (blank)-ed having a different (blank) than most other people. (Most often used in the phrase *differently abled*, not able to move as easily as most other people.) □ *The library has a wheelchair ramp for our patrons who are differently abled.* □ *This exercise class is specifically designed for the differently sized.*

difficult not obedient. □ *David is a rather difficult child in the classroom.* □ *The manager wondered what to do about the difficult employee.*

dilation and curettage AND **D&C** an abortion. (Note: dilation and curettage does not always have this meaning. Judge from the context.) □ *The doctor performed a dilation and curettage.* □ *She had a D&C last summer.*

direct action violent action. □ *If the logging company did not respond to their protests, the environmentalists considered taking direct action.* □ *"This initiative may require direct action. Are you prepared to do that?" the group leader asked.*

direct mail advertising sent through the mail. □ *The carpet-cleaning service advertised through direct mail.* □ *The postal service has special rates for direct mail.*

director a person who directs something. (Replaces *director* for men and *directress* for women.) □ *Susan Meadows is the director of the movie.* □ *Jim is director of the banking division.*

disability a difficulty or inability to do something. □ *Paula has a hearing disability.* □ *People with disabilities lobbied for more acceptance in the workplace.*

disabled not able to do something as easily as most other people. □ *John has been disabled since birth. He learned to use a wheelchair when he was a small boy.* □ *This bathroom stall is designed for disabled people to use.*

disadvantaged poor. (See also culturally disadvantaged, economically disadvantaged.) □ *Many of the children who attend this school are disadvantaged.* □ *He became a social worker because he wanted to help disadvantaged people.*

disappear someone to murder someone in secret. □ *The government disappeared the rebel leader's family.* □ *One by one, the new regime imprisoned or disappeared its opponents.*

discharge someone to fire someone. □ *The company discharged its chief financial officer for grave wrongdoing.* □ *If your work habits do not improve, I will have to discharge you.*

discharge something to fire a weapon. □ *The soldier discharged his weapon at the target.* □ *They discharged the cannon.*

discipline someone to punish someone. □ *The police officer was disciplined for his racist behavior.* □ *Don't be afraid to set limits and discipline your children when they go beyond those limits.*

discomfort pain. □ *The dentist said, "You may feel some discomfort as I begin to drill the cavity."* □ *Some of our passengers may experience motion discomfort as the plane moves through the area of turbulence.*

disincentive a reason not to do something. □ *The company's severe policy on theft was a strong disincentive for its employees to steal.* □ *The professor gave A's to almost every student. This practice was a disincentive for the students to work hard.*

disinformation propaganda. □ *The agents began a disinformation campaign aimed at destroying the president's reputation.* □ *The radio station was used to spread disinformation.*

disingenuous dishonest. □ *"I had no idea the car belonged to you," was her disingenuous reply.* □ *The mayor was being disingenuous, to say the least, when he claimed not to know that his chief of police was taking bribes.*

disinter someone remove someone's body from the grave. □ *The body was disinterred and medical tests were performed.* □ *In the course of the murder investigation, it was necessary to disinter the victim's body.*

disorder an illness. □ *He has a liver disorder.* □ *Her disorder makes it impossible for her to live without medication.*

disorderly house a house of prostitution. (Legal.) □ *The complaint alleges that the property at this address is a disorderly house.* □ *He was convicted on one count of keeping a disorderly house.*

dispatch someone to kill someone. □ *The spy was called upon to dispatch a minor official.* □ *The assassin quickly dispatched his target.*

dispense with someone's assistance to fire someone. (British.) □ *I'm afraid we must dispense with your assistance.* □ *If you can't be more punctual, we will have to dispense with your assistance.*

displaced person a refugee. □ *The aid organization provided medical care to the displaced persons in the camp.* □ *Tens of thousands of displaced persons crowded the temporary shelters.*

display figure a figure shaped like a person, used for displaying clothes. (Replaces *mannequin*.) □ *The dresser draped the skirt on the display figure.* □ *The display figures in that store were so realistic that I thought they were real people!*

disport oneself to have sexual intercourse. □ *Two cats were disporting themselves in the backyard all night long.* □ *I stumbled across a young couple disporting themselves on the beach.*

dispose of someone to kill someone. □ *She disposed of her husband for his insurance money.* □ *The ruthless dictator disposed of his opponents one by one.*

disrobe to undress. □ *She disrobed and got into the bathtub.* □ *The massage therapist asked me to disrobe and lie down on the table.*

disruptive noisy and disobedient. □ *Your daughter has been very disruptive in class this week. Is she having trouble at home?* □ *The diner's disruptive behavior caused the restaurant staff to escort him from the premises.*

dissolution death. (Formal.) □ *She faced illness and dissolution without fear.* □ *His heavy drug use led to his dissolution.*

distinguished old. □ *The distinguished gentleman with the white beard is Professor Martin.* □ *I am glad to see so many distinguished attorneys here today.*

distressed worn out. □ *The developer sought to bring businesses back to the distressed downtown area.* □ *This summer, distressed jeans are very fashionable.*

disturbed (in one's mind) mentally ill. (See also **troubled**.) □ *His family gradually realized that he was seriously disturbed and needed professional help.* □ *She's disturbed in her mind, poor thing.*

diversify to do many different kinds of business. □ *The head of the company decided it was time to diversify. It was time to move beyond food service and only food service.* □ *The company diversified in the 1980s, but in the 1990s, its business analysts recommended returning to its core competency, which was the manufacture of plastic kitchenware.*

diversity racial diversity. □ *We attended a training session about diversity in the workplace.* □ *Our town prides itself on its diversity. We have residents here from a large variety of ethnic backgrounds.*

divert something into someplace to steal something and keep it someplace. □ *He diverted the funds into a secret bank account.* □ *She diverted her clients' stock purchases into her own investment portfolio.*

divest to sell unpopular investments. □ *The university owned stock in several South African companies, and it was under pressure to divest.* □ *Because of the controversy over tobacco, the board of trustees debated whether or not to divest.*

do away with someone to kill someone. (**Do away with oneself** means *to kill oneself*.) □ *They say he did away with his poor sick mother.* □ *In despair, she did away with herself.*

dock worker a person who moves things on and off ships. (Replaces *longshoreman*, which does not include women. See also **longshore worker**.) □ *Maggie got a job as a dock worker.* □ *The shipping company is hiring dock workers for $8 an hour.*

doctor something to change something secretly and with bad intentions. □ *The scientist was disgraced when her colleagues learned she had doctored her data.* □ *He doctored the bank statements to hide the large amounts of money he had withdrawn.*

documented worker a foreigner who has official permission to live and work in the country. (Replaces *legal alien.* Compare with **undocumented person.**) □ *The company claimed that they employed documented workers only, not illegal aliens.* □ *His work visa allowed him to enter the country as a documented worker.*

do(-do) feces. (See also **poop.**) □ *There's a big dog do on the lawn.* □ *You need to clean the bird cage. It's covered in do-do.*

dog dirt dog feces. □ *The park is always full of dog dirt in the spring.* □ *He carefully scooped up the dog dirt with a shovel.*

doggone(d) damned. (A substitute for *goddamned.*) □ *I can't get the doggone remote control to work.* □ *I'm tired of your doggoned complaining!*

do it to have sex. (Slang.) □ *I hear that Bill and Jane did it in the back of his car.* □ *He did it for the first time when he was seventeen.*

domestic a servant. □ *She had worked as a domestic for forty years.* □ *To keep the mansion running, we had to maintain a large staff of domestics.*

domestic partner a person, often a lover, with whom you share your household. □ *Domestic partners are covered under our health care plan.* □ *Bill and I are not married, although we are domestic partners.*

domestic science the study of cooking, gardening, and shopping. (See also **home economics**.) ☐ *The community college offers a two-year certificate program in domestic science. Graduates of this program often find jobs in the hospitality industry, such as restaurants and hotels.* ☐ *He knows a lot about nutrition because he took several classes in domestic science.*

domestic violence violence done in the home, usually to women or children. ☐ *Many women in the town where I grew up were victims of domestic violence.* ☐ *The shelter aids those who are escaping from domestic violence.*

domestic worker a person who cleans houses. ☐ *Experienced domestic workers wanted for our cleaning service.* ☐ *What is the average wage for domestic workers in this area?*

domicile a house. ☐ *The suspect returned to her domicile at 7:02 P.M.* ☐ *The Army provided domiciles for the officers and their families.*

donate something to someone or something to give something to someone or something. ☐ *Can you donate five dollars to the relief fund?* ☐ *The church urges you to donate whatever you can spare to the homeless shelter.*

donation a fee. ☐ *Admission to the museum is free, but there is a suggested donation of $5 per person.* ☐ *We are asking a $10 donation for tonight's show.*

Don Juan a man who has sexual relations with many women. (See also **playboy**.) ☐ *Rumor has it that Michael is a real Don Juan.* ☐ *He was a Don Juan before he got married, but now he's settled down.*

do one's business to defecate or urinate. (See also **do one's duty**.) □ *Do you need to do your business before we get in the car?* □ *The cat did her business on the sofa again.*

do one's duty to defecate or urinate. (Usually used by adults talking to or about children. See also **do one's business**.) □ *We're not leaving this restroom until you do your duty.* □ *She did her duty in the potty, just like a big girl!*

do oneself harm AND **harm oneself** to commit suicide or try to commit suicide. □ *The doctor ordered Jim to be watched twenty-four hours a day. She was afraid that, in his depressed condition, he might do himself harm.* □ *Her friends feared she might harm herself.*

do (one's) time to serve one's sentence in prison. (Slang.) □ *Have you ever done time?* □ *I'm not a criminal. I did my time, and I intend to be a law-abiding citizen from now on.*

do someone in to kill someone. (Slang. **Do oneself in** means *to kill oneself*.) □ *The bank robbers did three people in on their way out of the bank.* □ *She did herself in with overwork.*

douceur a bribe. (French.) □ *He offered the judge a douceur.* □ *Her business did very well once she understood which officials required a douceur.*

downsize to fire a lot of people. (See also **reengineer something, reorganize, streamline**.) □ *I lost my job when the company downsized.* □ *The consultant said that the plant would have to downsize in order to remain competitive.*

Down's syndrome a genetic disease that limits intelligence. (Replaces *mongolism*.) □ *Our oldest boy has Down's syndrome.* □ *There are two kids with Down's syndrome in the third grade class this year.*

down there the genitals. □ *Did he touch you down there?* □ *When you take your shower, make sure you wash down there.*

down-turn AND **down-trend** a depression. □ *The down-turn in the economy resulted in a high level of unemployment.* □ *The stock market crash precipitated a long-term down-trend.*

drafter a person who draws plans for building things. (Replaces *draftsman*, which does not include women.) □ *The engineering department hired two new drafters.* □ *She is an experienced drafter.*

drat damn. □ *Drat that broken step!* □ *Oh, drat, I missed the bus!*

drawers underpants. (Folksy.) □ *I hung out my drawers on the clothesline.* □ *The little boy came running into the room without any drawers on.*

drink to drink alcohol. □ MICHAEL: *Would you like a beer?* BILL: *No thanks. I don't drink.* □ *Jane would be a good worker if she didn't drink so much.*

drinking driver a drunk driver. □ *The new law punishes drinking drivers severely.* □ *His daughter was killed in an accident with a drinking driver.*

droppings animal feces. □ *I found raccoon droppings in the basement.* □ *The car was covered with bird droppings.*

drown one's sorrows to drink a lot of alcohol in order to forget that one is unhappy. □ *After she lost her job, Jane spent every afternoon at the corner bar, drowning her sorrows.* □ *When his wife left him, he tried to drown his sorrows, but only succeeded in making his friends feel sorry for him.*

drumstick the leg of a bird. □ *BILL: Would you like white meat or dark meat? JOE: I'll take a drumstick.* □ *Save the chicken drumstick for me!*

dry not allowing the sale of alcohol. □ *You won't find a liquor store here. This is a dry town.* □ *If this law passes, the whole county will be dry.*

duff the buttocks. (Slang.) □ *Park your duff in that chair and tell me what happened.* □ *When I tried to ski, I just fell on my duff.*

dung animal feces. □ *It took all morning to shovel the dung out of the barn.* □ *The meadow was covered with horse dung.*

Dutch courage courage that comes from being drunk. (Possibly offensive to Dutch people. Use with caution.) □ *Two drinks at lunch gave him enough Dutch courage to ask his boss for a raise.* □ *I hoped that the gin would provide me with a certain amount of Dutch courage.*

dying process, the dying. □ *Anger is a natural part of the dying process.* □ *Joe is a counselor trained to help people and their families work through the dying process with dignity and honesty.*

dysfunctional unhealthy. □ *She was raised in a dysfunctional family. Her mother was an alcoholic, and her father was emotionally abusive.* □ *The supervisor's bad temper created a dysfunctional work environment.*

E

earth closet an outdoor toilet. (Compare to **water closet**.) □ *The cabin does not have indoor plumbing, just an earth closet in the back.* □ *At camp, we had to use an earth closet.*

ease oneself to defecate or urinate. □ *He stopped by the side of the road and eased himself in the bushes.* □ *I looked around for a bathroom. I badly needed to ease myself.*

easy woman AND **woman of easy virtue** a prostitute. (Old-fashioned. See also **fancy woman**.) □ *Mrs. Brown was a notorious easy woman.* □ *He spends all his money on easy women.* □ *Those outlandish clothes made her look like a woman of easy virtue.*

eating disorder a disease that causes one to eat too much or too little. □ *Jill is extremely thin because she has an eating disorder.* □ *A combination of medication and counseling helped Lucy overcome her eating disorder.*

eating for two pregnant. □ *Would you like another helping? You're eating for two, after all!* □ *Paula doesn't usually have such a big appetite, but now she's eating for two.*

eat-in kitchen a kitchen in a house or apartment that does not have a dining room. □ *This adorable starter home* *features an eat-in kitchen.* □ JANE: *Does your new apartment have a dining room?* JILL: *No, it has an eat-in kitchen.*

eccentric mentally ill. (Eccentric does not always have this meaning. Judge from the context.) □ *Uncle James is a touch eccentric, so we've hired a nurse to look after him.* □ BILL: *Why does your neighbor scream cuss words at everyone who walks by?* JILL: *She's eccentric, poor dear.*

ecdysiast a stripper. (Coined by the writer H. L. Mencken. See also **exotic dancer**.) □ *The Champagne Club features a number of lovely ecdysiasts.* □ *Jill had trained as a dancer, but could only find work as an ecdysiast.*

economical cheap. (See also **economy**.) □ *This is the most economical brand of dish soap.* □ *If the price on this car seems a bit high, perhaps you would like to look at some of our more economical models.*

economically disadvantaged poor. (See also **disadvantaged, culturally disadvantaged**.) □ *Many of the city's residents are economically disadvantaged.* □ *The charity gives food aid to economically disadvanged people.*

economically inactive unemployed. □ *Eleven percent of the town's residents are economically inactive.* □ *There is less chance of re-entering the job market if you have been economically inactive for three years or more.*

economical with the truth dishonest. □ *The mayor was known to be economical with the truth.* □ *I discovered that my boss had been economical with the truth when she said that the company was making money.*

economic insufficiency poverty. □ *This scholarship is designed to help those who, because of economic insufficiency,* would not otherwise be able to attend college. □ *The neighborhood suffered from economic insufficiency.*

economy cheap. (See also **economical**.) □ *I always fly economy. Business class is much too expensive.* □ *If you buy the economy size, you get two dozen rolls for three dollars.*

educator a teacher. □ *Educators from around the state attended the conference.* □ *She is a distinguished educator.*

effect change to change things. □ *We are looking for a dynamic executive who can effect change.* □ *These initiatives for corporate growth are designed to effect change.*

effective casualty radius the distance at which a weapon can kill people. □ *The device has an effective casualty radius of two hundred yards.* □ *Unfortunately, several civilians were within the effective casualty radius of the grenade.*

effeminate [of a man] homosexual. (Possibly offensive to homosexual men. Use with caution.) □ *That new teacher seems rather effeminate.* □ *Because James didn't like sports, the other boys thought he was effeminate.*

efficiency a one-room apartment. (See also **studio (apartment)**.) □ *I'm renting an efficiency near the university.* □ *I can show you several efficiencies that will be available July 1st.*

effing "fucking." □ *I'm so effing tired I can barely stand up.* □ *Who's making that effing noise?*

effluent an unpleasant or poisonous flowing liquid. □ *The effluent from the factory goes directly into the river.* □ *The broken sewer line poured thousands of gallons of effluent into the street.*

egad! "My God!" (Old-fashioned. Usually jocular.) □ *"Egad!" said the inspector, "the villain has escaped!"* □ *Egad! I believe you've discovered the answer!*

egress exit. □ *Locate your nearest means of egress from the building.* □ *This door is not available for egress.*

elderly old. □ *Many elderly people live in this apartment building.* □ *My next-door neighbor is an elderly gentleman.*

elder statesman an old politician. (See also **career politician**.) □ *Mr. Johnson is a respected elder statesman, who served as governor for four terms.* □ *A number of elder statesmen gave the candidate their support.*

electronic countermeasures hidden microphones used to spy on someone. □ *The police used electronic countermeasures to bust the drug ring.* □ *Electronic countermeasures were employed in the enemy's capital city.*

elevated drunk. (See also **high**.) □ *He was quite elevated when he came home from the party.* □ *The wine they had drunk at dinner left them feeling elevated.*

eligible unmarried. □ *John is good-looking and considerate and has a good job. And I hear he's eligible, too!* □ *I have a hard time meeting eligible women.*

eliminate to defecate or urinate. (A medical term.) □ *This laxative will help you eliminate.* □ *The patient is unable to eliminate.*

eliminate someone to kill someone. □ *The spy knew she had to eliminate her opponent.* □ *The criminal gang silently and ruthlessly eliminated their competitors.*

emasculate someone to remove someone's testicles. (Often used as a figure of speech.) □ *In ancient times, the ruling families emasculated young slave boys and trained them to be political advisors.* □ *Fred felt that his wife's constant criticism emasculated him.*

embarrassed without money. □ *I am temporarily embarrassed and unable to pay my debts.* □ *Rita has been embarrassed since the failure of her business.*

embonpoint fatness. (French.) □ *Her figure tends toward embonpoint.* □ *We specialize in clothing for ladies of embonpoint.*

embraces sex; copulation. □ *Her husband denied her his embraces, so she sought consolation from another man.* □ *He took to the embraces of a younger woman.*

embroider something to exaggerate something. (Often used in the expression *embroider the truth*.) □ *When Mary tells a story, she tends to embroider the truth.* □ *You know that Bob embroiders everything he says.*

emergency a war. □ *The troops were sent to contain the emergency.* □ *Our ally has asked us to provide military assistance in this emergency, and we must respond.*

emerging AND **emergent** [of a country] poor but building industry. (See also **developing, underdeveloped**.) □ *We want both the developed and the emerging nations of this hemisphere to make common cause with one another.* □ *He was the emergent country's first democratically elected leader.*

emolument payment. □ *The office of mayor involves a generous emolument.* □ *The emolument is more than sufficient to meet my needs.*

employee hour the work done by one person in an hour. (Replaces *man hour*, which does not include women.) □ *How many employee hours would we have to devote to the project?* □ *Your proposal said that your department could accomplish the task in forty-five employee hours.*

emporium a store. (Old-fashioned.) □ *Bailey's Hardware Emporium has all the tools and hardware you will ever need.* □ *Michael owns the clothing emporium on Main Street.*

empower someone to help or encourage someone. □ *We empower our employees by including their input in our decision-making process.* □ *The group home empowers its residents by insisting that they take responsibility for their own actions.*

enceinte pregnant. (French.) □ *Mrs. Hubbell is enceinte.* □ *Joan is enceinte. The happy event will take place in September.*

encore presentation a television rerun. □ *Tonight we are proud to bring you an encore presentation of last week's movie.* □ *The two-hour special is an encore presentation.*

encounter a battle. □ *The troops came off victorious in their encounter with the enemy.* □ *Our first encounter took place at 0500 hours, near the enemy encampment.*

end it (all) to kill oneself. □ *He had been depressed for months. He decided to end it all.* □ *I'm no good to anybody. I'm going to end it. Don't try to talk me out of it.*

end, the death. □ *Her children were with her at the end.* □ *His illness had been long and painful, and he was ready for the end when it came.*

enemy action bombing by the enemy. □ *There has been no enemy action in that sector for three days.* □ *The air strike was in response to enemy action in the capital.*

engagement a battle. (See also **engage with someone.**) □ *They lost the first few engagements, but in the end, they were able to take the city.* □ *We sustained heavy losses in that engagement.*

engage with someone do battle with someone. (See also **engagement.**) □ *We engaged with the enemy near the town of Huntsville.* □ *If you encounter enemy troops, do not engage with them. Maintain your distance.*

engineer a specialized worker. □ *One of our product engineers is working on that design.* □ *Joan is a software engineer.*

enhance something to make something appear more valuable than it really is. □ *He is very clever at enhancing old furniture.* □ *The forger enhanced several pictures and sold them as the work of old masters.*

enlistee an enlisted soldier. (Replaces *enlisted man,* which does not include women. See also **soldier.**) □ *The enlistees arrived at boot camp on a Saturday.* □ *Officers are not to fraternize with enlistees.*

enrichment program a set of advanced classes for schoolchildren. □ *After Jimmy gets out of his regular classes, he attends an enrichment program down at the high school.* □ *Students from our enrichment program have very high scores on college entrance exams.*

enslaved person a slave. □ *My ancestors were enslaved persons.* □ *These plantations were built and maintained by the labor of enslaved persons.*

entanglement a sexual relationship outside of marriage. □ *The rich boy's family wanted him to end his entanglement with the poor girl from the wrong side of town.* □ *I have done nothing I need be ashamed of, since my unfortunate entanglement with the young actor.*

entitlements welfare programs. □ *The legislature decided to cut back spending on entitlements.* □ *The proposed budget leaves entitlements at their current level of funding.*

entrenching tool a shovel. □ *The soldiers carried entrenching tools and other excavating equipment.* □ *Their first task was to dig a latrine with their entrenching tools.*

epicure a person who demands fine food. □ *I'm afraid to invite Jane over for dinner. She's an epicure, and my cooking is not all that good.* □ *The epicure published a guide to the city's best restaurants.*

episode a disaster. (See also **event, incident**.) □ *There was an episode at the restaurant tonight. One of the waiters punched a customer in the nose.* □ *The episode at the crack house left one police officer wounded.*

equal opportunity not discriminating on the basis of race or sex. □ *Jones Incorporated is an equal opportunity employer.* □ *The equal opportunity laws require that the percentages of women and minorities in your company reflect the percentages of women and minorities in the community.*

equestrian skills the ability to ride a horse. (Replaces *horsemanship*, which does not include women.) □ *Linda's equestrian skills are admirable.* □ *He won a prize for his equestrian skills.*

equipment 1. the penis and testicles. □ *When you play football, son, it's a good idea to wear a cup to protect your* *equipment.* □ *The city boy couldn't stop staring at the horse's equipment.* **2.** an airplane. □ *The flight has been delayed due to equipment failure.* □ *The pilot has discovered a slight problem with the equipment.*

equivocate to lie. □ *When Jim said he would have the project done on time, he was equivocating.* □ *I felt that if I told the truth, the consequences would be unpleasant, so I chose to equivocate.*

-era from the time of a certain war. □ *A number of Vietnam-era veterans spoke at the ceremony.* □ *The documentary showed some Persian Gulf–era interviews with the senator.*

erotica pornography. □ *He has a large and expensive collection of erotica.* □ *The bookstore specializes in erotica.*

err to have a sexual relationship outside of marriage. (See also **errant**.) □ *He erred once, when he was young, but he has been faithful ever since.* □ *He could not believe that his wife had erred.*

errant having sexual relations outside of marriage. (See also **err**.) □ *She forgave her errant husband on the condition that he remain faithful in the future.* □ *The errant wife felt great remorse for what she had done.*

erratum a mistake. (Latin. The plural is **errata**.) □ *The newspaper apologized for the erratum.* □ *A short list of errata was printed in the next edition of the magazine.*

erroneous report a lie. □ *There have been erroneous reports in the press about the mayor's financial situation.* □ REPORTER: *How can the company be in debt? You announced last month that you had a two-hundred-percent increase in sales.* EXECUTIVE: *That was an erroneous report.*

escalate something to increase a military activity, such as bombing. □ *The bombers escalated the number of sorties per day.* □ *The rebel troops have escalated their shelling of the city.*

escort service AND **escort agency** a service that provides prostitutes. □ *I was shocked when my business associate offered to call an escort service for me.* □ *The madam claimed that her escort agency had the most beautiful women in town.*

escort someone from the premises to force someone to leave. □ *The security guard escorted the unruly visitor from the premises.* □ *If you will not lower your voice, I must escort you from the premises.*

espionage spying. □ *He had been engaged in espionage against his own country's government.* □ *She was arrested and charged with espionage.*

estate a grave plot. □ *Our pre-need program includes the estate as well as all the funeral arrangements.* □ *It's never too soon to think about purchasing an estate for yourself or your loved ones.*

eternal life death. (See also everlasting life.) □ *He passed on into eternal life, leaving us behind to mourn.* □ *She is now at rest in eternal life.*

eternal rest See heavenly rest.

ethnic having to do with race, especially a non-ruling or minority race. □ *Ethnic humor is not acceptable in the workplace.* □ *There has been an increase in ethnic violence in the city.* □ *Are there any good ethnic restaurants in this neighborhood?*

ethnic cleansing the killing of people of a certain race; genocide. (This term came into use during the wars in the former Yugoslavia in the 1990s. It was how the Serbian forces described their killing of Muslims.) □ *The general ordered the troops to carry out ethnic cleansing in the region.* □ *At the war crimes tribunal, he was accused of participating in ethnic cleansing.*

euthanasia the killing of a sick person or animal. (See also **auto-euthanasia, mercy killing.**) □ *My dog was clearly suffering, and was not going to get better, so the veterinarian suggested euthanasia.* □ *The patient begged the doctor to help him die, but she said she opposed euthanasia.*

evacuate one's bowels to defecate. (Similarly: do a job, drop one's load, make a deposit, post a letter.) □ *After taking a jog around the block, Jill felt the need to evacuate her bowels.* □ *I am afraid my little boy is sick. He has not evacuated his bowels for several days.*

evasion a lie. □ *Much to her embarrassment, Kathy was caught in an evasion.* □ *I am tired of the evasions that I hear from the management. I want to know the truth.*

evening of life old age. □ *As she approached the evening of life, Sarah looked back on her accomplishments with satisfaction.* □ *The residents of this rest home are all in the evening of life.*

event a disaster. (See also **episode, incident.**) □ *In case of an explosion or other event, it will be necessary to evacuate the building.* □ *The event at the power plant took place at approximately 6:45 this morning.*

eventide home See **twilight home.**

everlasting life AND **the life everlasting** death. (See also **eternal life**.) □ *She has gone to her reward in everlasting life.* □ *We shall meet again in the life everlasting.*

everything the genitals. □ *She wasn't wearing any underwear, so when her skirt blew up, you could see everything.* □ *His shorts were so thin you could darn near see everything.*

exceptional either very intelligent or very unintelligent. (See also **special**.) □ *The school board voted in special funds for advanced classes for exceptional students.* □ *The school offers remedial programs for exceptional kids.*

excessive force extreme violence by the police. □ *The officer was judged to have used excessive force in apprehending the suspect.* □ *The suspect was not resisting arrest. Why did you use excessive force?*

exchange an exchange of nuclear bombs. □ *According to our calculations, eighty percent of the country's infrastructure would be destroyed in the first exchange.* □ *These missile silos should be capable of withstanding at least one exchange.*

exchange of ideas a conversation. □ *The opposing parties were able to participate in a civil exchange of ideas.* □ *The conference is an opportunity to include those of all cultures and creeds in an exchange of ideas.*

execute someone to kill someone. □ *The head of the gang ordered his thugs to execute the rival boss.* □ *The military leaders conspired to execute the president.*

executive a person who makes decisions in business. (Replaces *businessman* and *businesswoman*.) □ *The book includes advice from executives of several major companies.* □ *Jane and Frank are prominent executives.*

executive action the secret killing of a political opponent. □ *The agent received an order to carry out an executive action against the rebel leader.* □ *None of the government officials would admit having ordered the executive action.*

ex gratia payment a payment made to someone you have injured, before the injured party demands any payment. □ *The chemical company offered an ex gratia payment to the citizens of the town that had suffered from the pollution it had generated.* □ *The government made an ex gratia payment to the civilians whose lands the army had destroyed.*

exhibitionist a person who exposes his or her naked body in public. (See also **expose oneself**.) □ *Do you think the woman across the street is an exhibitionist? She seems to spend a lot of time standing naked in front of the window.* □ *The last time I walked through the park, I ran across an exhibitionist.*

exotic dancer a stripper. (See also **ecdysiast**.) □ *The club features beautiful exotic dancers.* □ *Bill's friends hired an exotic dancer to dance at his bachelor party.*

expectant mother a pregnant woman. (See also **expecting**.) □ *The doctor's waiting room was filled with expectant mothers.* □ *The magazine has articles of interest to young parents and expectant mothers.*

expecting pregnant. (Similarly: big, broken-legged, full of heir, have a belly full, in a fix, in the pudding club, knocked up, on the way, preggers, well along. See also **expectant mother**.) □ *Did you hear the news? Joan and Bob are expecting!* □ *Mary worked the whole time she was expecting.*

expectorate to spit. □ *The dentist said, "Please rinse your mouth and expectorate into the sink."* □ *I hate it when people expectorate on the sidewalk.*

expendable able to be killed without causing a military loss. □ *The general decided that the troops on the left flank were expendable.* □ *The infantry was considered expendable.*

experienced having sexual experience. □ *He was experienced by the time he was fifteen years old.* □ *She boasted to her friends that she was experienced, but in fact, she had never even kissed a boy.*

experientially enhanced old. (Usually jocular.) □ *We seek and respect the opinions of our experientially enhanced residents.* □ *So you're sixty years old today! How does it feel to be experientially enhanced?*

expire to die. (Literary.) □ *She expired with her beloved's name upon her lips.* □ *He turned his eyes to heaven and expired.*

expletive a swear word. (Sometimes used in the phrase *expletive deleted*, which can be used humorously in place of a swear word.) □ *She used a vigorous expletive when she dropped the hammer on her toe.* □ *I'm fed up with that expletive deleted landlord of mine.*

explicit See graphic.

expose oneself to show one's naked body or genitals in public. (See also **exhibitionist**.) □ *A man exposed himself to the children in the playground yesterday afternoon. Isn't that awful!* □ *The rock singer exposed herself onstage.*

expropriate something to take or steal something. □ *Ralph was caught expropriating office supplies from the supply room.* □ *The soldiers expropriated the farmer's truck.*

extended size a clothing size for large people. (See also plus size, queen-size(d), women's size.) □ *This dress shop specializes in extended sizes.* □ *Do you have underwear in extended sizes?*

extension class a night school class. □ *The university offers extension classes for non-traditional students.* □ *I am taking an extension class in economics.*

extortion blackmail. □ *The crime boss was convicted of extortion. He had made local businesses give him money to keep him from destroying their buildings.* □ REPORTER: *I won't publish the embarrassing story about you if you'll do me some favors.* POLITICIAN: *That's extortion!*

extracurricular involving sex outside of marriage. (Jocular.) □ *I heard a rumor that David is involved in some extracurricular activities. I wonder if his wife knows.* □ *Kathy's extracurricular adventures would fill a book.*

extralegal illegal. □ *Some of Paula's business activities were definitely extralegal.* □ *The goods were brought into the country in an extralegal fashion.*

extramarital involving sex outside of marriage. □ *He had an extramarital affair.* □ *Her husband found out about her extramarital activities.*

extremity an arm or leg. (Old-fashioned. Usually used in the plural.) □ *Frostbite attacks the extremities first.* □ *She felt pain in her extremities.*

fabrication a lie. □ *His claim to be a Harvard graduate was a fabrication.* □ *Her stories of adventures in Tibet were all fabrications.*

face in the moon the shapes on the surface of the moon that look like a face. (Replaces *man in the moon.*) □ *When the moon was full, the children could see the face in the moon.* □ *Go to sleep, little one, and the face in the moon will watch over you.*

face-lift surgery to remove fat and loose skin from the face. □ *She hoped the face-lift would make her look younger.* □ *Does your health insurance cover face-lifts?*

facetiae pornography. □ *The rare book dealer had a large selection of facetiae.* □ *She collects facetiae, some of it quite rare.*

facial tissue thin paper for blowing your nose. □ *These facial tissues come in six decorator colors.* □ *This is the softest brand of facial tissue you will find.*

facilitate something to lead something. □ *My name is Ralph, and I'm here to facilitate today's meeting.* □ *Susan facilitated the discussion.*

facilities, the the toilet. □ *Excuse me, can you tell me where to find the facilities?* □ JANE: *I need to use the bathroom.* BILL: *The facilities are down the hall and to your left.*

facility a building or group of buildings. □ *The new sports facility will be named for Mr. Williams, who donated the money for the project.* □ *The new water treatment facility was completed just last year.*

facts of life, the information about sex. (See also **the birds and the bees.**) □ *It is important to teach your children the facts of life when they are young.* □ *The seventh grade health class will cover the facts of life.*

fair bad. (You may see lists that rank things as *fair, good, very good,* or *excellent.*) □ *Kim is a fair student.* □ *Her performance on the test was fair.*

fair trade legally protected trade. □ *The senator promised to work for fair trade policies with Japan.* □ *The new fair trade regulations make it possible to increase our exports almost seventy percent.*

faith community a church, synagogue, or mosque. □ *This week we bring you a profile of St. Joseph's, one of the city's most prominent faith communities.* □ *To what faith community do you belong?*

fall to be killed in battle. (Literary.) □ *Twenty-four thousand men fell at Antietam that day.* □ *She learned that her son had fallen in the fighting at Maiwand.*

fall asleep to die. (See also **asleep (in Jesus).**) □ *After a long illness, Daddy fell asleep with his children gathered around him.* □ *She was ninety-two when she fell asleep.*

fallen woman a woman who has had sex outside of marriage. (Old-fashioned.) □ *The whole town knew she was a fallen woman. She made up her mind to leave.* □ *The ladies in polite society refused to have anything to do with her, because she was a fallen woman.*

fall off the wagon to start drinking alcohol again. (Slang. Compare with **on the wagon**.) □ *He swore he would stop drinking, but he fell off the wagon after just one month.* □ *She was determined not to fall off the wagon. She avoided bars and parties where she knew liquor would be served.*

falsehood a lie. □ *I have never told a falsehood in my life.* □ *His autobiography was full of falsehoods.*

family without any mentions of sex. □ *Are there any good family shows on TV?* □ *The video store has a large selection of family movies.*

(family) jewels AND **crown jewels** the testicles. (Jocular.) □ *We were playing soccer, and he kicked me right in the family jewels. Ouch!* □ *If you're going to play rugby, Andrew, you'd better wear an athletic supporter to protect the crown jewels.*

family planning birth control. □ *The book describes several methods of family planning.* □ *Family planning was not widely available in the rural areas.*

fancy house a house of prostitution. (Folksy. See also **fancy woman**.) □ *I heard they caught Mr. White going into a fancy house.* □ *She runs a fancy house, and she knows all the men in town.*

fancy woman AND **light woman** a prostitute. (Folksy. See also **easy woman, fancy house**.) □ *He keeps a fancy* *woman in a house outside of town.* □ *Folks say she's a light woman. I'd avoid her if I were you.*

fanny the buttocks. (In British English, **fanny** means *the female genitals*. Use with caution.) □ *She patted him on the fanny.* □ *That dress barely covers her fanny!*

far gone drunk. □ *After the party, we were all pretty far gone.* □ *He is too far gone to drive. I'll call him a cab.*

farmhand a person who works on a farm. (Replaces *hired man*, which does not include women.) □ *In the harvest season, we hire about ten farmhands.* □ *Jim, Mary, and Frank worked as farmhands when they were younger.*

farrier a person who makes horseshoes and puts them on horses. (Replaces *blacksmith*, which may be offensive to black people.) □ *The farming museum has a farrier who will show you how horseshoes are made.* □ *The riding stable employs two farriers.*

fatality a death. □ *There were two fatalities as a result of the accident.* □ *There has been a shooting here, with one fatality.*

father of lies, the the Devil. □ *The father of lies throws temptation in our way.* □ *His impulse to go into that liquor store must have come straight from the father of lies.*

father-to-be the father of an unborn child. (See also **mother-to-be**.) □ *Congratulations! I hear you're a father-to-be!* □ *The young father-to-be was very protective of his pregnant wife.*

faux false; fake. (French.) □ *This lovely faux diamond ring can be yours for only $39.99.* □ *The faux marble finish on that* *table is just the dramatic touch you need for your dining room.*

faux pas a mistake, especially a social mistake. (French.) □ *She committed a terrible faux pas. She left the party without thanking the host.* □ *Jim boasted about his raise in front of Mark, who didn't get one. That was a faux pas.*

favors sexual attentions. □ *She enjoyed the young man's favors all summer long.* □ *He begged for his sweetheart's favors.*

feeling no pain drunk. □ *After two beers, I was feeling no pain.* □ *A group of young people staggered down the street, singing and laughing loudly. Clearly, they were feeling no pain.*

fellow traveler a person who sympathizes with the Communist Party but does not belong to it. □ *In the 1950s, his career was ruined because of rumors that he was a fellow traveler.* □ *Because of her liberal opinions, she was called a fellow traveler.*

felony augmentation the practice of giving the longest possible prison sentence to a convicted criminal. □ *The judge said, "I believe felony augmentation is appropriate in this case. I sentence you to fifteen years."* □ *The district attorney argued for felony augmentation, because of the cruelty of the murders.*

female identified AND **female oriented** [of a woman] homosexual. (See also **male identified**.) □ *I attended a retreat for female identified women.* □ *Although I have not had a relationship with a woman, I consider myself female oriented.*

female-intensive occupation a job usually done by women. □ *Office work is a female-intensive occupation.* □ *Although paralegal work has historically been a female-intensive occupation, we are seeing more and more men joining the profession.*

female oriented See female identified.

female trouble a disease of the uterus, ovaries, or vagina. (Old-fashioned and possibly offensive to women. Use with caution.) □ JOHN: *I heard Paula had to go to the hospital. What's wrong with her?* BILL: *Some kind of female trouble, I think.* □ *Maria has had various female troubles ever since she was a young woman.*

feminine having to do with the vagina. (**Feminine** has this meaning in only a few contexts.) □ CUSTOMER: *Where can I find sanitary napkins?* STORE CLERK: *Feminine hygiene products are in aisle 7.* □ *This cream relieves feminine itching on contact.*

fertilizer animal feces. □ *I spread fertilizer on the lawn.* □ *She bought a twenty-five-pound bag of fertilizer at the garden store.*

festival seating AND **general seating** the practice of selling seats "first come, first served." □ *There was festival seating for the rock concert, and many fights broke out over the best seats.* □ *There will be general seating for the show, so you will want to arrive early to get a good seat.*

fib a lie. □ CHARLES: *You said you liked my cooking.* LINDA: *I'm afraid that was a fib.* □ *To cheer her up, I told her a little fib. I said she was looking much better.*

fiction a lie. □ *The bank discovered a number of fictions in Jim's accounts.* □ *Her story about where she had been all night was certainly a fiction.*

fiddlesticks 1. nonsense. □ BILLY: *Janie said I was stupid!* FATHER: *Fiddlesticks. You're very smart.* □ MARK: *You shouldn't have gone to all this trouble.* MARY: *Fiddlesticks. I'm happy to do it.* **2.** "I wish that had not happened!" □ *Oh, fiddlesticks! I dropped the eggs.* □ *Fiddlesticks! I missed my TV show!*

figure the breasts and hips. □ *Nancy got her figure when she was thirteen years old.* □ *She has a lovely figure.*

fille de joie a prostitute. (French.) □ *He spent all his time drinking and carrying on with filles de joie.* □ *When she was sixteen, poverty drove her to the life of a fille de joie.*

filler a cheap substance added to food to increase its volume. □ *This dog food is made with pure beef. There is some corn meal as filler.* □ *Is it true that clay is used as a filler in some foods?*

fill out [for a young person] to develop an adult body. (Usually used to describe a girl developing breasts. See also **develop, round out.**) □ *Little Paula has really filled out since I saw her last.* □ *Jimmy was a skinny little boy, but this year, he has filled out.*

final curtain, the death. (Refers to the curtain that falls at the end of a play.) □ *He faced the final curtain with courage.* □ *And so the final curtain fell for Stanley.*

(final) disposition the place a dead body is going to be put; the way a dead body is to be disposed of. □ *Do you have any preferences for the final disposition of the deceased? Would you prefer earth burial, or interment in a mausoleum?*

☐ *Uncle Ned's will clearly stated his wishes about disposition. He wanted to donate his body to a medical school.*

final process of life, the death. ☐ *The hospice is a resource for those undergoing the final process of life.* ☐ *Facing the final process of life is often the greatest challenge we will have.*

finances money. ☐ *He was without finances.* ☐ *My finances are somewhat limited.*

financial aid AND **financial assistance** a gift or loan of money. (See also **assistance**.) ☐ *The college offers financial aid to qualified students.* ☐ *I received financial assistance from my family.*

financial services the lending of money and selling of stocks. ☐ *Our bank provides a full line of financial services, from auto loans to retirement planning.* ☐ *Financial services are now available to all our account holders.*

finesse something to succeed at something through lying or tricks. ☐ *I hadn't studied for the test, but I managed to finesse it.* ☐ *She was able to finesse her way past the security guards.*

finish someone off to kill someone. ☐ *The gang members beat their victim, and then the gang leader finished him off with a shot to the head.* ☐ *She was ill for a long time, and then the stroke finished her off.*

fink a worthless person. ☐ *I'm sick of that lousy fink.* ☐ *You're a fink, do you hear me? A fink!*

firefighter a person who puts out fires. (Replaces *fireman*, which does not include women.) ☐ *The town employs* *five full-time firefighters.* □ *I bought a ticket to the firefighters' annual picnic.*

first strike the first attack with nuclear bombs. □ *How much of our industry would we lose in the first strike?* □ *Now that they have developed a uranium industry, the country is now capable of a first strike.*

First World Western Europe and North America. (Possibly offensive to people from countries outside these regions. Use with caution. See also **industrial(ized), Third World**.) □ *It is the responsibility of the industrialized nations of the First World to foster democracy throughout the globe.* □ *Adequate food and shelter are often taken for granted by residents of the First World.*

first-year student a student in the first year of high school or college. (Replaces *freshman*, which does not include women. See also **freshperson**.) □ *The dean made a speech to welcome the first-year students.* □ *Jean and Bill are two of the most promising first-year students at the college.*

fiscal having to do with money. □ *The mayor has a conservative fiscal policy.* □ *The treasurer handles all our fiscal decisions.*

fiscal health the amount of money someone or something has. □ *The organization's fiscal health was not good.* □ *The treasurer is responsible for keeping an eye on the fiscal health of the company.*

five-o'clock shadow a day's growth of beard. □ *To prevent five-o'clock shadow, Jim shaved twice a day.* □ *That five-o'clock shadow makes you look sloppy. You should shave.*

fixed income a small income from a pension or the government. □ *Many senior citizens in our city live on fixed incomes.* □ *Her fixed income did not allow her to buy a car.*

fixer-upper a house in bad condition. (See also handyman's special.) □ *This beautiful old Victorian is a fixer-upper with lots of potential.* □ *The young couple bought a fixer-upper and did all the work themselves.*

fix something 1. to remove the uterus or testicles of a pet animal. □ *We took Fluffy to the veterinarian to have her fixed.* □ *The animal shelter fixes all animals that come there, to prevent overpopulation.* **2.** to pay money in secret to have something turn out the way you want. □ *The Boss fixed all the horse races in the county.* □ *After the gun-control bill failed to pass, there were rumors that the gun lobby had fixed the legislature.*

flamboyant [of a man] homosexual. (Possibly offensive to homosexual men. Use with caution.) □ *Jill's piano teacher was a flamboyant young man who always called her "darling."* □ *On TV, the actor played a macho detective, but in his private life, he was, shall we say, flamboyant.*

flatter someone's figure to make someone look thin. □ *The princess lines of this dress really flatter your figure.* □ *The trousers had a full cut that flattered Maria's figure.*

flexible loose; without morals. □ *Paula is a fairly flexible person, so I think she will be open to our proposal, even though it involves a few extralegal activities.* □ *His flexible approach to business made many enemies, and a great deal of money.*

flight attendant a person who takes care of passengers on a plane. (Replaces *steward* for men and *stewardess* for women.) □ *If you need a flight attendant, just press the* *button on the arm of your seat.* □ *The flight attendant asked me if I wanted anything to drink.*

floor clock AND **tall clock** a tall clock in a wooden case that rests on the floor. (Replaces *grandfather clock* and *grandmother clock*.) □ *A handsome floor clock stood in the living room and chimed on the hour.* □ *Don't forget to wind the tall clock before you go to bed.*

floral tribute flowers sent to a funeral. □ *The church was filled with floral tributes.* □ *Did you wish to make any arrangements for floral tributes at your grandmother's funeral?*

flower carrier a child who carries flowers in a wedding ceremony. (Replaces *flower girl,* which does not include boys.) □ *Billy and Sally will be the flower carriers at my wedding.* □ *The flower carrier at the wedding was a darling little four-year-old.*

fluffy large; fat. (Cute.) □ *This exercise class is especially for fluffy women.* □ *He started to get a little fluffy once he stopped jogging.*

food product processed food. □ *"I always buy Squeeze brand cheese food product," said the smiling actor in the TV commercial.* □ *Our company manufactures a number of food products, including Yummy Up grape drink and Squeeze brand cheese.*

foot! AND **fudge!** "I wish that had not happened!" (A very mild replacement for "fuck!") □ *Oh, foot! I spilled the tomato sauce all over the clean floor!* □ *Fudge! I forgot to call Maria! Now she'll be upset!*

foreign national a foreigner. □ *These tax regulations apply to foreign nationals living in the United States.* □ *Victor is not a citizen. He is a foreign national.*

foreperson (of the jury) the leader of a jury. (Replaces *foreman (of the jury)*, which does not include women.) □ *The jury members selected Ms. Oakes as their foreperson.* □ *The foreperson of the jury said, "We find the defendant guilty on all counts."*

forget oneself to act rudely or shamefully. (Old-fashioned and literary.) □ *He so far forgot himself as to take the Lord's name in vain.* □ *Under the influence of drink, she forgot herself completely, and made indecent proposals to all the men in the room.*

fornicate to have sexual intercourse outside of marriage. (Because this word is used to describe sexual relations in English translations of the Bible, it is often so used by Christian fundamentalists.) □ *The Lord will punish those who fornicate.* □ *Young people today fornicate without giving it a second thought.*

for your convenience inconveniently. □ *For your convenience, we are rebuilding the pedestrian walkways. They will not be available for use during the rebuilding period.* □ *For your convenience, we accept only cash and credit cards. No checks.*

foster care the care of someone other than the parents. □ *When she went to prison, her children were put in foster care.* □ *Our group home provides foster care for children under the age of twelve.*

foul play murder as the cause of death. □ *I hear Jones was killed last night. Is there any suspicion of foul play?* □ *When* *the Boss turned up dead, everyone was sure it was foul play, even though there was not a single mark on his body.*

foul something to defecate or urinate on something. □ *The cat keeps fouling the rug.* □ *She had a sudden attack of diarrhea in the middle of the night, which caused her to foul the bedsheets.*

foul something up to ruin something. (A mild replacement for *fuck something up*.) □ *Every time I ask John to do something, he fouls it up.* □ *If the exchange rate drops, that will foul everything up.*

foundation (garment) a tight garment that squeezes the stomach to make it look smaller; a girdle. □ *I have to wear a foundation if I'm going to squeeze into that dress.* □ *Today's foundation garments are light and comfortable, not like the girdles your mother used to wear.*

Founders, the the people who founded a country. (Replaces *Founding Fathers*, which does not include women.) □ *The Supreme Court debated the intentions of the Founders in the First Amendment.* □ *We honor the Founders on Independence Day.*

four-letter word a swear word. □ *The comedian's routine was full of four-letter words.* □ *I heard a stream of four-letter words coming from the garage as Jane worked on fixing the car.*

fragmentation device a grenade. □ *Pull the pin from the fragmentation device.* □ *The soldier lost his arm when a fragmentation device exploded near him.*

fragrant 1. bad-smelling. □ *The baby's diapers are rather fragrant. I think she needs changing.* □ *They live next to a fragrant hog farm.* **2.** pregnant. (Cute.) □ *You're going to be* *a grandfather soon. I'm fragrant! □ I hear Jill is . . . well . . . fragrant.*

frank depicting sex plainly. □ *The book was praised for its frank description of teenage sexuality. □ Some of the frank scenes in the movie are not suitable for young viewers.*

fraternize with someone to have sex with someone. □ *We discourage our employees from fraternizing with each other. □ Officers may not fraternize with enlistees.*

free beach a nude beach. (See also **clothing optional.**) □ *If you want to sunbathe in the nude, there's a free beach a few miles down the coast. □ The first time I went to a free beach, I felt embarrassed about taking off my swimming suit.*

freedom fighter a rebel fighter. □ *The senator proposed sending military aid to the freedom fighters in the communist country. □ Many of the freedom fighters were trained in the United States.*

free enterprise private business. □ *"These trade regulations are the enemy of free enterprise," said the company's chief executive officer. □ The formerly communist country was now interested in encouraging free enterprise.*

free gift something extra given to you when you buy something else. □ *When you order your magazine subscription, this book is yours to keep as our free gift. □ This canvas tote is a free gift for everyone who opens an account at our bank today!*

free love the freedom to have sexual relations outside of marriage. □ *The members of the community practice free love. □ The social reformer argued in favor of free love.*

free spirit a person who does not obey rules. □ *Jane is a real free spirit. She never lives in one place for more than a year or two. She goes wherever she feels like going.* □ *The old man was a free spirit who refused to act his age.*

Free World the United States and its allies. (Possibly offensive to people from countries that do not fit this description. Use with caution.) □ *The president pledged to keep communism from spreading into the Free World.* □ *She runs a company that does business throughout the Free World.*

freeze a stoppage; a refusal to increase. (See also **hiring freeze, wage freeze**.) □ *The company hoped that a spending freeze would increase profits.* □ *The group lobbied for a nuclear weapons freeze.*

French kiss 1. a kiss given with the tongue. (Possibly offensive to French people. Use with caution.) □ *He gave her a French kiss.* □ *The picture showed the young couple engaged in a French kiss.* **2.** to kiss with the tongue. □ *He wanted to French kiss on our first date!* □ *He had never French kissed before.*

French letter a condom. (Old-fashioned. Possibly offensive to French people. Use with caution.) □ *He went to the city to purchase a supply of French letters.* □ *She had heard that a French letter could prevent the spread of disease.*

freshen up to urinate or defecate. (Suggests that you are going into the bathroom only to wash or groom yourself.) □ *Would you like to freshen up before dinner?* □ *Excuse me while I freshen up.*

freshperson AND **fresher** a student in the first year of high school or college. (Replaces *freshman*, which does not include women. See also **first-year student**.) □ *All freshers* *received a bulletin from the principal.* □ *Freshpersons are housed in the dormitories.*

friend 1. a sexual partner. □ *Our daughter brought her friend to our cabin for the weekend. We didn't allow them to stay in the same bedroom.* □ *This is my friend, Michael. We've been together for three years now.* **2.** a menstrual period. □ *"I always feel a little sleepy on the first day when my friend comes," Jill said with a yawn.* □ *My friend was late this month. I thought I might be pregnant.*

friendly fire the shooting or bombing from troops on one's own side. □ *He was killed in friendly fire.* □ *Our commander learned that the shelling was friendly fire.*

frigging worthless. (A replacement for *fucking*.) □ *My neighbor's loud music must have kept the whole frigging apartment building awake.* □ *That was the hardest frigging test I have ever had.*

fringe not widely accepted. □ *She is the leader of a fringe political party.* □ *Dr. Redmond considers homeopathy a fringe science.*

front the breasts. □ *Mrs. Ferris had an enormous front.* □ *I spilled coffee all down my front.*

frontage a big belly. □ *He has a pretty good frontage on him.* □ *I can't get my jacket to close over my frontage.*

fudge! See foot!

full-figured fat; large. □ *We offer lingerie for the full-figured woman.* □ *Jane is a handsome, full-figured lady.*

fun 1. sex. □ *Hey, baby, want to have some fun?* □ *Cheryl and I had some fun together when we were kids.* **2.** violence.

☐ *"Let's have some fun," said Big Dave, slipping another round into his pistol.* ☐ *The Boss says we're going to go across the river and have some fun with Lefty's boys.*

functional limitation a disability. ☐ *Please leave these seats free for passengers with functional limitations.* ☐ *Is your hotel fully accessible for guests with functional limitations?*

fundament the buttocks. ☐ *He gives me a pain in the fundament.* ☐ *The fall left a big bruise on my fundament.*

fundamentalist a believer in the literal truth of a religious text. ☐ *The host of the radio show is a fundamentalist preacher.* ☐ *The politician's conservative platform appealed to fundamentalists.*

funding AND **funds** money. ☐ *The funding for this documentary was provided by a grant from the Marshall Corporation.* ☐ *His parents supplied him with funds.*

funeral chapel a place where funerals are held. (See also **funeral home**.) ☐ *Services will begin at six o'clock at the funeral chapel.* ☐ *The professional staff at our funeral chapel will assist you with every aspect of the arrangements.*

funeral coach a hearse; a vehicle for carrying dead bodies to the grave. (See also **professional car**.) ☐ *The widow and children of the deceased rode in the funeral coach.* ☐ *My father drives a funeral coach for a living.*

funeral director a person who prepares dead bodies for burial and who conducts funerals; an undertaker. (See also **mortician**.) ☐ *Please speak with the funeral director to make the arrangements.* ☐ *The funeral director showed the mourners into the chapel.*

funeral facilitator a person who leads funerals. □ *The conference on grief and loss was attended by funeral facilitators both lay and clergy.* □ *As a community leader, I am often asked to serve as a funeral facilitator.*

funeral home AND **funeral parlor** a place where funerals are held and bodies are prepared for burial. (See also funeral chapel.) □ *The reviewal will take place at the funeral home.* □ *The family gathered at the funeral parlor for the wake.*

funeral service practitioner AND **funeral service professional** a person who conducts funerals and prepares dead bodies for burial or cremation; an undertaker. (See also mortician.) □ *One of our funeral service professionals will help you with every aspect of the arrangements.* □ *Funeral service practitioners must pass a licensing examination in this state.*

furlough someone to fire someone. □ *The auto plant furloughed five hundred workers.* □ *Managers were encouraged to furlough as many employees as they could.*

f-word, the "fuck." (See also s-word, the.) □ *Mommy! Billy used the f-word!* □ *The radio host was fired for using the f-word on the air.*

gadzooks "What a surprise!" "How amazing!" (Old-fashioned or jocular. A replacement for "My God!") □ *Gadzooks! Thou art yet alive!* □ *Gadzooks! What a party!*

gal Friday AND **guy Friday** AND **man Friday** AND **woman Friday** a secretary and helper. (From *Friday*, the name of Robinson Crusoe's helper in the book by Daniel Defoe. **Gal Friday, woman Friday** refer to a woman, and **guy Friday, man Friday** refer to a man.) □ *The want ad said that an up-and-coming executive was looking for a guy or gal Friday.* □ *Gina is my gal Friday. She takes care of everything from plane reservations to checking my grammar.* □ *I could use a man or woman Friday to help me organize my files.*

game management the killing of unwanted animals. □ *The game warden is responsible for game management in the wildlife area.* □ *The workers in charge of game management shot over a hundred deer this fall.*

gamestership the ability to play games well. (Replaces *gamesmanship*, which does not include women.) □ *The negotiators demonstrated their expert gamestership in the business talks.* □ *The leader of the chess team praised the gamestership on both sides of the match.*

gaming gambling. □ *Visit our gaming casinos for an exciting Las Vegas–style weekend!* □ *The state gaming commission is in charge of the lottery.*

garçon a waiter. (French.) □ *Ask the garçon to bring us our check, please.* □ *And how is the salmon meunière tonight, garçon?*

garden niche a space for storing the ashes of a dead person. □ *After the inurnment, the cremains will be placed in the garden niche you have selected.* □ *You may take the urn with you, or deposit it here, in a garden niche.*

garden of honor a graveyard for military veterans. □ *He was laid to rest in the garden of honor.* □ *This section of the memorial grounds is the garden of honor.*

gay homosexual. (**Gay** is the term preferred by many homosexual people.) □ *Is Bob gay?* □ *I felt out of place at the party. All the other men there were gay.*

G.D. "Goddamned." □ *Shut up and listen for just one G.D. minute!* □ *I can't find my G.D. car keys!*

gee "Wow!" (A very mild replacement for *Jesus!*) □ *Gee! What a surprise!* □ *Gee, I didn't know that.*

gee whiz "How surprising!" (A mild replacement for *Jesus!*) □ *Gee whiz, guys, I wish you would have told me you were going to the movies.* □ *Gee whiz! Look at the rain come down!*

gender sex. □ *The law forbids discrimination on the basis of gender.* □ *I could not tell that young person's gender by looking at him or her.*

gender-free language language that does not have a bias against women. □ *The university encourages its scholars to use gender-free language in any publications.* □ *The handbook on gender-free language suggests using* they, *or* he or she, *instead of* him, *for a generic pronoun.*

generalist a person who does many kinds of work. (Replaces *jack-of-all-trades*, which does not include women.) □ *Jill paints houses, does carpentry, and repairs cars as well. She's a generalist.* □ JOB INTERVIEWER: *Are you a specialist in hardware or software?* CANDIDATE: *I'm a generalist, really. I can do both.*

general seating See festival seating.

generously proportioned fat; large. □ *She is generously proportioned, and her face is lovely.* □ *Although he is generously proportioned, he is in good physical condition.*

genitals AND **genitalia** the sex organs. □ *Warts appeared on the patient's genitals.* □ *The diagram showed the location of the bird's genitalia.*

gentleman cow a bull. (Old-fashioned. See also **he-cow.**) □ *All of these calves were fathered by the same gentleman cow.* □ *The farmer sent the gentleman cows to be slaughtered.*

gentleman friend a male sexual partner. (See also **lady friend.**) □ *Mr. Holt is my grandmother's gentleman friend.* □ *By all means come to the party, and bring your gentleman friend.*

gentrification the practice of repairing old buildings in poor neighborhoods, so that poor people can no longer afford to live there. □ *Gentrification has begun in this neighborhood, and there is an uneasy mix of rich and poor ten-*

ants. □ *The neighbors disagreed about whether or not gentrification was a good thing.*

gents' (room) a toilet for men and boys. (See also **ladies' (room)**.) □ *Where's the gents'?* □ *Excuse me. I need to use the gents' room.*

gestational mother the woman who carries and gives birth to a child. (See also **surrogate mother**.) □ *The adoptive parents paid the gestational mother's medical expenses.* □ *Although Linda provided the ovum necessary to conceive the baby, she was not the gestational mother.*

get cold feet See **have cold feet**.

get physical to have sex. (Slang.) □ *They had been going out for months before they started to get physical.* □ *Somehow I knew tonight was the night. We were going to get physical.*

get something pay for something. □ *No, no. Put your purse away. I'll get lunch.* □ *Let me get the movie, and you can get the popcorn and drinks.*

getting on (in years) old. □ *Mom is getting on. She can't travel as much as she used to.* □ *Mrs. Hathaway is getting on in years, but she is still perfectly able to take care of herself.*

ghost (writer) a person who writes something for someone else. □ *He didn't write that autobiography. He hired a ghost.* □ *I heard a rumor that the novelist doesn't really write her own books anymore. She has a whole team of ghost writers.*

gifted intelligent or talented. □ *The school has afternoon programs for gifted students.* □ *Sylvia is a gifted violinist.*

gingerbread cookie AND **gingerbread figure** a spicy cookie shaped like a person. (Replaces *gingerbread man,* which does not include women.) □ *Every holiday season, our family cuts out and decorates gingerbread cookies and brings them to children at the hospital.* □ *The bakery window was full of cute little gingerbread figures.*

girl a prostitute. □ *The madam had six girls working for her.* □ *Three girls stood outside the movie theater, soliciting the men who walked by.*

give (one's) notice to quit one's job. □ *Did you hear that James is leaving? He gave his notice yesterday.* □ *Lisa gave notice today. She got a job offer from another company.*

give up the ghost to die. (Often used to describe machines breaking down.) □ *The old man gave up the ghost.* □ *My poor old car finally gave up the ghost.*

glamour photograph a sexually provocative photograph. (See also **boudoir photograph**.) □ *She posed for a set of glamour photographs and gave them to her boyfriend.* □ *The photographer specializes in glamour photographs. He has a number of sexy costumes for you to choose from.*

glands the testicles. (Similarly: bobbles, clock-weights, (family) jewels, gonads, marbles, nads, testimonials, vitals.) □ *His glands swelled up. It was really painful.* □ *You can't hire a woman just because she's pretty. Stop thinking with your glands.*

glass ceiling the job level beyond which women are not promoted. □ *The glass ceiling in our company is sadly obvious. There are dozens of female assistant vice presidents, but not one female vice president, and of course, the president is a man.* □ *The professor argued that there is no glass ceiling in the university.*

glow to sweat. (Cute.) □ *She was really glowing after our brisk walk.* □ *The hot bath made me glow.*

gluteus maximus the buttocks. □ *Get your gluteus maximus out of my chair.* □ *The dog bit him right in the gluteus maximus.*

go 1. to defecate or urinate. □ *Mommy, I have to go.* □ *I had drunk a big glass of water at breakfast, so by the time I got to the office, I really had to go.* **2.** to die. □ *When I go, I want you to have my china plate collection.* □ *George hasn't been the same since his wife went.*

go all the way to have sexual intercourse. (Slang.) □ *I hear Betty and Frank went all the way.* □ *Is it true that you and your boyfriend go all the way?*

go Dutch [for each person] to pay for him- or herself. □ *I don't want you to pay for my ticket. Let's go Dutch.* □ *Is it still considered a date if you go Dutch?*

go home AND **be taken home** to die. □ *She's been suffering a long time. She's ready to go home.* □ *When I go home, the Lord will meet me.* □ *I'm calling to tell you that Aunt Lucy was taken home last night.*

golden ager an old person. (See also golden years.) □ *We offer special tours for golden agers.* □ *Our retirement community is full of lively golden agers.*

golden handshake the money that a company pays someone who has been fired. □ *His contract included a $50,000 golden handshake.* □ *They let her go, but they gave her a golden handshake to soften the blow.*

golden parachute a contract requiring an employer to pay an employee a certain amount of money if the employee is fired. □ *Jane: I heard Sarah lost her job. Poor woman. Jill: Don't feel bad for her. She had a golden parachute.* □ *The manager's golden parachute was the equivalent of a year's salary.*

golden years old age. (See also **golden ager**.) □ *To enjoy your golden years to the fullest, start planning for retirement now.* □ *Many people take up a new hobby in their golden years.*

gold star mother the mother of a soldier killed in war. □ *The parade honored gold star mothers.* □ *She was a gold star mother twice over. Two of her sons fell in the European theater.*

golly (Moses) "Wow!" (A very mild replacement for "My God!" See also **gosh**.) □ *Golly! Will you look at that beautiful car!* □ *Golly Moses, that was fun!*

gone 1. dead. □ *"There was nothing we could do. I'm afraid he's gone," said the doctor.* □ *Harry is a widower. His wife has been gone for ten years.* **2.** pregnant. (Usually used in the expression *so many months gone*.) □ *Sarah: Jill is about due, isn't she? Jane: No, she's only six months gone.* □ *Maria's only three months gone, but she's starting to show already.*

gone before AND **gone ahead** dead; having died before. □ *My Daddy is gone before.* □ *Her husband is gone ahead.*

good grief AND **good gravy** "How amazing!" (A mild substitute for "good God!") □ *Good grief! This movie is going to be three hours long!* □ *Good gravy, are my feet tired!*

go over to leave one's country and go to an enemy country; to defect. □ *When the ballet company visited New York, two of the dancers decided to go over.* □ *He had been spying for the Americans for many years, and he finally went over.*

go pee(-pee) See pee.

gosh "Wow!" (A mild replacement for "God!" See also golly (Moses).) □ *Gosh, that's a big tomato!* □ *Oh, my gosh! I forgot to put salt in the soup!*

goshdarn worthless. (A mild replacement for *goddamned.*) □ *It's too dark out. I can't see a goshdarn thing.* □ *That's a goshdarn shame. I'm sorry.*

go steady with someone See go with someone.

go the way of all flesh to die. □ *In her eighty-eighth year, she went the way of all flesh.* □ *He is no longer living. He has gone the way of all flesh.*

go through some hard times 1. to be depressed. □ *JILL: Bill really looks bad. MARIA: He's been going through some hard times since his dad died.* □ *Try to treat Lisa with extra consideration. She's going through some hard times, and as her friends, we should let her know we care.* **2.** to have no money. □ *Susie lost her job, so her family is going through some hard times.* □ *They've been going through some hard times ever since the flood destroyed their house.*

go to a better place AND **go to a better world** to die. □ *Don't cry. She's gone to a better place.* □ *I took comfort in the thought that my child had gone to a better world.*

go to bed with someone to have sexual intercourse with someone. □ *Harry wants to go to bed with me.* □ *How many men have you gone to bed with?*

go to join someone to die, and therefore join someone who is dead. □ *She went to join her beloved husband.* □ *Don't be sad for me. I'm going to join my darling wife.*

go to meet one's Maker to die. □ *Grandpa went to meet his Maker.* □ *Shortly after giving birth, the poor woman went to meet her Maker.*

go to one's (last) reward AND **go to one's just reward** to die. □ *After a long and useful life, she went to her last reward.* □ *When I go to my reward, I hope you'll look after my kids for me.* □ *He was a good and faithful servant, and he has gone to his just reward.*

go under [for a business] to fail. (Slang.) □ *That restaurant on the corner will never go under. Their food is too good.* □ *When the big discount store opened up, a lot of little shops went under.*

go upstairs to urinate or defecate. (Refers to the location of the toilet in some houses.) □ *He excused himself to go upstairs.* □ *Excuse me a moment. I must go upstairs.*

gourmand a person who likes to eat a lot; a glutton. (French.) □ *This restaurant is a gourmand's paradise. They serve large portions.* □ *I'm a gourmand when it comes to seafood.*

go wee(-wee) AND **wee** to urinate. (Baby talk.) □ *Do you need to go wee-wee?* □ *I have to go wee.* □ *I need to wee. Real bad.*

go West to die. (Sometimes used to describe a machine breaking down.) □ *She lived to the age of ninety-seven, and then she went West.* □ *That computer has really gone West. There's nothing I can do to fix it.*

go with someone AND **go steady with someone** to have a romantic relationship with someone. (Can also imply *to have sex with someone.*) □ *Sally has been going with*

Mark for two months now. □ *He wants to go steady with her. He doesn't want her to see other guys.*

gracious (me)! "How surprising!" (A very mild replacement for "My God!") □ *Gracious me! You cleaned all the windows!* □ *Gracious! It's hot out!*

graft taking bribes. □ *The newspaper article accused the mayor of graft.* □ *When the official's graft was discovered, it cost her her job.*

grande dame a fat woman. (French.) □ *It is difficult to find tailored clothes for the grande dame.* □ *The store sells dresses and accessories for grandes dames.*

grant-writing skills the ability to write grant proposals that get money. (Replaces *grantsmanship*, which does not include women.) □ *We need a development associate with outstanding grant-writing skills.* □ *Susan's grant-writing skills were legendary in the arts community.*

graphic AND **explicit** showing sex or violence plainly. □ *The graphic scenes in the movie are not suitable for children.* □ *The stories in the dirty magazine were very explicit.*

gratification sexual intercourse; sexual satisfaction. □ *Since she could not get gratification at home, she decided to seek it elsewhere.* □ *Gratification was the most important thing in Harry's life.*

gratify someone's desires to have sex with someone. □ *The prostitute promised to gratify her customer's desires.* □ *That night, he gratified her desires.*

gratuity a tip. □ *A fifteen percent gratuity will be added to the bill for parties of six or more.* □ *It is customary to leave a gratuity for the housekeeper in your hotel.*

great certainty, the death. □ *We must all face the great certainty.* □ *She knew she was nearing the great certainty.*

great leveler, the death. (Literary.) □ *The great leveler makes us all equal.* □ *The great leveler deals alike with great people and small.*

Great Scott! "Wow!" (A replacement for "Good God!") □ *Great Scott! What a terrible thunderstorm!* □ *Great Scott! I've lost my wallet!*

Greek society a college fraternity or sorority. (Replaces *fraternity* for a men's organization and *sorority* for women's.) □ *Many of our students choose to join a Greek society.* □ *The Greek societies had a reputation for throwing wild parties.*

Grim Reaper, the death. (Death is personified as a harvester or reaper, cutting people down with a sickle.) □ *The Grim Reaper will come for us all.* □ *She narrowly escaped the Grim Reaper in that car accident.*

groin the genitals. □ *The football player had been kicked in the groin.* □ *The native people wear small aprons that barely cover their groins.*

group home a house for people who cannot live on their own. □ *Michael lives in a group home for developmentally disabled adults.* □ *The group home helps recovering addicts learn to live a drug-free life.*

growth a cancer. □ *The doctor found a growth in Paula's breast.* □ *Unfortunately, the growth is malignant.*

growth experience AND **growth opportunity** AND **learning experience** an unpleasant experience. □ *This job has been a growth experience for me. I've learned so* much. □ *I looked at the loss of my home as a growth opportunity.* □ *Jim said that his trip to Mexico turned out to be a real learning experience.*

guest worker a migrant worker. □ *The melon plantation employed over a hundred guest workers every summer.* □ *A number of guest workers come to work in the factories here.*

guff nonsense. (Old-fashioned.) □ *I don't trust Harry. He always talks a lot of guff.* □ *Don't you believe any of her guff.*

gunner a soldier who maintains and fires heavy guns. (Replaces *artilleryman*, which does not include women.) □ *Sarah and Michael both trained as gunners.* □ *The unit had five gunners.*

guy Friday See gal Friday.

hair loss the process of going bald. □ *Men, do you suffer from hair loss?* □ *This new treatment can actually reverse hair loss.*

hairpiece a wig. □ *Jim is pretty thin on top, so he wears a hairpiece.* □ *When he started to go gray, his hairpiece no longer matched his hair.*

(hair) stylist a person who cuts and styles hair; a barber. □ *I made an appointment with my hair stylist.* □ *One of our stylists will be with you shortly.*

halfway house a place for people to live who have just left a prison or hospital. □ *After she got out of jail, she was in a halfway house for awhile.* □ *The halfway house helped its residents to find jobs and permanent places to live.*

Halifax Hell. (Old-fashioned.) □ *He was really making me mad, so I told him to go to Halifax.* □ *If she keeps living an evil life, she's going to go straight to Halifax.*

halitosis bad breath. □ *These mint drops will put an end to halitosis.* □ *Halitosis may be a sign of tooth decay.*

handicappism a bias against people with handicaps. (See also **ableism**.) □ *The new law was intended to do away with handicappism in hiring practices.* □ *"Handicappism comes out in some small, strange ways," said Brian, who uses a wheelchair. "For instance, if I'm with an able-bodied person, other able-bodied people will talk to my companion, but not directly to me."*

handyman's special a house in bad condition. (See also fixer-upper.) □ *A handyman's special can be a good value for your money, if you're willing to put a little work into it.* □ *By the time I paid for a new roof, new plumbing, and new electrical wiring, my handyman's special cost me as much as a brand-new house.*

hanky-panky sexual intercourse. □ *Unless I'm mistaken, those two are up to some hanky-panky.* □ *The resident manager would not tolerate any hanky-panky in the dorm rooms.*

Hansen's disease a disease that damages the skin, face, and limbs. (Replaces *leprosy*.) □ *The doctor is working on a new treatment for Hansen's disease.* □ *Many people with Hansen's disease come to this clinic.*

happen to be to be. □ *Linda is a Muslim who happens to be of European descent.* □ *Most of the single parents in our support group happen to be women.*

happy drunk. (Slang.) □ *I get pretty happy after just one beer.* □ *Bill is way too happy to drive, I think.*

happy event the birth of a child. □ *I hear you're expecting. When is the happy event?* □ *The happy event will take place sometime in February.*

happy hour a time, usually in the afternoon or evening, when alcoholic drinks are sold cheaply at a bar or restaurant. □ *Let's go to happy hour at Sonny's.* □ *The gang from the office goes to happy hour every Friday.*

happy release death, especially death after a painful illness or injury. □ *Don't cry because Mama's gone. It was a happy release.* □ *The sick man yearned for his happy release.*

harass someone to make unwanted sexual advances to someone. □ *He was fired for harassing a female employee.* □ *He denied that he was harassing her. He said he had only asked her for a date.*

harbor chief AND **harbor superintendent** the person in charge of a harbor. (Replaces *harbormaster*.) □ *Before you enter the harbor, you have to check with the harbor chief.* □ *The harbor superintendent informed me that the ship had departed three hours earlier.*

hard of hearing deaf or nearly deaf. □ *I'm a little hard of hearing. Could you repeat that, please?* □ *She wears a hearing aid in each ear because she is hard of hearing.*

hardware weapons. □ *The gang members had better hardware than the police who were supposed to arrest them.* □ *They have sufficient hardware to launch a terrible nuclear attack.*

harlot a prostitute. (Because **harlot** is used for this meaning in English translations of the Bible, it is often used by Christian fundamentalists.) □ *Mine eyes are offended by the young women dressed as harlots.* □ *Repent! Fornicators and harlots!*

harm oneself See do oneself harm.

harvest something to kill or hunt something. □ *The game wardens harvest the deer every fall.* □ *If we don't harvest the rabbits, they will destroy all the plants in the area.*

have a baby on the way AND **have another on the way** to be pregnant. □ *Lisa is taking good care of herself because she has a baby on the way.* □ *Bill and Nancy have two kids, and another on the way.*

have a bun in the oven to be pregnant. (Cute.) □ *JILL: Are you going to Linda's baby shower next week? JANE: My goodness! I had no idea Linda had a bun in the oven!* □ *I called to tell you our happy news. I have a bun in the oven!*

have a drinking problem See have an alcohol problem.

have a few too many See have one too many.

have an accident 1. to urinate in one's clothes. □ *Little Billy had an accident and had to go home and change his pants.* □ *Her bladder condition kept her inside. She was afraid of having an accident if she left home.* **2.** to become pregnant without planning to. □ *They were taking precautions, but they had an accident, so they had to get married.* □ *She had an accident when she was sixteen. She gave the baby up for adoption.*

have an alcohol problem AND **have a drinking problem** to be a drunkard. □ *He has an alcohol problem. It got so bad that he almost lost his job.* □ *If you have a drinking problem, our clinic can help.*

have another on the way See have a baby on the way.

have a reputation to have a reputation for being willing to have sex. (Usually used to describe young people, especially girls.) □ *She isn't a nice girl. She has a reputation.*

□ *I know she has a reputation, but she seems like a sweet person.*

have a roving eye to be interested in having sexual relations outside of marriage. (Usually used to describe men.) □ *Poor Maria. Her husband has a roving eye.* □ *When they were first married, he had a roving eye.*

have a weight problem to be fat; to be heavy. □ *He had a weight problem when he was a teenager, but he slimmed down once he started exercising.* □ *She has a weight problem, but she's a lovely woman.*

have carnal knowledge of someone to have had sex with someone. (Formal.) □ *The complaint alleged that he had had carnal knowledge of a minor child.* □ *She had never before had carnal knowledge of a man.*

have cold feet AND **get cold feet** to be too afraid to do something. □ *The bridegroom got cold feet on the day of the wedding.* □ *Sally said I should try the high diving board, but I had cold feet.*

have intimate relations with someone to have sex with someone. □ *I understand that Jim once had intimate relations with Sarah.* □ *Rumor has it that she has had intimate relations with someone other than her husband.*

have one's hand in the till AND **have one's finger in the till** to steal money from one's employer. □ *James couldn't afford that car on just his salary. He must have his hand in the till.* □ *Sally was outraged when she found that one of her sales clerks had his finger in the till.*

have one's name inscribed in the book of life to die. □ *He was a beloved father, brother, and friend, and he has his name inscribed in the book of life.* □ *By the time she* *was twenty, her parents, brothers, and sister had all had their names inscribed in the book of life.*

have one's way with someone to have sexual relations with someone, possibly against that person's will. □ *He invited her up to his apartment, hoping to have his way with her.* □ *Now that you have had your way with me, do I mean nothing to you?*

have one too many AND **have a few too many** to be drunk. □ *He had one too many, and now he's throwing up.* □ *You'd better not drive. I think you've had a few too many.*

have relations with someone to have sexual relations with someone. □ *While engaged to Mary, he was having relations with at least two other women.* □ *She was having relations with one of her employees, which was strictly against policy.*

have to get married [for a couple] to get married because the woman is pregnant. □ *They didn't have a long engagement. They had to get married, you see.* □ *They had to get married, and their first baby was born seven months later.*

have words to argue. □ *From the sound of things, Bill and his father had words last night.* □ *We had words on the subject of money.*

head the person in charge of a private school. (Replaces *headmaster* for men and *headmistress* for women.) □ *If you continue to misbehave, you'll have to go explain yourself to the head.* □ *Rita is the head of Mount Maple Academy.*

head brewer the person in charge of a brewery. (Replaces *brewmaster*.) □ *Our head brewer has studied beer making in Germany.* □ *The head brewer personally inspects every batch.*

health care medicine. □ *It's sometimes hard to get good health care in rural areas.* □ *Our clinic believes in preventive health care and health maintenance.*

healthy 1. fat; large. □ *I like to see healthy young folks with some meat on their bones.* □ *She's a big, healthy woman.* **2.** big-breasted. □ *He prefers women with healthy figures.* □ *My, she's quite a healthy girl, isn't she?*

hearing impaired deaf or nearly deaf. □ *This program is closed-captioned for our hearing-impaired viewers.* □ *His mother happens to be hearing impaired, so he learned to sign at an early age.*

heated violently angry. □ *They exchanged heated words, and then Larry stomped out of the room and slammed the door.* □ *Their argument soon became heated.*

heavenly rest AND **eternal rest** death. □ *Our loved one has gone to his heavenly rest.* □ *I think of her at peace, in eternal rest.*

heavy going boring. □ *The first part of the movie is heavy going, but the second half is well worth it.* □ MICHAEL: *How did you like Pearson's new novel?* JAMES: *To be honest, I found it pretty heavy going.*

heavy(-set) fat; large. □ *Did you see John when you were at the office? He's about my height, kind of heavy, brown hair, glasses?* □ *She may be heavy-set, but she sure can move fast.*

he-cow a bull. (See also **gentleman cow.**) □ *I've got six heifers and five he-cows.* □ *Look out for that old he-cow. He's got a nasty temper on him.*

heir a person who inherits something. (Replaces *heir* for men and boys and *heiress* for women and girls.) □ *Maria* *is the heir to a large fortune.* □ *When I die, my sons and daughters will be my heirs.*

help servants. □ *We don't socialize with the help, dear.* □ *She hired some help for the big party.*

help oneself to something to steal something. □ *She helped herself to the cash in her father's wallet and left the house.* □ *The burglars helped themselves to my jewelry and all my silverware.*

hemorrhage to bleed. □ *She was hemorrhaging internally.* □ *The doctors tried to prevent the injury from hemorrhaging.*

hereafter, the death. □ *We shall meet again in the hereafter.* □ *She has gone to join her loved ones in the hereafter.*

hero a person or character who does good deeds. (Replaces *hero* for men and boys and *heroine* for women and girls.) □ *She is a hero. She saved the lives of those children.* □ *The hero of the story is a young boy named Frank.*

herstory the history of women. (A play on words. *History* can be divided into the words *his story*, the story of men, and so *her story* or *herstory* is the story of women.) □ *The herstory of our foremothers is often ignored in school textbooks.* □ *We must reclaim our herstory by celebrating women who have done great things.*

high intoxicated; drunk or having taken drugs. (Slang. See also **elevated**.) □ *The young man was obviously high when he was arrested.* □ *You sound funny. Are you high?*

Higher Power God. □ *On this spiritual retreat, you may commune with your Higher Power, whatever you understand it to be.* □ *I place my trust in a Higher Power.*

highlight something to bleach something, especially hair. □ *My stylist highlighted my hair in a few places.* □ *We can highlight your bangs to make your face look narrower.*

high scorer the person who scores the most points in a game. (Replaces *point man*, which does not include women.) □ *Trish was the high scorer in the basketball tournament.* □ *This season's high scorer will win a trophy.*

highway robber a person who robs travellers. (Replaces *highwayman*, which does not include women.) □ *"Stand and deliver!" cried the highway robber.* □ *The mail coach was held up by a highway robber.*

hind end the buttocks. □ *The sand at the beach was so hot that I burned my hind end.* □ *Quit that, or I'll slap you on your hind end.*

hindquarters the buttocks. □ *The bee stung me in my hindquarters, so I can't sit down comfortably.* □ *Those pants make your hindquarters look pretty broad.*

hiring freeze a stoppage in hiring people. (See also **freeze, wage freeze**.) □ *We really need a secretary, but we can't advertise for one because of the hiring freeze.* □ *As a cost containment measure, the company instituted a hiring freeze, effective immediately.*

hirsute hairy. □ *He was quite hirsute. His beard grew almost up to his eyes.* □ *Jim has hirsute hands.*

historic [of a building or neighborhood] old. □ *Visit our historic district.* □ *This beautiful, historic home is a handyman's special.*

hit a murder. □ *He was the victim of a gang hit.* □ *"Joey and Pretty Boy will take care of the hit," said the Boss.*

hogwash nonsense. (A mild replacement for *bullshit.*) □ *Jill's plan is just hogwash.* □ *You can't believe the hogwash you read in the papers these days.*

hoist operator a person who operates lift equipment. (Replaces *hoistman,* which does not include women.) □ *When the miners had entered the lift, they would signal the hoist operator that they were ready to go down.* □ *James and Paula are the hoist operators on the night shift.*

hold someone back to require someone to repeat a year of school. □ *If you can't pass any of your classes, we will have to hold you back.* □ *Because she needed extra time to learn, her teachers decided to hold her back a year.*

holiday having to do with Christmas. (**Holiday** sometimes has a more general meaning, including other winter religious holidays such as Chanukah and Kwanzaa. Judge from the context.) □ *We have a wide selection of holiday ornaments.* □ *Wrap a present to bring to the holiday gift exchange.*

Hollander a person from Holland. (Replaces *Dutchman* and *Dutchwoman.*) □ *This town was originally settled by Hollanders.* □ *If you want to do business in Holland, it is wise to have a Hollander for a business partner.*

Holy cow! AND **Holy cats!** AND **Holy Moses!** "How amazing!" (A mild replacement for "My God!") □ *Holy cow! Did you hear that thunder?* □ *Holy cats! How many books did you* buy? □ *Holy Moses! Look at the size of that squirrel!*

home 1. a house. □ *The real estate agent said, "I can show you a number of homes in that price range."* □ *This is a lovely home, built in 1926.* **2.** an institution for taking care of people who are old or mentally ill. □ *Grandpa can't take care of himself anymore, but I just can't bring myself to put him* *in a home.* □ *When her depression was very bad, Maria spent some time in a home.*

home economics the study of cooking, cleaning, sewing, and shopping. (See also **domestic science.**) □ *I have a degree in home economics.* □ *My background in home economics was very helpful when I first started working in the hotel industry.*

home equity loan a new mortgage; a loan against the money you have paid for your house. □ *They took out a home equity loan to finance their daughter's education.* □ *Isn't it time you took that worldwide cruise you've been planning? Consider a home equity loan from our bank to help make your dreams a reality.*

homely ugly. □ *She has a homely face, but a lovely figure.* □ *He's a homely man, but he's very sweet.*

homemade made in the same place where it is sold. □ *Our restaurant features homemade pies.* □ *The billboard said, "Try our homemade ice cream."*

homemaker a person who cooks, cleans, mends, and shops for his or her family. (Replaces *housewife.*) □ BILL: *What do you do, Jane?* JANE: *I'm a full-time homemaker.* □ *The economic study looked at homemakers and other unwaged workers.*

homicide a murder. □ *The officer was investigating a homicide.* □ *Three homicides took place in this precinct last year.*

honorarium a payment. □ *The budget for the conference includes an honorarium for the invited speaker.* □ *The lecturer was given an honorarium for her talk.*

hooker a prostitute. (Slang.) □ *I had to walk past several hookers to get from my car to the hotel.* □ *He picked up a hooker in the bar.*

horizontally through having sex. □ *I'm told she earns her living horizontally.* □ *I've heard the rumors. I know people think I made my way to the top horizontally.*

hormones the menstrual cycle. □ *"My mood goes up and down with my hormones," said Lucy.* □ *Her hormones made her gain and lose weight every month.*

horse apple AND **road apple** the feces of a horse. (Folksy.) □ *Someone's been riding a horse on this road. I just saw a pile of horse apples.* □ *Be careful. Don't step in that road apple.*

horsefeathers nonsense. (A mild substitute for *bullshit*.) □ BILL: *Fred told me that tomatoes are poisonous.* JANE: *Horsefeathers. Tomatoes are good for you.* □ *Those rumors are just a load of horsefeathers.*

hospitality alcoholic drinks. □ *The conference fee includes hospitality at the party on the last night.* □ *Hospitality is available in the lounge.*

host a person who entertains guests. (Replaces *host* for men and *hostess* for women.) □ *Jerry and Louisa are the hosts of the party.* □ *Maria is a famous talk-show host.*

hostess a prostitute working in a nightclub. (**Hostess** does not always have this meaning. Judge from the context.) □ *One of our lovely hostesses will see to your every need.* □ *She used to walk the streets, but now she works as a hostess.*

housebroken See house-trained.

house-cleaning the firing of a lot of people in order to reduce corruption. □ *The new head of the agency began a thorough house-cleaning.* □ *When it became clear that charges would be brought against several of the company's officials, the board of directors performed a house-cleaning.*

household technician a person who cleans houses or other buildings. (See also **housekeeper**.) □ *The hotel is hiring household technicians.* □ *I hired a household technician to help me with the spring cleaning.*

housekeeper a person who cleans houses or hotels. (Replaces *maid*. See also **household technician**.) □ *Make sure to leave a tip for the housekeeper.* □ *I have a housekeeper who comes in twice a week.*

house of correction a prison. □ *He was sentenced to five years in the county's house of correction.* □ *The Jones House of Correction was built in the 1950s, when violent crime was much less common here.*

house of ill repute AND **house of ill fame** a house of prostitution. (See also **bawdy house, bordello**.) □ *The sign says "Health Club," but everyone knows it's a house of ill repute.* □ *He made a lot of money by running a house of ill fame.*

houseparent a person who supervises a place where groups of young people live, such as a college dormitory. (Replaces *housemother*, which does not include men.) □ *I work as a houseparent in a group home for homeless youth.* □ *Be sure to notify the houseparent if you are going to be out all night.*

house-trained AND **housebroken** [of a pet animal] trained not to urinate or defecate inside the house. □ *These* *puppies are already house-trained. □ Is your dog house-broken?*

(housing) project apartments or houses built by the government for poor people. □ *I grew up in a housing project.* □ *My mother knew every kid who lived in the project by name, and she knew which ones were up to no good.*

humankind the human race. (Replaces *mankind*, which does not include women.) □ *Her research may be a great benefit to humankind.* □ *Humankind is unique in its ability to change the environment for its own purposes.*

human-made made by people. (Replaces *manmade*, which does not include women.) □ *Those rocks almost look like human-made structures.* □ *Nylon is a human-made material.*

human resources having to do with employment. □ *One of our human resources specialists will contact you for an interview.* □ *The human resources department investigates all complaints of harassment in the workplace.*

hygienically challenged [of a person] dirty. (Jocular.) □ *Bill always smells terrible. He must be hygienically challenged.* □ *A couple of the kids in my class are, let us say, hygienically challenged.*

I

ice-cream vendor a person who sells ice cream from a truck or a stand. (Replaces *ice-cream man*, which does not include women.) □ *Whenever the children heard the ice-cream vendor's bell, they begged their parents for money for a treat.* □ *Sally worked as an ice-cream vendor last summer.*

if anything should happen AND **if anything happens** "If a disaster happens." □ *I'll give you the phone number of my hotel, so that you can reach me if anything happens.* □ *If anything should happen, I want you to look after my children.*

I hear you "I disagree with you." □ *JANE: This budget does not include enough money for salaries. It is not acceptable. BILL: I hear you. But I think we need to consider the long range.* □ *BILL: That secretary is incompetent and rude. He should be fired. JANE: I hear you. But I think you'll find that most people's experience with him has been different.*

I'll be hanged "I'll be damned." (An exclamation of surprise.) □ *Well, I'll be hanged. She really did send me the check.* □ *I'll be hanged! You were right after all!*

illegitimate born of unmarried parents. (Replaces *bastard*.) □ *He has two illegitimate children.* □ *Technically, the* *baby was illegitimate, but her parents got married shortly after she was born.*

illicit having to do with sexual intercourse outside of marriage. □ *She had an illicit affair.* □ *He tried to hide his illicit activities.*

I'll let you go "It is time to end this phone conversation." □ *Well, I'll let you go. It's getting late.* □ *I have to go to work early tomorrow, so I'll let you go.*

imaginative untruthful. □ *"The young reporter's imaginative journalism has done a great deal of damage to my reputation," the politician claimed.* □ *Paula's imaginative bookkeeping kept her theft from being detected for many months.*

imbibe to drink alcohol. □ *She has imbibed rather a bit too much.* □ *He has been known to imbibe at parties, but seldom drinks at other times.*

immediate burial a burial without a funeral ceremony before it. □ *Immediate burial is certainly one of the less costly arrangements we can provide.* □ *The deceased's family chose immediate burial.*

immediate need See at-need.

immolate oneself to kill oneself. (Formal.) □ *He immolated himself as a gesture of protest against the war.* □ *The villagers immolated themselves rather than surrender to the enemy.*

impaired lacking an ability to do something. (See **visually impaired, hearing impaired, mobility impaired**.) □ *I teach learning-impaired children.* □ *The therapist worked with the speech-impaired young man.*

impediment a handicap. □ *She has a speech impediment.* □ *The crutches help him with his impediment.*

improper sexual. (Old-fashioned.) □ *He made improper advances to his host's daughter.* □ *She grinned and made an improper suggestion.*

impropriety a sexual relationship outside of marriage. (Old-fashioned.) □ *There was some hint of impropriety in the lady's past.* □ *He had committed an impropriety with a woman beneath his station.*

improvident poor and unable to earn money. □ *She supported the family when her improvident father could not.* □ *The improvident young man was always asking his friends for money.*

in AND **inside** in prison. (Slang.) □ *I was in jail once myself, and I can always spot someone who has been inside.* □ *How long are you in for?*

in (a) conference See in a meeting.

in a delicate condition pregnant. □ *Are you sure you're up for this hike? I know you're in a delicate condition.* □ *She shouldn't be lifting those boxes. She's in a delicate condition.*

in a meeting AND **in (a) conference** not willing to talk to you. (See also **unavailable**.) □ *I'm sorry, Ms. Smith is in a meeting. Would you like to speak to her voice mail?* □ *Bob is in a conference right now. Would you like to leave a message?* □ *I'm sorry, Mr. Farrell is in conference. I can take a message if you would like.*

inamorata a female sexual partner. (Italian.) □ *His inamorata is twenty-five years younger than he is.* □ *Bob says that his inamorata is starting to hint about marriage.*

in an interesting condition pregnant. (Somewhat old-fashioned.) □ *Young Mrs. Appledore is in an interesting condition.* □ *The bride appeared to be in an interesting condition.*

inappropriate wrong, rude, or illegal. □ *I thought that was an inappropriate remark on Bill's part.* □ *Using the office phone for personal calls is highly inappropriate.* □ *He made inappropriate demands of his employees.*

incentive something given to reward extra work. □ *Our pay scale includes special incentives for the top three salespeople every month.* □ *The trip to the Mediterranean was an incentive for executives who met their hiring goals.*

incident a disaster. (See also **episode, event**.) □ *If an incident occurs, notify the appropriate authorities.* □ *The eyewitnesses' accounts of the incident suggested that the gunman had been carrying at least two weapons.*

inclement [of weather] bad. □ *We had inclement weather during most of our stay.* □ *Aside from one or two days of inclement weather, it was sunny the whole time I was in Paris.*

inclusive without bias. □ *You should strive to use inclusive language in your reports. For instance, do not refer to* policemen. *Refer to* police officers. *Some of them may be women.* □ *The neighborhood association strove to be inclusive, to reach out to people of color and whites alike.*

income bracket the level of money someone makes. □ *Most of the people who bought this car model were in middle or high income brackets.* □ *The survey found that the show's viewers were in the lower income brackets.*

income level the amount of money someone makes. □ *He was sure that a college degree was necessary to guarantee* *a decent income level.* □ *The income levels in this neighborhood are generally low.*

income maintenance welfare. □ *Sixty percent of the families in this neighborhood depend on income maintenance to make their rent payments.* □ *Without some form of income maintenance, the majority of my constituents would soon be homeless.*

incontinence the inability to hold one's urine or feces. □ *Ever since her surgery, she has suffered from incontinence.* □ *He found these attacks of incontinence terribly embarrassing.*

incontinence pad a piece of paper or cloth for absorbing an adult's urine. □ *I have to wear an incontinence pad to protect my clothes.* □ *The nurse's aide changed the patient's incontinence pad.*

incontinent unable to hold one's urine or feces. □ *The stroke left her incontinent, poor dear.* □ *He was severely developmentally disabled. He was incontinent and unable to speak.*

inconvenience a problem. □ *Not knowing how to speak the language was a major inconvenience on our trip to Portugal.* □ *The lack of a computer may be an inconvenience.*

inconvenienced crippled. (Old-fashioned.) □ *He is inconvenienced by the loss of one hand.* □ *Although inconvenienced by her weak spine, she never complained.*

incursion an invasion. □ *The incursion of the rebel troops sent a panic through the city.* □ *The enemy has made several incursions, mostly unsuccessful, into our territory.*

in custody in jail. □ *The police have two suspects in custody.* □ *You cannot keep my client in custody without bringing a charge against her.*

indecency 1. nudity. □ *The man who exposed himself in the park was arrested for public indecency.* □ *She took her shirt off to get a suntan and was arrested for indecency.* **2.** anal or oral sex. (Somewhat old-fashioned and possibly offensive to homosexual people.) □ *He committed acts of indecency with other young men.* □ *As a woman of the streets, she had become familiar with a number of kinds of indecency.*

independent contractor a worker without a steady job. (See also **consultant**.) □ *I was downsized from my last job, and I've been working as an independent contractor.* □ *We've hired several independent contractors to help us with this programming project.*

independent means a lot of inherited money. (See also **means**.) □ *She is a woman of independent means.* □ *He is able to write poetry full-time because he has independent means.*

independent school a private school. □ *They sent their kids to independent schools, although they believe very strongly in public education.* □ *The independent school offers special classes in the arts.*

indigenous people the people who lived in a region before invaders settled there. (Replaces *natives* or *native people*.) □ *The indigenous people of Taiwan were conquered by the Chinese.* □ *The conquistadores did not respect the religions or cultures of the indigenous peoples they encountered.*

indigent poor. □ *Most of the clinic's patients are indigent.* □ *The shelter helps indigent women learn skills with which to support themselves and their children.*

indigestion an upset stomach; nausea. □ *Do you suffer from indigestion? Insta-Calm gives instant relief.* □ *I ate too much too fast, and I got indigestion.*

indiscretion 1. sexual relations outside of marriage. □ *When she found out about her husband's indiscretions, she was furious.* □ *When she was a young woman, she committed several indiscretions.* **2.** the act of eating or drinking too much. □ *If food or drink indiscretions cause indigestion, this antacid gives instant relief.* □ *She woke with a headache from her indiscretions of the night before.*

indisposed 1. sick. □ *The day after the party, I was somewhat indisposed.* □ *A slight cold left her indisposed.* **2.** defecating or urinating. (Often used to explain why someone cannot come to the telephone or the door. Jocular.) □ *He can't come to the phone right now. He is indisposed.* □ *Sorry I didn't come to the door right away. I was indisposed.*

individual a person. □ *A number of individuals will be made redundant.* □ *I saw a suspicious-looking individual hanging around in front of the store.*

indulge to do something enjoyable that may be bad for you, such as drink alcohol or eat fatty foods. (See also **overindulge**.) □ *Larry: Champagne? Jane: I don't usually indulge, but I'll drink a glass in honor of the occasion.* □ *Scott brought a positively sinful chocolate cake to the party and told us all to indulge.*

(industrial) dispute AND **industrial action** a strike. □ *An industrial dispute arose between the bus drivers' union and the management.* □ *Owing to the garbage workers' dispute, garbage was not picked up in the city for over four weeks.* □ *The union leaders threatened an industrial action.*

industrial(ized) having industries. (See also **First World**, **Third World**. Replaces *advanced*. Compare with **non-industrialized**.) □ *Most of the world's wealth is in the hands of the industrialized nations.* □ *Historically, this country has had an agricultural economy, but it is gradually becoming industrial.*

industrial relations relations between management and labor. □ *The steel company prides itself on its healthy industrial relations.* □ *All of our arbitrators have strong backgrounds in industrial relations.*

inebriated drunk. □ *I'm sorry, sir, but I can't serve you another drink. You're already inebriated.* □ *How can she be inebriated? She had only two glasses of wine!*

in extremis about to die. (Latin.) □ *The patient was in extremis and had asked for a priest.* □ *In the doctor's judgment, the patient was in extremis.*

infidelity sexual relations outside of marriage. (See also **unfaithful**.) □ *He could not believe that his wife would commit infidelity.* □ *She accused him of infidelity.*

in flagrante (delicto) in the act of sexual intercourse. (Latin.) □ *He caught his wife and her lover in flagrante delicto.* □ *The photograph showed the two of them in flagrante.*

inflated exaggerated; false. □ *He has an inflated sense of his own importance.* □ *Her book contained an inflated account of her involvement with the famous trial.*

informant a person who tells secrets, especially to the police. (Replaces *informer*.) □ *My informant seemed pretty sure that there would be some gang activity here tonight.* □

The police had an informant who kept them aware of the gang's activities.

in heaven dead. □ *He explained to his little girl that her mother was in heaven.* □ *Our beloved brother is in heaven. We shall see him on the other side.*

inmate a prisoner. □ *There are three hundred inmates in this facility.* □ *There is an education program available for the inmates.*

inner city 1. a poor part of a city; a slum. □ *Pastor Middleton's church is in the inner city.* □ *She grew up in a housing project in the inner city.* **2.** having to do with the poor part of a city. □ *The camping program allows inner city children to enjoy outdoor activities.* □ *The clinic serves several inner city neighborhoods.*

in one's altogether AND **in the altogether** naked. □ *A man just ran down the street in his altogether!* □ *On weekends, she walks around the house in the altogether.*

in one's mid-years over the age of 40. □ *The magazine marketed itself to readers in their mid-years.* □ *You should begin planning for retirement well before you are in your mid-years.*

inoperable [of a disease] not able to be cured by surgery and therefore probably not curable. □ *I'm afraid the cancer is inoperable.* □ *Although your condition is inoperable, drug therapy may be of some help.*

inoperative 1. untrue. □ *The mayor's earlier statement is now inoperative.* □ *The promises I made on that occasion may be regarded as inoperative.* **2.** dead. □ *He rendered the enemy agent inoperative.* □ *I am pleased to report that both of our opponents are now inoperative.*

in recovery trying to give up alcohol or drugs. □ *When you are in recovery, it is important to take things one day at a time.* □ *Don't offer Alice a drink. She's in recovery, and she's having a hard time of it.*

inside See in.

insides internal organs, especially the stomach and intestines. □ *The roller coaster always ties my insides in knots.* □ *She went to the doctor. She's got some problem with her insides.*

insolvent without money. (A legal term.) □ *After only six months, the company was insolvent.* □ *My cousin is always insolvent and asking me for money.*

institute an organization. □ *The Willard Institute offers training in auto mechanics, data entry, and electronics repair.* □ *The study was published by the Institute for American Values.*

institution a mental hospital. □ *After being diagnosed with clinical depression, I spent three years in an institution.* □ *Thomas is a danger to himself and others. He should be in an institution.*

institutionalize someone to put someone in a mental hospital. (See also **commit someone**.) □ *They were heart-broken when the doctor said they ought to institutionalize their son.* □ *If she can't control herself, we may have to institutionalize her.*

intake room a room where prisoners wait. □ *The attorney went to the intake room to speak with her client.* □ *I spent fifteen hours in the intake room before they finally processed me and sent me to a cell.*

integration a mixture of people of different races. (Compare with **segregation**.) □ *The court order said that the town must achieve integration in its public schools.* □ *There is a high level of integration in our neighborhood.*

intelligence having to do with spying. (See also **counterintelligence**.) □ *The professor used her academic job as a cover for her intelligence work.* □ *The national intelligence agency had collected several thousand pages of information about the rising young politician.*

intelligence community in the United States, the Federal Bureau of Investigation and the Central Intelligence Agency. □ *The radical activist was well-known to the intelligence community.* □ *Some elected officials felt that the intelligence community had too much influence over national policy.*

intercourse the sexual joining of two individuals. □ *Although they had kissed and petted, they had never attempted intercourse.* □ *The health class taught that condoms prevent the spread of disease through intercourse.*

interfere with someone to sexually touch or have sexual intercourse with a child. □ *The teacher had been interfering with several students.* □ *Her stepfather had interfered with her when she was young.*

interment burial. □ *Interment will take place following the service.* □ *We drove out to the cemetery for the interment.*

interment industry, the the business of burying dead people. □ *We sell digging equipment and concrete vaults for the interment industry.* □ *The magazine has articles of interest to funeral service practitioners and other members of the interment industry.*

intern a prisoner. □ *The interns were put to work building a road.* □ *The reporter estimated there were two thousand interns in the prison camp.*

international crisis a war. □ *The military must be constantly alert in times of international crisis.* □ *This gross disregard of the treaty may result in an international crisis.*

internment camp a prison camp. □ *Prisoners of war were herded into unsanitary internment camps and kept on a starvation diet.* □ *The captured civilians were put in an internment camp outside of the city.*

intern someone to put someone in prison. □ *The dictator interned all the journalists in the country.* □ *We are going to intern you for your own protection.*

interrogate someone to question someone under torture. □ *The police interrogated the prisoner for seventy-two hours straight.* □ *They interrogated him, and he broke down.*

inter someone to bury someone. (See also **inurnment**. Often used in the passive voice.) □ *We will inter the deceased at Greenlawn Cemetery.* □ *He wanted to be interred next to his wife.*

intervention an invasion. □ *Our intervention into the country was at the request of its democratically elected leader.* □ *A multinational force will lead the intervention.*

intestinal fortitude courage. (Replaces *guts*. Coined by John W. Wilce, a football coach at Ohio State University.) □ *Standing up to the boss like that really took intestinal fortitude.* □ *What he lacks in intelligence, he makes up for in intestinal fortitude.*

in the altogether See in one's altogether.

in the black making money. (See also **in the red**.) □ *The company was in the black for the first time this year.* □ *After I pay off my student loan, I'll be in the black!*

in the Common Era AND **C.E.** after the year 1 according to the Western calendar. (Replaces *Anno Domini* and A.D. Compare with **Before the Common Era**.) □ *The comet was last seen in the year 1986 in the Common Era.* □ *The Huns invaded Gaul in 451 C.E.*

in the family way pregnant. (Folksy.) □ *Mary is in the family way again.* □ *The young couple was in the family way.*

in the red losing money. (See also **in the black**.) □ *State government has been operating in the red for five straight years.* □ *What with all those car repairs, we're going to be in the red this month.*

intimate apparel women's underwear. (See also **lingerie**.) □ *"You'll find bras and body shapers in the intimate apparel department," said the sales clerk at the department store.* □ *The catalog features intimate apparel for the grande dame.*

intoxicated drunk. (Often used as a legal term. Similarly: afloat, awash, bent out of shape, blind, blitzed, blotto, bombed, comfortable, dead to the world, decks awash, elevated, hammered, in liquor, in one's cups, loaded, plastered, seeing double, tight, tight as a tick, toasted, wasted.) □ *The driver was obviously intoxicated.* □ *Several of the passengers were intoxicated at the time they boarded the aircraft.*

in transition AND **transitional** going from poor to rich and therefore unstable. □ *It is a developing country, currently in transition.* □ *It is possible to get good real estate values in transitional neighborhoods such as this one.*

intrigue a secret sexual relationship. □ *He was carrying on an intrigue with his boss.* □ *I suspected that Bill and Maria were involved in an intrigue.*

in trouble pregnant without wanting to be. (Slang.) □ *He got his girlfriend in trouble.* □ *When Shirley was in trouble, her parents paid for her to have an abortion.*

intrusion detector AND **intruder detector** a burglar alarm. □ *The security guard kept an eye on the intrusion detector.* □ *An intruder detector can increase your sense of security as well as add value to your home.*

Inuit having to do with tribal people native to Greenland, Alaska, Canada, and Siberia. (Replaces *Eskimo*.) □ *The Inuit hunters were very familiar with that part of the coast.* □ *She learned the old stories from her Inuit grandfather.*

inurnment the placing of a dead person's ashes into an urn. (See also **inter someone**.) □ *The inurnment will immediately follow the cremation service.* □ *Only the immediate family will be present at the inurnment.*

inventory leakage AND **inventory adjustment** a loss from theft. (See also **shrinkage**.) □ *We anticipate an inventory leakage of about ten percent.* □ *The inventory adjustment was due both to shoplifting and to employees helping themselves.*

investigator a detective. □ *They hired a private investigator to find out who had been writing the obscene notes.* □ *The investigator was able to give me some very interesting background on several of my co-workers.*

invite someone to resign to fire someone. (See also **resign**.) □ *The board of trustees has invited me to resign.* □ *I resigned before my boss had a chance to invite me to resign.*

involved with someone having sexual relations with someone. □ *Is it true that Ron is involved with Tina?* □ *It is usually not a good idea for a manager to get involved with an employee.*

involvement a sexual relationship. □ *Her involvement with Bruce was years ago.* □ *I'm not ready for another involvement. I'd like to be by myself for awhile.*

irregular, an a paid soldier; a mercenary. □ *A unit of German irregulars was also involved in the battle.* □ *He was a highly trained irregular who had fought in several European and African conflicts.*

irregularities signs of something illegal. □ *The investigation found a number of irregularities in the company's finances.* □ *The article alleged that there were irregularities in some of the contributions made to the senator's campaign.*

irregularity the inability to defecate. (Replaces *constipation.*) □ *I recommend oatmeal for irregularity.* □ *This medication relieves irregularity within four hours.*

issue a problem. □ *The family has several issues, including alcohol dependency and domestic abuse.* □ *It is clear that there are issues with the product we have received from that vendor.*

it is all up with someone AND **it is all over with someone** someone is about to die. □ *I am afraid it is all up with Aunt Sarah. Her last surgery did not go well at all.* □ *The doctor told us that it was all over with Daddy. We sat for a moment in shock.*

jeepers (creepers) "What a surprise!" (A mild replacement for *Jesus Christ!*) □ *Jeepers creepers! You surprised me!* □ *Jeepers! Your dog certainly has grown!*

jeez (Louise) "Wow!" (Slang. A mild substitute for *Jesus Christ!*) □ *Jeez Louise, am I hungry!* □ *Well, jeez, you didn't have to do all that.*

Jellinek's disease alcoholism. □ *The clinic has several programs for the treatment of Jellinek's disease.* □ *As in many cases of Jellinek's disease, the entire family felt the effects of one person's drinking.*

Jezebel a prostitute. (From Jezebel, a Biblical character.) □ *The drunkards and the Jezebels filled the street after midnight.* □ *She made up her face and dressed like a Jezebel.*

Jiminy Cricket(s) "Wow!" (Slang. A very mild replacement for *Jesus Christ!*) □ *Jiminy Crickets, it's hot out there!* □ *Jiminy Cricket, what a lot of work I have to do!*

job an act of defecation. □ *I was finally able to do a job this morning. The oatmeal really helped.* □ *He hasn't done his job for several days, and I'm worried, doctor.*

job turning a decrease in pay and prestige that takes place when women begin doing a given job. □ *Many jobs in the insurance industry have undergone job turning in the last decade.* □ *Job turning in computer programming has made the field less attractive to many men.*

jock itch a fungus that grows on the penis and testicles. (See also **male itch(ing)**.) (Slang.) □ *Whenever I use the showers at the gym, I always wind up getting jock itch.* □ *He bought some medicated cream for his jock itch.*

john a toilet. (Slang.) □ *Excuse me. I need to go to the john.* □ *Where's the john?*

John Barleycorn alcohol. □ *John Barleycorn has been the downfall of many a man.* □ *She loved John Barleycorn better than life.*

journey worker a person who is learning a skill. (Replaces *journeyman*, which does not include women.) □ *As an actor, Beth is still a journey worker, but she has a lot of promise.* □ *The master carpenter had several journey workers on the crew.*

Judas Priest "What an unpleasant surprise!" (A replacement for *Jesus Christ!*) □ *Judas Priest! Do you have to wreck everything?* □ *Judas Priest! I can't believe how hard that test was!*

juice harp AND **mouth harp** a musical instrument made of wire and played by holding it in the mouth and plucking one end. (Replaces *Jew's harp*, which may be offensive to Jewish people.) □ *Sally played the guitar, and Bill accompanied her on the juice harp.* □ *He played a lively rhythm on the mouth harp.*

junket a pleasure trip disguised as a business trip. □ *The senator's junket included stops in Florida and the Bahamas.* □ *The medical conference was held in a popular skiing resort, so making the trip to attend it was in the nature of a junket.*

Junoesque [of a woman] fat; large. (From *Juno*, the Roman goddess of marriage, who is often depicted as a tall, fat woman.) □ *She had a Junoesque figure and beautiful skin.* □ *The dress was designed for Junoesque women.*

just good friends not having a sexual relationship. (Can imply the opposite.) □ *The movie star and her director insisted that they were just good friends.* □ *My goodness, no. Not at all. Tom and I are just good friends.*

juvenile a young criminal. (Note: juvenile does not always have this meaning. Judge from the context.) □ *The burglary was committed by a juvenile.* □ *The perpetrator was a juvenile.*

keep banker's hours to work for less than eight hours a day. □ *The advertising agency keeps banker's hours. They are only open until four.* □ *James doesn't really work full-time. He keeps banker's hours.*

kept woman a prostitute who works for only one customer. □ *His wife discovered he had a kept woman in the city.* □ *She found the life of a kept woman to be very lonely.*

kickback a bribe. (Slang.) □ *The congressman was taking kickbacks from the lumber companies.* □ *The police officer got kickbacks from the drug dealer.*

kleptomaniac a thief. □ *The kleptomaniac had plenty of money, but she stole things anyway.* □ *When so many things were missing from the office, I suspected that one of the employees must be a kleptomaniac.*

know someone biblically to have sexual intercourse with someone. (Some English translations of the Bible use *know someone* to mean *have sexual intercourse with someone.*) □ *Yes, Bill knows Sally. He knows her biblically, if you know what I mean.* □ *Is it true that you know that man biblically?*

labor organizer a person who urges workers to join a union. □ *Conditions at the plant were so bad that it was easy for the labor organizer to win support.* □ *Some workers claimed that the labor organizers had threatened them with violence if they refused to sign a union card.*

ladies' (room) a toilet for women and girls. (See also gents' (room).) □ *She excused herself and went to the ladies' room.* □ *I need to use the ladies'.*

lady dog a female dog. (Replaces *bitch*.) □ *All the male dogs in the neighborhood knew when that lady dog was in season.* □ *Is your dog a male or a lady dog?*

lady friend a female sexual partner. (See also **gentleman** friend.) □ *May I bring a lady friend to the party?* □ *I met Bill's new lady friend yesterday.*

lady of the evening a prostitute. □ *I saw several ladies of the evening down on Main Street.* □ *He was approached by a lady of the evening.*

landfill a place where garbage is buried. (Replaces *dump*.) □ *Our neighborhood borders on the town landfill.* □ *You may not dump batteries in the landfill.*

land of no return death. □ *He has gone to the land of no return.* □ *She has left us for the land of no return.*

landscape architect a gardener. □ *We hired a landscape architect to do something interesting with the yard.* □ *The landscape architect put in a lovely fish pool and that little weeping willow tree.*

language arts AND **communication arts** the study of English. □ *Paula got a good grade in language arts.* □ *We aim to give our students a solid background in communication arts and numeracy skills.*

large medium-sized. □ *On that soft drink, did you want regular, large, or jumbo?* □ *The boxes of detergent come in two sizes, large and economy.*

larger fat. □ *The catalog has elegant clothes for the larger woman.* □ *The shop caters to larger and taller men.*

last mile, the the path to a death chamber. □ *The priest walked with the prisoner down the last mile.* □ *The convicted man was weeping as he walked the last mile.*

late dead. □ *I knew your late father very well.* □ *This picture was painted by the late Mary Burford.*

late developer a young person who has not reached puberty. □ *It's hard for her to see all her girlfriends get figures, when she's a late developer.* □ *He was a late developer, but he certainly filled out well.*

late unpleasantness, the the U.S. Civil War. □ *The town courthouse was burned in the late unpleasantness.* □ *Many of my ancestors lost their lives in the late unpleasantness.*

latrine a toilet, especially an outdoor toilet. (A military term.) □ *The soldiers dug a latrine.* □ *I had to get up in the middle of the night to use the latrine.*

launder money to make money from an illegal source appear to come from a legal source. □ *The company was a front for laundering money.* □ *He used a number of foreign bank accounts to launder money.*

lavatory a toilet. (British.) □ *Is there a public lavatory anywhere near here?* □ *I am in urgent need of a lavatory.*

lavender having to do with homosexual people or homosexuality. □ *The lavender film festival takes place this weekend.* □ *There are two lavender newsletters in the city.*

law enforcement policing. □ *Bill is thinking of working in law enforcement if he can pass the entrance exams to the police academy.* □ *Law enforcement in the city was very lax.*

law-enforcement officer a police officer. □ *If approached by a law-enforcement officer, do not take flight.* □ *Three law-enforcement officers arrived at the scene of the crime.*

Laws! "What a surprise!" (Folksy. A mild replacement for *Lord!*) □ *Laws! How you scared me!* □ *Laws! How steep those stairs are!*

lay down one's life for something to die for something. □ *The soldier laid down his life for his country.* □ *She laid down her life for her children.*

layperson 1. a person who is not a member of the clergy. (See also **member of the laity.**) □ *Some parts of the church service were performed by laypeople.* □ *He had said he wanted a layperson to lead his funeral, so we obeyed his* *wishes.* **2.** a person without special knowledge of a subject. (Replaces *layman*, which does not include women.) □ *Can you describe your research in terms that a layperson would understand?* □ *This astronomy book is intended for the intelligent layperson.*

lay someone off AND **lay off someone** to fire someone. □ *The plant laid two hundred people off.* □ *There were rumors that they were going to lay off fifty more.*

lay someone to rest to bury a dead person. (See also at **rest**.) □ *They laid her to rest by her mother and father, out in the old churchyard.* □ *We gather together today to lay our beloved son to rest.*

learning disorder an inability to learn easily. (See also **behavior disorder**.) □ *Billy has a learning disorder and needs special help with his reading homework.* □ *The school offers a special class for children with learning disorders.*

learning experience See growth experience.

(learning) resource center a library. □ *The students can check out books, watch educational films, and log onto the Internet in the school's learning resource center.* □ *She spent the afternoon in the resource center, researching her report on freshwater fishes.*

leave of absence the act of leaving one's job because one has done something wrong. □ *Ms. Takaguchi is on an indefinite leave of absence while the charges are being investigated.* □ *His leave of absence is expected to end in his resignation.*

leave-taking a burial. □ *If you wish to join us at the cemetery for the leave-taking, please follow the funeral coach.* □ *The departed woman's daughter wept all through the leave-taking.*

legal aid having to do with getting a lawyer's help for free. (See also **pro bono**.) □ *In addition to her busy practice, Terry works at the legal aid clinic two nights a week.* □ *The attorney was able to help a legal aid client obtain a divorce.*

less active not active; sedentary. □ *Less active people could benefit from introducing exercise into their daily routine.* □ *We have personal care assistants to help the less active residents of our nursing facility.*

less affluent poor. □ *Many of the less affluent people in the community rely on some form of government aid.* □ *Less affluent families spend a higher percentage of their income on housing.*

less attractive ugly. □ *It's true, James is one of the less attractive men I know, but he has a heart of gold.* □ *Makeup can sometimes do wonders for less attractive women.*

less fortunate poor. □ *Help make the holidays a joyful time for the less fortunate people in our community.* □ *I have a great deal of sympathy for my less fortunate neighbors, but what can I possibly do to help?*

less than not. □ *I get the feeling that Bob has been less than honest with me.* □ *I'm afraid Mary is less than happy with the project we did for her.*

let someone go to fire someone. □ *They let Rita go from her job.* □ *I'm afraid we're going to have to let you go.*

letter carrier a person who delivers mail. (Replaces *mailman*, which does not include women.) □ *The post office is hiring letter carriers to work in your area.* □ *I put the letter in my mailbox for the letter carrier to pick up.*

leveraged in debt. □ *He is very highly leveraged and needs to generate some cash flow.* □ *The company had to be leveraged in order to pay for the new divisions it had acquired.*

liaison a sexual relationship. □ *He formed a liaison with his employer's daughter.* □ *There had been a liaison between Bill and Joan before she married.*

liberate something 1. to steal something. □ *I liberated the old computer that was sitting in the hall at work.* □ *As far as I could tell, no one was using that bicycle, so I liberated it.* **2.** to conquer something. □ *The army announced that it had successfully liberated the city.* □ *"We will liberate our neighbor from its oppressors!" cried the general.*

lie in state [for a dead body] to be on display in public. □ *The president will lie in state in the Capitol Rotunda.* □ *Mourners filed past the leader where he lay in state.*

life everlasting, the See everlasting life.

life insurance insurance that is paid when you die. □ *Consider your family's needs when purchasing life insurance.* □ *The police suspected she had killed her husband for his life insurance.*

life preserver a club. (Old-fashioned.) □ *When I go out at night, I carry a life preserver, just in case.* □ *He assaulted me, so I gave him a crack across the head with my life preserver.*

lifestyle (choice) the choice of sexual partners. □ *Jim's parents were not comfortable with his lifestyle, and refused to accept his partner Frank as a member of the family.* □ *We do not discriminate on the basis of lifestyle choice. Heterosexuals, homosexuals, and bisexuals are all welcome here.*

life, the prostitution. (See also **trade, the**.) □ *"I'm getting tired of the life," the prostitute sighed.* □ *The life was wearing her out.*

lift one's hand to someone See raise one's hand to someone.

light-fingered AND **sticky-fingered** having the habit of stealing things. (Slang.) □ *One of the sales clerks was rather light-fingered and made off with several hundred dollars' worth of merchandise.* □ *The suspicious boss was sure that all her employees were sticky-fingered.*

light woman See fancy woman.

like one's food AND **like one's meals** to eat too much. □ *No, I'm not pregnant. I just like my food.* □ *He's a growing boy, and he likes his meals.*

like that homosexual. (May be offensive to homosexuals.) □ *Jane's oldest boy is like that, you know, so she won't get any grandchildren from him.* □ *Until I met his boyfriend, I had no idea that James was like that.*

limited intelligence a lack of intelligence; stupidity. □ *The way Stanley dealt with the problem showed limited intelligence.* □ *You must put things in very simple terms so that readers of limited intelligence will understand you.*

lineworker a person who puts up and fixes electrical lines. (Replaces *lineman*, which does not include women.) □ *After the storm, lineworkers worked night and day to restore power to all parts of the city.* □ *Steve, Jane, and John are all experienced lineworkers.*

lingerie women's underwear. (French. See also **intimate apparel**.) □ *She put on a set of black lace lingerie.* □ *Do you have lingerie in petite sizes here?*

liquidate someone to kill someone. □ *The Boss gave orders for James the Arm to liquidate Pretty Boy.* □ *The ruthless dictator liquidated all opponents.*

liquidity crisis a lack of money. □ *A liquidity crisis forced the company to downsize.* □ *If you cannot generate income quickly, you will be facing a liquidity crisis.*

listening device a hidden microphone. (Replaces *bug*.) □ *The listening device recorded all conversations that took place in the suspect's office.* □ *The agent ordered listening devices to be placed in the subject's home.*

litter box AND **sand box** a box in which a pet cat urinates and defecates. □ *The litter box is starting to smell bad.* □ *I think Puff needs to use the sand box.*

little boys' room a toilet for men and boys. (Cute. See also **little girls' room**.) □ *The little boys' room is just up the stairs.* □ *JANE: Where's Bob? JILL: I think he went to the little boys' room.*

little girls' room a toilet for women and girls. (Cute. See also **little boys' room**.) □ *Where's the little girls' room? I need to powder my nose.* □ *I need to find the little girls' room.*

little people, the fairies; small supernatural beings. □ *Don't walk in the woods under the full moon. The little people may be out.* □ *When I was a child, I used to hope to meet the little people out in the meadow.*

little room, the See **smallest room, the**.

little stranger a new baby. □ *Soon after my nephew was born, I went to my sister's house to meet the little stranger.* □ *The expectant mother looked forward to the little stranger's arrival.*

little visitor a flea. □ *Uh-oh. Looks like the dog has a little visitor.* □ *How disgusting! I found some little visitors in my socks.*

live as man and wife to live together and have sexual intercourse with one another. □ *Although they had never married, they lived as man and wife.* □ *The actor and his inamorata are living as man and wife, and are expecting their first child in the spring.*

lived-in [of a room or a house] messy. □ *Her apartment looks lived-in.* □ *Their house has a comfortable, lived-in appearance.*

live in sin to live together and have sexual intercourse with someone outside of marriage. (See also **live together, cohabit, roommate.**) □ *Maria just about died of shame when she found out that her daughter is living in sin.* □ *Sally and Frank are living in sin.*

live together to live together and have sexual intercourse with one another outside of marriage. (See also **live in sin, cohabit, roommate.**) □ *Sally and Frank have been living together for ten years.* □ *My boyfriend says he wants us to live together.*

live with someone to live together and have sexual intercourse with someone outside of marriage. □ *Is Frank living with his girlfriend?* □ *Sandy is living with her domestic partner.*

living alive. □ *Are your parents living?* □ *She has one brother still living.*

living will a document that records a person's wish not to be kept alive by the use of machines. □ *My physician has a copy of my living will.* □ *Before you have the surgery performed, you may wish to consider making out a living will, just as a precaution.*

logger a person who cuts down trees and delivers them to the sawmill. (Replaces *lumberjack*.) □ *The loggers planned where the tree would fall.* □ *The paper company employs a large number of loggers.*

loins the genitals. □ *He felt a stirring in his loins.* □ *Her loins ached for him.*

longer-lived, the old people. □ *The clinic specializes in medical care for the longer-lived.* □ *Many of the longer-lived lead very active lives.*

longshore worker a person who loads and unloads freight from ships. (Replaces *longshoreman*, which does not include women. See also **dock worker**.) □ *The longshore workers piled the boxes onto a platform.* □ *The shipping company is hiring longshore workers.*

loo a toilet. (British slang.) □ *Which way to the loo?* □ *The loo in the train was awfully cramped.*

lookism AND **looksism** a bias against ugly people. □ *Lookism is impossible to avoid in the acting business. Pretty people get all the parts.* □ *The lawsuit argued that the company practiced lookism by hiring only good-looking men and women for receptionist jobs.*

loose bowels the inability to hold one's feces; diarrhea. □ *I ate too much fruit, and got loose bowels as a result.* □ *Loose bowels were a symptom of the virus.*

loose woman a prostitute. □ *He drank, he gambled, and he hung out with loose women.* □ *He thought the party would not be complete without loose women to entertain all his men friends.*

lord of the flies the Devil. □ *The lord of the flies hungers for our souls.* □ *The lord of the flies ruled over that evil man's sinful life.*

lose someone have someone die. □ *He lost his father last year.* □ *Ever since she lost her husband, she hasn't been the same.*

loss of life death, especially the death of many people. □ *The chemical spill resulted in a great loss of life.* □ *The loss of life in that one battle was tremendous.*

loss reserve something that can be sold cheaply in order to convince people to come into a store. (Replaces *loss leader.*) □ *Canned goods were the grocery store's loss reserve.* □ *The department store had a couple of specials as a loss reserve, and planned to make their money back selling big-ticket items.*

lounge 1. a toilet. □ *You'll find a diaper-changing station in the ladies' lounge.* □ *There are paper towels in the gentlemens' lounge.* **2.** a bar. □ *A live band plays in the hotel lounge every night.* □ *I stopped for a drink at a friendly looking lounge.*

love to have sexual intercourse. □ *They loved for the first time that night.* □ *Let me love you. It will be so beautiful.*

love child a child born to unmarried parents. (Replaces *bastard.*) □ *She had a love child when she was twenty.* □ *Bill was a love child, and never knew his father.*

loved one a dead person. □ *Do you need to make arrangements for a loved one?* □ *Did you wish an earth burial for your loved one?*

love handles fat sides. □ *You should exercise more. You're starting to get love handles.* □ *Her love handles slopped over the top of her pants.*

love life sexual activity. □ *His love life has been pretty tame since he broke up with his last girlfriend.* □ *The magazine article has hints for spicing up your love life.*

love that dare not speak its name homosexual love. (From a poem by Alfred Douglas, made famous by Oscar Wilde.) □ *He had experienced the love that dare not speak its name.* □ *She wanted to tell her co-workers about her new lover, but hers was the love that dare not speak its name.*

low depressed. □ *She has been very low since she lost her job.* □ *He is very low, and could use some support from his friends.*

low-income poor. □ *Our agency distributes clothing to low-income families.* □ *The project will include six units for low-income renters.*

lump a cancer. □ *She found a lump in her breast.* □ *The doctor discovered a lump in his colon.*

-ly advantaged having a lot of something, such as fat, age, etc. □ *Don't say he's fat. Say he's quantitatively advantaged.* □ *We value the experience of our chronologically advantaged employees.*

madam the manager of a house of prostitution. □ *The madam insisted on payment up front.* □ *The madam had six girls working for her.*

magdalene a prostitute. (Old-fashioned. From Mary Magdalene, a biblical character.) □ *The magdalene sought to leave her wicked life.* □ *The fallen woman found herself among the magdalenes of the great city.*

mainstream someone to put someone who has trouble learning in a regular classroom. □ *The school district plans to mainstream the learning disabled students.* □ *The deaf child's parents insisted that the school mainstream him.*

maintenance worker a person who cleans and repairs a building. (Replaces *janitor.*) □ *A staff of fifty maintenance workers is responsible for the day-to-day care of the building.* □ *We need a maintenance worker to fix the furnace.*

make a deposit to defecate or urinate. □ *Excuse me while I make a deposit.* □ *I need to make a deposit. I'll be back in a minute.*

make an honest woman of someone to marry a woman. □ *Say, Sally, when is Frank going to make an hon-*

est woman of you? □ *You've been going out with Mary for three years now. You ought to make an honest woman of her.*

make away with someone to kill someone. □ *Pretty Boy made away with the cop who was giving him a hard time.* □ *I am so afraid that someone has made away with my daughter.*

make away with something to steal something. □ *While I was in the grocery store, someone made away with my car!* □ *He suspected the servants of making away with his fine liquors.*

make it to live. □ *For awhile, we were afraid Pat wasn't going to make it, but he's going to be fine.* □ *Do you think she'll make it, doctor?*

make it worth someone's while to bribe someone. □ *I made it worth the waiter's while to give us good service.* □ *If you'll throw a few contracts my way, I'll make it worth your while.*

make love to have sex. (Similarly: bump uglies with someone, couple with someone, do the nasty with someone, play doctor with someone, score, tumble.) □ *Do you want to make love?* □ *They rented a hotel room and made love all night.*

make out with someone to kiss and caress someone. (Slang. See also **pet with someone**.) □ *He made out with his girlfriend in the back seat of the car.* □ *There was a couple making out with each other right there in the middle of the park!*

make someone redundant to fire someone. (British.) □ *The company made seventy people redundant.* □ *We are forced to make a number of employees redundant.*

make the arrangements to arrange a funeral. □ *A funeral services practitioner will be happy to help you make the arrangements.* □ *When my father died, I was the one who made the arrangements.*

make water AND **pass water** to urinate. (Similarly: drain one's radiator, evacuate one's bladder, kill a tree, piddle, take a leak, take a whiz, void.) □ *I could hear him making water in the bathroom.* □ *I felt an urgent need to pass water.*

maladjusted disobedient. □ *Several maladjusted students created a discipline problem for the teacher.* □ *The school social worker has had some success working with maladjusted teens.*

maladroit clumsy. □ *She is somewhat maladroit in social situations.* □ *A maladroit person should not consider a career as a mechanic.*

malefactor a criminal. (Formal.) □ *The inspector vowed to apprehend the malefactor.* □ *That quarter of the city was full of thieves, murderers, and malefactors of all descriptions.*

male identified AND **male oriented** [of a man] homosexual. (See also female identified.) □ *The support group is for male identified men who have not yet acted on their feelings.* □ *He edits a male oriented magazine.*

male-intensive occupation a job held mostly by men. (See also female-intensive occupation.) □ *At present, most jobs involving mechanically skilled labor are male-intensive occupations.* □ *She wanted to make it easier for women to enter traditionally male-intensive occupations such as construction and forestry.*

male itch(ing) a fungus that grows on the penis and testicles. (See also **jock itch**.) □ *Men, are you troubled by male itching?* □ *This preparation soothes male itch on contact.*

male oriented See **male identified**.

mammary glands the breasts. □ *If the neckline on her dress was any lower, her mammary glands would be on full display.* □ *She had well-developed mammary glands.*

man Friday See **gal Friday**.

manhood the penis and testicles. □ *He felt his manhood shrivel up with fear.* □ *His rival made a scornful comment about his manhood.*

manure animal feces. □ *I shoveled manure out of the barn.* □ *Work the manure into the soil.*

marginalized excluded. □ *Women's experiences have been marginalized for too long.* □ *Several employees of color complained that they felt marginalized in group meetings led by whites.*

marital aid a sex toy. □ *He looked at the marital aids in the catalog and wondered how they were used.* □ *She considered using a marital aid to enliven her sex life.*

marital relations sexual relations within marriage. (See also **conjugal relations**.) □ *Mr. and Mrs. Thompson had not had marital relations in three months.* □ *She complained that her marital relations were not satisfying.*

marker a gravestone. □ *The funeral service practitioner can help you select a marker.* □ *We engrave all our markers here on the premises, and would be happy to add any special text that you would like.*

marketing selling. □ *I work in marketing.* □ *Our marketing needs to appeal to women as well as men.*

market value a price on the public market. □ *What is the market value of these shares?* □ *He was able to buy fine wines for less than their market value.*

massage parlor a house of prostitution. □ *The cops busted the massage parlor for being a disorderly house.* □ *The neighbors fought to close down the massage parlor on the corner.*

massage something to falsify something. □ *The scientist had massaged her data.* □ *If we massage the sales figures just a bit, it will look like we're doing OK.*

materiel weapons or ammunition. □ *The Communist regime supplied the rebels with materiel.* □ *The arms dealer promised to deliver the materiel.*

maternity having to do with pregnancy or giving birth. □ *Is this maternity dress OK for business wear?* □ *Kelly will go on maternity leave in September.* □ *The expectant father hurried through the hospital to the maternity ward.*

matinee sexual intercourse during the day. (Slang.) □ *The lovers slipped out at lunchtime for a matinee.* □ *The weekend was a good opportunity for a matinee with his girlfriend.*

mature old. (See also **of mature years**.) □ *We are seeking a mature, responsible individual to do light bookkeeping three days a week.* □ *He is a mature gentleman and is beginning to think of retiring.*

mature figure a fat female body. □ *We offer career wear for the mature figure.* □ *Ladies with mature figures do not always look their best in shorter skirts.*

mausoleum a building for holding dead bodies. □ *The family mausoleum sat on a hill in the cemetery.* □ *He built a mausoleum for himself, his wife, and their three children.*

May I be excused? "May I leave to use the toilet?" □ *Nature calls. May I be excused?* □ *The student raised her hand and said, "Teacher, may I be excused?"*

means money. (Similarly: bread, buckage, capital, dough, moolah, pennies. See also **independent means**.) □ *She lacked the means to go to college.* □ *He certainly has the knowledge to go into business for himself, but does he have the means?*

medical center a hospital. □ *He had his surgery at the county medical center.* □ *The ambulance took her straight to the medical center.*

medical examiner a person who examines dead bodies; a coroner. □ *The medical examiner found signs of poison in the deceased's system.* □ *The detective read the medical examiner's report.*

medication a drug. □ *She is taking medication for her condition.* □ *Are you currently on any medication?*

mellow drunk. □ *The beer he had had at lunch left him feeling mellow.* □ *After the cocktails, the guests were all quite mellow.*

member 1. a penis. (Similarly: bone, ding-dong, dingle, dingus, doodad, gadget, jock, John Thomas, male member, membrum virile, part, pizzle, privy member, thingamabob, third leg, whatsis, wick, **willy**, woccus.) ☐ *The office reported that the young man had displayed his member in public.* ☐ *He seemed to feel insecure about the size of his member.* **2.** a person who has given money for something. ☐ *This program was made possible by the members of Channel Five.* ☐ *Please become a member of the Save the Wildlife Foundation.*

member of Congress a person who has been elected to Congress. (Replaces *Congressman* for men and *Congresswoman* for women.) ☐ *She is one of two new members of Congress from our state.* ☐ *How many members of Congress sit on that committee?*

member of the clergy a person of religious authority, such as a priest, minister, rabbi, or imam. (Replaces *clergyman*, which does not include women.) ☐ *There are special tax regulations for members of the clergy.* ☐ *She was ordained as a member of the clergy.*

member of the laity a person who does not belong to the clergy. (See also **layperson**.) ☐ *Members of the laity assisted in the communion service.* ☐ *I am not a pastor. I am a member of the laity.*

memorial having to do with death or burial. ☐ *He purchased a memorial estate for himself and his wife.* ☐ *The memorial service will be held on Monday.*

memorial park a graveyard. ☐ *The memorial park where Dad is has been very well kept up.* ☐ *There is a cinerarium on the north side of the memorial park.*

memorial service a funeral service where the dead body is not present. ☐ *His body was lost at sea, and so there was a memorial service instead of a funeral.* ☐ *Only the immediate family attended the funeral, but everyone who knew her came to the memorial service.*

memory image AND **memory picture** the appearance of a dead person in his or her coffin. □ *The mourners will appreciate the memory image of their loved one.* □ *She looks so peaceful. A lovely memory picture, don't you think?*

ménage à trois sexual relations involving three people. (French.) □ *Imagine my surprise when the couple invited me to participate in a ménage à trois!* □ *Because she did not care to form part of a ménage à trois with her husband and his mistress, she left him for good and all.*

men's magazine a pornographic magazine for homosexual men. □ *His mother was shocked to discover a drawer full of men's magazines in his room.* □ *He is a photographer for a men's magazine.*

menstruate [for a woman] to bleed monthly. □ *At what age did you begin to menstruate?* □ *Cindy gets bad cramps when she menstruates.*

mental disability See mental impairment.

mental fatigue depression. □ *She went through an episode of mental fatigue after she flunked out of school.* □ *The new medication seems to be helping him with his mental fatigue.*

mental hospital AND **psychiatric hospital** a hospital for mentally ill people. (Replaces *lunatic asylum* and *madhouse*.) □ *His psychiatrist suggested a stay in a mental hospital.* □ *After her third suicide attempt, her family committed her to a psychiatric hospital.*

mental impairment AND **mental disability** an inability to learn easily. (Replaces *mental retardation*.) □ *My son was born with a mental impairment.* □ *Although she has a slight mental disability, she is able to lead a full and independent life.*

merchandize something to sell something. □ *We can merchandize the product more effectively if we target our advertising to specific genders and age groups.* □ *The new ad campaign merchandizes the car by appealing to the buyer's desire for high status.*

Mercy! "Wow!" □ *Mercy! Just look at that mess!* □ *Mercy! These stairs are steep!*

mercy killing the killing of a sick and suffering person or animal. (See also **euthanasia**.) □ *She claimed that murdering her sick grandmother was a mercy killing.* □ *The patient begged for help to end his life, but the doctor said she would not participate in a mercy killing.*

Merde! "Shit!" (French.) □ *Merde! I've lost my car keys.* □ *Oh, merde! Now I've broken it.*

mess the feces of a pet animal. □ *That dog has left a mess on the carpet again.* □ *I love my dog, but she does tend to make a mess whenever she gets excited.*

message a commercial. □ *Tonight's special presentation will return after these messages.* □ *And now, a message from our sponsor.*

meter reader AND **meter attendant** a person who checks parking meters. (Replaces *meter maid*, which does not include men. See also following entry.) □ *I hope the meter reader hasn't ticketed my car.* □ *The meter attendant saw that there was still fifteen minutes left on the parking meter.*

meter reader a person who checks gas or electric meters. (Replaces *meter man*, which does not include women.) □ *Leave the basement door unlocked so that the meter reader* *can get in.* □ *I can't believe we used that much electricity last month! The meter reader must have made a mistake.*

MIA See missing in action.

micturate to urinate. □ *He had drunk too much beer and urgently needed to micturate.* □ *She squatted down in the ditch and began to micturate.*

middle the belly. □ *She has a rather fat middle.* □ *He felt a pain in his middle.*

middle age the middle of an average lifetime. (Middle age can be used to describe any age between about thirty-five and sixty-five. See also **midlife**.) □ *She is a woman of middle age and is at the head of her profession.* □ *When he reached middle age, he began to feel regret over things he had done in his youth.*

middle-aged spread the fat that comes after the age of thirty. □ *He's starting to show a bit of middle-aged spread.* □ *After she turned forty, she exercised and dieted with a will, hoping to fight middle-aged spread.*

Middle Eastern dance a dance style from the Middle East, involving swaying and shaking of the hips, belly, and breasts. (Replaces *belly dance*.) □ *The Sahara Cafe features Middle Eastern dance on Friday and Saturday nights.* □ *She teaches and performs Middle Eastern dance.*

middleperson a person who goes between buyers and sellers. (Replaces *middleman*, which does not include women.) □ *I decided to start buying my shoes directly from the factory and eliminate the middleperson.* □ *The publisher asked the author to come to a meeting without her agent. "No need for a middleperson to be involved, is there?" the publisher said.*

midlife having to do with the middle of an average life-time. (See also **middle age**.) □ *She went through the usual midlife process of taking stock of her life.* □ *He had a severe midlife crisis, and left his wife and children to join a monastery.*

midriff the belly. □ *Her outfit featured a bare midriff.* □ *These exercises will trim and tone the midriff.*

midsection the belly. □ *He received a blow to the midsection.* □ *She has quite a muscular midsection.*

migrant immigrant. (In the United States, **migrant** is usually used to describe Central and South American people who come to the United States to work.) □ *The grapes were harvested by migrant workers.* □ *In the harvest season, the town's population swells with migrant families.*

military adviser a soldier. □ *The United States has sent two hundred military advisers to the troubled region.* □ *The officers are military advisers only and have not gone there to fight.*

military diver a member of the military who is trained to dive and work underwater. (Replaces *frogman*, which does not include women.) □ *Military divers worked to recover pieces of the wrecked plane.* □ *A military diver inspected the underside of the ship.*

minority a non-white person or group of people. (Possibly offensive to people who are not white. Use with caution.) □ *How many minorities are represented in your workforce?* □ *James was one of the first minorities elected to the state senate from this district.*

misadventure a disaster. □ *A surgical misadventure resulted in the demise of the patient.* □ *A number of misadventures with the equipment alerted us to its unsafe nature.*

misappropriate something to steal something, especially a large amount of money. (See also **appropriate something**.) □ *One of the managers had been misappropriating the funds allocated to her department.* □ *The member of Congress resigned in disgrace, under suspicion of having misappropriated public money.*

miscarriage the birth of a fetus before it is old enough to live. (Replaces *spontaneous abortion.*) □ *Her first two pregnancies ended in miscarriage.* □ *She had a miscarriage, and it left her very weak.*

miscommunication a failure to communicate. □ *I think there must have been a miscommunication about the time of the meeting.* □ *Perhaps there was some miscommunication on my part as to what I expected you to do.*

miscreant a wrongdoer. □ *The teacher plotted to catch the miscreant who had been writing cuss words on the chalkboard every morning.* □ *It turned out that Ben was the miscreant who had left his computer on all night.*

misdeed a crime or other bad deed. □ *I forgave him for his childish misdeeds.* □ *Harrison's misdeeds landed him in a federal prison.*

misleading false. □ *The report was full of misleading statistics.* □ *The company president made a misleading speech about the organization's financial health.*

misplace something to lose something. □ *I seem to have misplaced my notebook.* □ *Because he had misplaced his umbrella, Jim got wet on his way to work.*

misrepresentation a lie. □ *The article contained several misrepresentations.* □ *Her resume was found to be full of misrepresentations and outright fictions.*

missing in action AND **MIA** killed or taken prisoner in battle. □ *Tom was reported missing in action.* □ *Sixty men were killed and five were MIA.*

misspeak to lie or say something wrong. □ *Did I say Jane had an advanced degree? If I did, then I misspoke.* □ *I misspoke when I said that the deadline was Monday. The deadline is really Wednesday.*

misstatement a lie. □ *I wish to correct my earlier misstatement.* □ *His boss accused him of making deliberate misstatements in his report.*

mixed bad. □ *The movie got mixed reviews.* □ *The reactions to the president's announcement were mixed.*

mixed breed not of a pure breed. (Usually used to describe dogs. Replaces *mongrel* and *mutt*.) □ *JILL: What a cute dog! What kind is he? JANE: He's a mixed breed.* □ *Mixed breed puppies for sale.*

mobile home a small building that can be moved by a truck. (Replaces *trailer*.) □ *When we first got married, we lived in a mobile home.* □ *Their mobile home was destroyed by the storm.*

mobility impaired not able to move easily. (Replaces *crippled*.) □ *Linda is mobility impaired and uses a wheelchair.* □ *This bathroom stall is designed for people who are mobility impaired.*

model a prostitute. (Model does not always have this meaning. Judge from the context.) □ *The club features hot young models.* □ *He hired a model for the evening.*

moderator a person who leads a meeting. (Replaces *chairman*, which does not include women.) □ *Susan is the moderator for this session.* □ *Our first item of business will be to elect a moderator.*

modest 1. not good. □ *His musical talents are modest.* □ *Her modest academic record would not allow her to attend a first-rate college.* **2.** not large. □ *A private bathroom is available for a modest fee.* □ *They have a very modest home.*

molest someone to touch sexually or have sexual intercourse with someone against his or her will. □ *I can't believe that nice man would molest a little girl.* □ *He was fired for molesting a young employee.*

moment of silence a prayer time. □ *After the Pledge of Allegiance, the students bowed their heads in a moment of silence.* □ *The courts decreed that public schools could not hold prayers, and so the schools allowed time for a moment of silence every morning before class.*

monitor someone or something to spy on someone or something. □ *The company president hired an investigator to monitor the suspicious vice president.* □ *The intelligence agency was monitoring all of the activist's phone conversations.*

monkey business wrongdoing, especially sexual or business wrongdoing. □ *He suspected his wife was carrying on some kind of monkey business.* □ *The investigation of the company's finances revealed some rather serious monkey business.*

monument a gravestone. □ *She selected a granite monument for her husband's grave.* □ *Her name was engraved on the monument, with her dates of birth and death.*

Morals Division the part of a police force that enforces laws against prostitution, gambling, and drugs. (Replaces *Vice Squad*.) □ *The Morals Division shut down the house of ill fame.* □ *He was arrested by the Morals Division for running a betting operation.*

moribund dying. □ *The textile industry in this area is clearly moribund.* □ *The nurse believed that the patient was moribund.*

morning-after pill a drug that prevents pregnancy when a woman takes it after having sex. (Slang.) □ *We had forgotten to use precautions, so I hurried to the doctor for a morning-after pill.* □ *"The morning-after pill should not be used as a routine method of contraception," said the nurse.*

morning after, the 1. the morning after a night of drinking too much alcohol. □ *The morning after found her with a splitting headache.* □ *It was well into the afternoon before the effects of the morning after wore off.* **2.** the morning after a night of sex. □ *They had made love passionately all night, but on the morning after, they found they had nothing to say to each other.* □ *The morning after was full of regrets for both of them.*

mortality death. □ *What is the mortality rate for white males in this area?* □ *When her mother died, she had to face her own mortality.*

(mortal) remains a dead body. □ *We hereby consign our loved one's mortal remains to the earth.* □ *The police could not discover what had become of the murder victim's remains.*

mortician a person who prepares dead bodies for burial or cremation. (See also **funeral service practitioner.**) □ *The mortician will pick up the deceased at the hospital.* □ *The mortician was very kind and helped us so much with all the arrangements.*

mortuary a place where dead bodies are prepared for burial or cremation. □ *Our mortuary has been serving those in need since 1956.* □ *The mortician will bring your loved one from the mortuary to the funeral chapel.*

mother-to-be a pregnant woman. (See also **father-to-be.**) □ *The article contains loads of health advice for mothers-to-be.* □ *You need to take good care of yourself, now that you are a mother-to-be.*

mouth harp See **juice harp.**

Mrs. Warren's profession prostitution. (From *Mrs. Warren's Profession*, a play by George Bernard Shaw. See also **oldest profession, the.**) □ *I believe that my neighbor is active in Mrs. Warren's profession, if you know what I mean.* □ *He associated mainly with women of Mrs. Warren's profession.*

muck something up to ruin something. (A replacement for *fuck something up.*) □ *I should never have trusted Jim with the repair work. He was bound to muck it up.* □ *I asked her to take over for me while I was gone, and she really mucked it up.*

muscle-powered powered by people. (Replaces *man-powered*, which does not include women.) □ *Bicycles or other muscle-powered vehicles are allowed on the trail.* □ *She learned to fly a muscle-powered aircraft.*

My foot! AND **My eye!** "I do not believe it at all!" (A mild replacement for *my ass!*) □ JILL: *Bob says he can't come to the party because he has to visit a sick friend.* JANE: *Sick friend, my foot! He just doesn't think my party will be any fun.* □ *The boss says I can't get a raise because there is a wage freeze on. Well, wage freeze, my eye! Brenda got a raise just last month!*

My word! "How surprising!" (A mild replacement for *My Lord!*) □ JILL: *Did you hear the news? Jane ran away and got married!* BILL: *My word! Did she really?* □ *My word! That was a funny story!*

nation a country. □ *We live in the strongest and best nation on Earth.* □ *We reach out the hand of friendship to all nations.*

natural child a child born to unmarried parents. □ *The king's natural children were not in line for the throne.* □ *William the Conquerer was the natural child of Duke Robert.*

natural functions defecation and urination. (See also bodily functions, private function.) □ *A stomach disorder had interrupted his ability to perform the natural functions.* □ *Let us please not discuss the natural functions at the dinner table.*

naturist a person who is in the habit of going naked. (Replaces *nudist*.) □ *The camp is for naturists of all ages.* □ *My parents were naturists and often brought all of the kids to naturist gatherings.*

naughty sexual. □ *She whispered a naughty suggestion in his ear.* □ *The video showed three or four people doing some rather naughty things.*

necessary, the a toilet. □ *I have to use the necessary.* □ *You will find the necessary down the hall and on the left.*

needs of nature the need to urinate or defecate. (See also call of nature.) □ *She was overcome by the needs of nature and had to leave the meeting.* □ *As soon as I had left the rest stop behind me, I began to feel the needs of nature.*

needy poor. □ *Your contributions of food will be distributed to the needy in your area.* □ *The charity collected money for holiday celebrations for the needy.*

negative less than zero. □ *The company experienced a negative increase in sales last quarter.* □ *The market has taken a negative turn.*

negative growth a decrease. □ *The negative growth of the stock market is a cause for concern.* □ *The company experienced a negative growth of its assets. We are therefore forced to downsize.*

negative patient care outcome the death of a patient. □ *The therapeutic misadventure resulted in a negative patient care outcome.* □ *The new policy seeks to limit negative patient care outcomes for this particular procedure.*

negative reinforcement punishment. □ *The counselors use negative reinforcement to help their clients stop smoking.* □ *With enough negative reinforcement, the children learn not to leave a mess behind them.*

negative saver a person in debt. □ *Many of the bank's customers are negative savers.* □ *The money management program teaches negative savers to pay off existing debts and save money for the future.*

neoplasm a cancer. □ *The surgeon will remove the neoplasm during the procedure.* □ *The mole on your skin may be a sign of neoplasm.*

(nervous) breakdown an episode of mental illness. □ *After her daughter's death, Helen suffered a nervous breakdown.* □ *I heard that Michael had some kind of a breakdown and spent six months in a mental hospital.*

nether parts the genitals. □ *Her skirt barely covered her nether parts.* □ *He carefully applied the jock-itch cream to his nether parts.*

network to meet new people in hopes that they will help you in your business. □ *I went to the party and networked like mad. I must have given out twenty business cards.* □ *The gym can be a great place to network.*

neutralize someone to kill someone. □ *The agent planned to neutralize the popular politician.* □ *Once the agent's identity was discovered, we were able to neutralize him.*

news management the practice of controlling which facts are made public. □ *Ms. Young is in charge of news management for the governor's office. You may address all your questions to her.* □ *After the incident at the power plant, the power company had a team of lawyers and public relations people working full-time on news management.*

(news)paper carrier a person who delivers newspapers. (Replaces *paper boy* and *paper girl*.) □ *The newspaper carrier will collect your payment at the end of each month.* □ *Lisa got her first job as a paper carrier.*

next world, the death. (See also world to come, the.) □ *We will meet in the next world.* □ *He believed he had made contact with spirits from the next world.*

nick someone or something to remove the testes from someone or something; to castrate someone or something.

(Slang.) □ *We'll have to nick that bull calf before he gets too much older.* □ *The vet nicked our dog for us.*

nightcap an alcoholic drink taken at night. □ *Care to come in for a nightcap?* □ *After the party, we went to Jim's for a nightcap.*

night soil AND **night earth** feces produced during the night. (Old-fashioned.) □ *In the days of chamber pots, it was the servants' job to collect and remove the night soil.* □ *The nurse removed the bedpan and dumped the night earth into the water closet.*

nightstick a club. □ *The officer used his nightstick to subdue the suspect.* □ *The security officers do not carry guns, but they do have nightsticks.*

nocturnal emission a release of semen during sleep. □ *Have you been experiencing nocturnal emissions?* □ *The doctor explained that nocturnal emissions were nothing to be embarrassed about.*

no longer young old. □ *Although no longer young, he is still very active in the business.* □ *You are no longer young, Uncle Ralph, and you should behave with dignity.*

nominal [of an amount of money] small. □ *A copy of the song lyrics may be had for a nominal fee.* □ *He lives with his uncle and pays a nominal rent.*

non compos (mentis) mentally ill. (Latin.) □ *She acted in such a strange way that we suspected she was non compos mentis.* □ *His family judged that he was non compos and had him institutionalized.*

noncustodial punishment imprisonment in one's own house. □ *Because he was a first offender, the judge sentenced* him to noncustodial punishment. □ *Overcrowding in the state's prisons made noncustodial punishment a popular option.*

non-dairy not made from milk or cream. □ *The fast food restaurant serves non-dairy frozen treats.* □ *I can't get cream for my coffee here, only this non-dairy creamer.*

nondisabled able-bodied. (See also **temporarily abled**.) □ *Both nondisabled and disabled patrons will find the new entrance to the library very easy to use.* □ *The wheelchair activist hoped to help nondisabled people understand the challenges faced by the disabled.*

nonhuman animal an animal. (Emphasizes that human beings are also animals. Used mostly by proponents of legal rights for animals.) □ *The proposed law seeks to ensure a minimum standard of living for nonhuman animals.* □ *Beth thought it was not fair for people to keep nonhuman animals as pets.*

nonidentical twins twins who grew from two separate eggs, instead of one egg that split in two. (Replaces *fraternal twins*, which does not include females.) □ *Are Sally and Jill nonidentical twins or identical twins?* □ *Obviously, John and Mary are nonidentical twins. Identical twins are always of the same sex.*

non-industrial(ized) [of a country] not having industries. (Compare with **industrial(ized)**.) □ *Although a non-industrialized nation, it does possess considerable natural resources.* □ *Representatives from several non-industrial countries were also present at the environmental summit.*

non-performing asset something that does not earn any money. □ *That particular stock was a non-performing asset this quarter.* □ *When reviewing the list of non-*

performing assets in your investment portfolio, keep in mind that your investment plan is intended to perform over the long term.

non-traditional casting the practice of having actors play roles that were written for someone of a different race. □ *Having an Asian actor play Othello was definitely a piece of non-traditional casting.* □ *The theater's policy of non-traditional casting allows it to choose the strongest possible actor for every role, regardless of race.*

non-traditional student a college student over the age of twenty-two. (See also **returning student**.) □ *Many non-traditional students attend the university's extension courses.* □ *Most of our non-traditional students have full-time jobs in addition to their coursework.*

non-white not of European descent. (Use with caution. **Person of color** is the term currently preferred by many people of African, Asian, or Native American descent.) □ *We have more non-white students in our school district than white students.* □ *The store had shown a bias against hiring non-white people.*

no-pops kernels of popcorn that fail to pop. □ *I won't buy this brand of popcorn again. Just look at all those no-pops!* □ *You shouldn't try to eat the no-pops. They'll hurt your teeth.*

no scholar a bad student; not learned. □ *Jim is no scholar. He's lucky he managed to graduate from high school.* □ *I'm no scholar, but I know that William Wordsworth wrote poetry.*

no spring chicken old. □ *That actress is no spring chicken, but she does a pretty good job of playing a twenty-year-old girl.* □ *JANE: How old do you think Robert is? JILL: Well, he's certainly no spring chicken.*

not a kid anymore old. □ *You can't keep partying all weekend, every weekend. You're not a kid anymore.* □ KATHY: *Bill is just as wild as ever, I hear.* JANE: *Bill needs to realize that he's not a kid anymore.*

not as (blank) as one might wish not (blank). □ *My assistant is not as bright as one might wish.* □ *The hotel was not as clean as one might wish.*

not as young as one used to be getting old. □ *Aunt Lila isn't as young as she used to be. She can't take a lot of trips anymore.* □ *Don't walk so fast! I'm not as young as I used to be. It takes me awhile to catch up.*

not available right now See unavailable.

not doing well dying. □ JANE: *How's your dad?* BILL: *He's not doing well, I'm afraid.* □ *The doctor says that Paula is not doing well, and we should be prepared for the worst.*

not going to win any beauty contests ugly. □ *Fred isn't going to win any beauty contests, but he's smart and considerate and he does well at his job.* □ *This old truck of mine is not going to win any beauty contests, but I wouldn't trade it for anything.*

not (quite) right fake-looking. □ *The expert looked at the painting and said, "I doubt it's really Titian. Something's not right about those skin tones."* □ *I almost bought the antique chair, but the finish on it was not quite right.*

not quite right mentally ill. (Similarly: a few bricks short of a load, a few cards short of a full deck, a few enchiladas short of a combination plate, have bats in the belfry, loony, loopy, mental, nuts, nutty, off one's rocker, round the bend.) □ *She can't depend on her brother. He's not quite* *right, you know.* □ *He isn't quite right. He hasn't been all there since he lost his wife, really.*

not what we had hoped bad. □ *His performance on the test was not what we had hoped.* □ *The results of the experiment were not what we had hoped.*

nuclear capability the possession of nuclear bombs. □ *How many nations have nuclear capability?* □ *The United States has had nuclear capability since 1945.*

nuisance urine or feces. □ *The cat has left a nuisance in the middle of the bed.* □ *I'm tired of cleaning up that dog's nuisances.*

number one urine. □ *Daddy, I need to do number one.* □ CHILD: *I have to go to the bathroom.* MOTHER: *Number one or number two?*

number two feces. □ *I take a laxative to help me do my number two.* □ *The dog did a number two on the rug.*

nurse to suck milk from a mother. □ *The puppies nursed at their mother.* □ *The baby nursed happily.*

nurse's aide AND **nursing assistant** a person who helps a nurse by lifting, feeding, and bathing patients. (Replaces *aide*, which was used mostly for women, and *orderly*, which was used mostly for men.) □ *If you would like the nurse's aide to help you out of bed, just press this button.* □ *The nursing assistant helped me with the bedpan.*

nurse someone to allow someone to suck milk from one's breasts. □ *She went into the back room to nurse her baby.* □ *Did you nurse your first baby, or did you bottle-feed?*

nursing home a place where old or sick people pay to live and be taken care of. □ *Grandpa just can't take care of himself. We'll have to put him in a nursing home.* □ *She was so weak and ill after her surgery that she had to spend several months in a nursing home.*

obituary a death announcement. □ *Georgia Jones died. I saw her obituary in the paper.* □ *The author's obituary listed the books he had published.*

obsequies a funeral. □ *Her obsequies were well attended.* □ *All of his friends and relations and business associates gathered at the synagogue for the obsequies.*

of a certain age over the age of thirty-five. (Usually used to describe women.) □ *Many women of a certain age either think about making a career change or actually make one.* □ *The clothing in that store appeals to women of a certain age.*

of classic proportions fat; large. (Used to describe women.) □ *She is a lady of classic proportions.* □ *I design my gowns for women of classic proportions.*

off-color [of stories or jokes] having to do with sex. □ *After a few drinks, the off-color jokes start to fly.* □ *It is in poor taste to tell off-color stories in the workplace.*

offender a criminal. □ *The punishment of sex offenders was a topic of current debate.* □ *She was a first offender, so her sentence was light.*

offense a crime. □ *A parking violation is not considered a severe offense.* □ *This is not the first offense of this type on his record.*

offensive an invasion. □ *The offensive into enemy territory will take place at 0700.* □ *General Stevens led the offensive.*

off the record in secret and not to be published. □ *What I'm telling you is strictly off the record.* □ POLITICIAN: *Is this off the record?* JOURNALIST: *Absolutely.*

of mature years old. (See also mature.) □ *My employer is a man of mature years.* □ *The professor, a woman of mature years, is planning to retire at the end of the school term.*

older old. □ *Some of our older residents appreciate the hand rails in all the halls.* □ *Many older people choose to sell their homes so that they don't have to worry about maintaining them.*

oldest profession, the prostitution. (See also Mrs. Warren's profession.) □ *Uneducated and friendless, she fell back on the oldest profession as a way to support herself.* □ *The oldest profession is alive and well on Lake Street.*

old Harry, the the Devil. □ *It must have been the old Harry whispering in my ear and telling me to take that money.* □ *He's a bad so-and-so, and he'll go to old Harry when he dies.*

old man's friend pneumonia. (Old-fashioned.) □ *He died of the old man's friend.* □ *The old man's friend finally carried him off.*

Old Nick the Devil. (Slang.) □ *She has the Old Nick in her for sure.* □ *Old Nick may catch you if you don't watch out.*

old soldier's home, the a toilet. (Jocular.) □ *He excused himself and retired to the old soldier's home.* □ *I must go to the old soldier's home.*

ombuds a person who responds to complaints. (Replaces *ombudsman*, which does not include women.) □ *The student took her complaint about the dormitory to the ombuds.* □ *The ombuds is here to help you if you have any trouble with the medical care you receive here.*

onanism masturbation. (From Onan, a Biblical character who masturbated rather than father children.) □ *He practiced onanism in secret.* □ *His only relief was in nightly acts of onanism.*

one "I." □ *One doesn't like to have to argue with people, does one?* □ *One feels uncomfortable having to say this sort of thing.*

one of those homosexual. (Possibly offensive to homosexual people. Use with caution.) □ *Bill isn't interested in girls. You know. He's one of those.* □ *I would never have guessed that Jane was one of those.*

one's all one's naked body. □ *She took off her robe and revealed her all.* □ *When he took his pants off at the beach, his swim trunks came off, too. There he was, displaying his all to an admiring crowd.*

one's last resting place one's grave. □ *Daddy has gone to his last resting place.* □ *I want to be beside her in her last resting place.*

one's person one's penis and testicles. □ *One can scarcely scratch one's person in public, can one?* □ *It's a good idea to wear a cup to protect your person.*

one's sunset years one's old age. □ *Many people in their sunset years love to travel.* □ *Now is the time to think about financial planning for your sunset years.*

one-upping the act of showing that one is better than someone else. (Replaces *one-upsmanship*, which does not include women.) □ *I'm not interested in getting into a game of one-upping.* □ *Jane is an expert in one-upping. She always has or does or knows something better or more than you do.*

on one's back having sexual intercourse. (Usually used to describe women.) □ *There were ugly rumors that she earned her promotion on her back.* □ *She has a new boyfriend, so I bet she spent the whole weekend on her back.*

on the (blank) side very (blank). □ *She's about five foot six and on the heavy side.* □ *He's on the slow side. You have to explain everything to him five or six times before he gets it.*

on the side outside of marriage. (To *have someone on the side* or *have something on the side* is to be having sex with someone outside of marriage.) □ *I hear George has a little something on the side.* □ *Can you believe it? Paula has a man on the side!*

on the town drinking alcohol. □ *Looks like Charlie had a night on the town.* □ *Come on, you guys! Let's go out on the town!*

on the up and up honest and legal. (Usually used in the negative.) □ *I am not sure that Bill's business is entirely on the up and up.* □ *Stay away from that car dealer. She isn't exactly on the up and up.*

on the wagon not drinking alcohol. (Compare with **fall off the wagon**. To *go on the wagon* is to stop drinking alcohol.) □ *No, I don't care for a cocktail. I'm on the wagon.* □ *Bob's old drinking buddies complained that he was no fun when he went on the wagon.*

open enrollment the practice of allowing anyone to enroll who wants to. □ *There are no admissions requirements at Mainway Community College. We have open enrollment.* □ *Because of our policy of open enrollment, we attract students of a wide variety.*

open housing making housing available to people of all races. □ *The open housing law means you can't refuse to rent to Hispanics.* □ *The investigators tested the open housing policies of the major apartment complexes in the city.*

open marriage a marriage in which both partners are allowed to have sexual relations with other people. □ *Jim's affairs don't bother me. We have an open marriage.* □ Bob: *I can't sleep with you. You're married.* Jane: *Don't be silly. We have an open marriage.*

open shop a company in which the employees do not belong to a union. □ *We pride ourselves on our good labor relations, which have allowed us to maintain an open shop.* □ *The labor organizer wanted to win over the employees in the open shop.*

operative a spy. (See also **operator**.) □ *How many operatives do we have in Mexico City?* □ *The operatives were working independently, so that if one of them was caught, he or she would know nothing of the other's activities.*

operator a spy. (See also **operative**.) □ *She was an operator for the Chinese government.* □ *How could they know that? They must have an operator within the agency!*

ordnance weapons and ammunition. □ *We will use heavy ordnance against the enemy position.* □ *Once the ordnance was in place, the shelling began.*

ordnance success the ability of a weapon to kill people and destroy things. □ *This particular weapon had a high rate of ordnance success.* □ *The ordnance success of the missiles was not what we had hoped.*

organization, the a criminal organization. (See also syndicate.) □ *"You shouldn't talk to the cops, Pretty Boy,"* said the Boss. *"It ain't good for the organization."* □ *The organization profited from all the prostitution and gambling in the city.*

organize someplace to persuade the people who work someplace to join a union. □ *Kathy wants to organize the nursing home where she works.* □ *The union successfully organized several factories in the town.*

otherly abled not able to do something easily. (Replaces crippled.) □ *This bathroom is accessible for otherly abled users.* □ *Otherly abled people would have difficulty getting up these stairs.*

other place, the Hell. □ *If you're good, you'll go to Heaven, and if you're bad, you'll go to the other place.* □ *If she keeps up her drinking and gambling, she's headed to the other place for sure.*

other side of the tracks AND **wrong side of the tracks** the poor part of a town or city. □ *He was a rich boy, and she was a girl from the other side of the tracks.* □ *You don't want to buy a house in that neighborhood. It's on the wrong side of the tracks.*

other side, the death. □ *We shall meet our dear departed on the other side.* □ *She's gone to the other side. I hope she is at rest.*

other than honorable discharge a dishonorable discharge from the military. □ *His drinking and drug use resulted in an other than honorable discharge.* □ *The soldier was threatened with an other than honorable discharge.*

other woman, the a woman with whom a married man is having sex outside of marriage. □ *I love Jim, but I refuse to be the other woman.* □ *Tell me about the other woman. Is she prettier than me?*

outcall service a prostitution service. □ *He phoned the outcall service and asked to have someone come to his room.* □ *Our outcall service is very discreet.*

outhouse an outdoor toilet. □ *I hate having to go out to the outhouse in the rain.* □ *I put a roll of toilet paper in the outhouse.*

outplacement help finding jobs for people who have been fired. □ *Although we are letting you go, we do provide outplacement for up to six months.* □ *The human resources department is also responsible for outplacement.*

outside sexual contact sexual relations outside of marriage. (A medical phrase.) □ *As for the source of the infection, have you or your partner had any outside sexual contact within the last year or so?* □ *Her husband is infertile. Therefore, her pregnancy must be the result of outside sexual contact.*

outsource something to pay someone outside the company to do something. □ *We don't do any computer programming in-house anymore. We outsource all of it.* □ *By* *deciding to outsource word processing, we were able to down-size all of our word processing and secretarial staff.*

overcome extremely drunk. □ *Several of the wedding guests were overcome by the end of the reception.* □ *Jim, overcome, passed out on the bar.*

overdue more than nine months pregnant. □ *Sally's over-due, isn't she? I thought she was supposed to have her baby two weeks ago.* □ *Poor Emma. She's overdue, and she's had such a hard time of it, too.*

overfly someplace to spy on someplace from an air-plane. □ *The pilot overflew the disputed territory.* □ *Why was a private plane overflying a Soviet country?*

overindulge to eat or drink until you are sick. (See also indulge.) □ *The food was so good, and there was so much of it, that several of us overindulged.* □ *I overindulged last night. I have a hell of a headache today.*

over-tired drunk. □ *I'll drive him home. He's over-tired.* □ *I was rather over-tired after the party last night.*

overweight fat. □ *She was overweight when she was younger, but she's really slimmed down now.* □ *My doctor says I'm overweight and should get more exercise.*

pacify someone or something to attack someone or something. □ *Troops were sent to pacify the region.* □ *The president threatened to send in the National Guard to pacify the demonstrators.*

package store a store that sells alcohol. □ *Is the package store on the corner open on Sundays?* □ *The package store sells a large variety of beers.*

page-style hairdo a hair style with straight sides between chin- and shoulder-length and short bangs in front. (Replaces *pageboy*, which does not include adults or girls.) □ *All the band members had page-style hairdos.* □ *In the fifties, page-style hairdos were popular.*

pain management the practice of treating pain with large doses of drugs. □ *Pain management is an important aspect of terminal care.* □ *The hospice nurses were trained in pain management.*

painted woman a prostitute. (Old-fashioned.) □ *He spent all his money on painted women.* □ *Painted women and worn-out gamblers lived in that part of town.*

panties girl's or women's underpants. □ *They have cotton panties on sale at the department store.* □ *Her pants were so tight that you could see the outline of her panties.*

parallel pricing the practice of all sellers setting the same price for something. (Replaces *price fixing*.) □ *Parallel pricing in the airline industry made it hard to get a good deal on a ticket.* □ *The journalist suspected that the dairy farmers were engaging in parallel pricing.*

paramilitary trained to fight, but not part of the military. □ *The gunman belonged to a paramilitary group that believed in states' rights.* □ *Johnson ran a paramilitary organization that was loyal to him, not to the government.*

paramour a sexual partner. □ *Dave's latest paramour is a redhead.* □ *Her parents disapproved of her paramour.*

pardon my French "Please excuse my swearing." □ *God damn it! Pardon my French.* □ *He's a bastard, if you'll pardon my French.*

parentalism the practice of claiming that you know what is best for someone else. (Replaces *paternalism*.) □ *People in developing countries often resent the parentalism of aid workers from industrial countries.* □ *Jane thought she was giving Bob helpful advice. Bob thought she was displaying offensive parentalism.*

parental leave time off from work in order to care for a new baby. (Replaces *maternity leave*, which does not include fathers.) □ *James will take two months' parental leave when his baby is born.* □ *Two of our staff members are on parental leave right now.*

partially sighted not able to see well. (See also **visually impaired**.) □ *Carrie is partially sighted, but she is not able* *to see well enough to read.* □ *I am not blind. I am partially sighted.*

particular the female genitals. (Old-fashioned. Similarly: Cape of Good Hope, cleft, conundrum, crumpet, fanny, happy valley, Holy of Holies, honey-pot, love chamber, Low Countries, muff, nonesuch, secret parts, temple of Venus.) □ *He was inexperienced in the ways of love, and had never before entered the particular.* □ *As they caressed one another, his hand strayed near her particular.*

partner a sex partner to whom you are not married. (Sometimes used to refer to homosexual sex partners who live with one another.) □ *Jim and his partner bought a house.* □ *My name is Lisa. This is my partner, Beth.*

pass (away) AND **pass on** AND **pass over** to die. (Similarly: answer the final summons, buy the farm, cash in one's chips, curl up one's toes, drop off the hooks, fade, join the great majority, perish, slip one's cable.) □ *Jim's dad passed away last year.* □ *I was so sorry to hear about your sister. When did she pass?* □ *My first wife passed on ten years ago.* □ *Her parents passed over when she was very young.*

pass gas to release intestinal gas through the anus. (Similarly: back talk, flatulence, flatus, make a raspberry, make a rude noise, pass wind, puff, step on a frog.) □ *Someone on the bus had passed gas. It smelled awful.* □ *Something I ate at lunch made me pass gas all afternoon.*

passive euthanasia the act of killing someone by removing machines that are keeping him or her alive. (Compare with **active euthanasia**.) □ *The doctor would not consider active euthanasia, but believed that passive euthanasia was not wrong.* □ *His relatives wanted to end his suffering by passive euthanasia.*

pass on See pass (away).

pass over See pass (away).

pass water See make water.

patriot a trained fighter who opposes the government. (Refers specifically to antigovernment fighters, typically white men, who became prominent in the United States in the 1980s and 1990s.) □ *The local group of patriots published a newsletter claiming that the government was poisoning everyone's drinking water.* □ *The patriots refused to pay their taxes. When officials came to collect their taxes, the patriots met them with guns.*

patron a customer. □ *The restaurant was full of patrons.* □ *The librarian helped the patron find the book she wanted.*

pay a visit to urinate or defecate. □ *JILL: Where did Jane go? BILL: She needed to pay a visit.* □ *I stopped at the gas station to pay a visit.*

paying guest a person who rents a room. (British.) □ *I have two paying guests staying with me at the moment.* □ *Vera cooks and cleans for her family and their paying guest as well.*

pay one's debt to society to serve one's prison sentence. □ *I've paid my debt to society, and I'm ready to be a responsible person.* □ *You can't hold Harry's crime against him forever. He paid his debt to society.*

pay one's last respects (to someone) to go to someone's funeral. □ *I paid my last respects to Mr. Kantor yesterday.* □ *Scores of people came to pay their last respects.*

peace-keeper a soldier. □ *Two hundred United Nations peace-keepers were sent to the troubled region.* □ *One French peace-keeper was killed and three others were injured in the attack.*

peace-keeping mission a military occupation. □ *The troops were sent on a peace-keeping mission.* □ *The peace-keeping mission was composed of a multinational force.*

peace officer a police officer. □ *A call to 911 brought the nearest peace officers to the scene.* □ *The peace officer broke up the fight.*

peculation theft. (Formal.) □ *The senator denied that she had been involved in any peculation.* □ *The mayor was accused of graft and peculation.*

peculiar institution slavery in the United States. □ *The Emancipation Proclamation abolished the peculiar institution.* □ *Many white southerners owed their wealth to the peculiar institution.*

pee AND **go pee(-pee)** urine. (Pee-pee is baby talk.) □ *Do you have to go pee-pee?* □ *Daddy, I need to go pee.* □ *The meeting kept going on and on, and I really needed to pee!*

pellets feces in the form of small balls. □ *The lawn was covered with rabbit pellets.* □ *The goat left pellets all over her pen.*

penetrate someplace to break into someplace. □ *An intruder had penetrated the building.* □ *We estimate that the burglars penetrated the domicile at approximately one in the morning.*

penitentiary a prison. □ *The state penitentiary is in Joliet.* □ *He was sentenced to the federal penitentiary.*

people's republic a Communist country. □ *Have you ever visited the People's Republic of China?* □ *The victorious workers declared that the country was now a people's republic.*

perdition Hell. (Folksy. Can also be used to replace the exclamation, "Hell!") □ *If you continue in your sinful ways, you will perish in the fire of perdition.* □ *Perdition! I can't get this car to start nohow.*

perform 1. to have an erection of the penis. □ *When his wedding night finally arrived, he found himself unable to perform.* □ *He hoped that medical treatment would help him perform.* **2.** to have sex. □ *She was afraid that she would not be able to perform to his satisfaction.* □ *He bragged that he was able to perform for hours and hours at a time.*

perinatal mortality the death of a baby at birth. □ *The rate of perinatal mortality was slowly decreasing in that area.* □ *The pregnancy ended in a perinatal mortality.*

period a menstrual period. □ *I don't feel like jogging today. I got my period.* □ *It had been forty days since her last period. She was sure she was pregnant.*

permissive permitting sexual activities and the taking of drugs. □ *Anything goes, it seems, in this permissive society.* □ *His parents were much too permissive when he was a young man. They should have disciplined him more.*

perpetrator a criminal. (A police term.) □ *How did the perpetrator enter the premises?* □ *The victim was able to give us a good description of the perpetrator.*

perpetual care a payment for the care of a grave. □ *Our pre-need plan includes perpetual care.* □ *I pay thirty dollars a month for perpetual care for Mother.*

-person a person who works in or with a particular field. (Replaces *-man*. See **selectperson, committeeperson, chair(person)**.) □ *My name is Mary. I'm your new mailperson.* □ *What day does the garbageperson come around?*

personal flotation device a life jacket. □ *Place the personal flotation device over your head and fasten the buckles on the sides.* □ *Each boat passenger must wear a personal flotation device.*

personhole a hole in the street leading to a sewer. (Jocular. Replaces *manhole*.) □ *Are you visually impaired or something? Look down the personhole and see what's clogging the sewer!* □ *Gosh darn it, I almost fell down that personhole! They ought to make sure to put the personhole covers on those things.*

personhood one's identity as a human being. (Replaces *manhood* or *womanhood*.) □ *We must learn to value the personhood of others, even if they come from very different traditions.* □ *Jim may choose to express his personhood through sports activities, while Ron prefers artistic self-expression. Both are valid choices.*

personnel people, especially soldiers or employees. □ *We'll need heavy artillery and the necessary personnel.* □ *We may have to limit the number of new personnel we bring on board.*

person of color a person of African, Asian, or Native American descent. □ *The apartment manager clearly discriminated against people of color. He would only rent to whites.* □ *As a person of color, I felt threatened by the racist jokes that my co-worker told.*

person with a disability a person who is unable to do something easily. □ *Many people with disabilities depend on* *the bus to get where they need to go.* □ *There are two people with disabilities on the library staff. Mary is visually impaired, and Jim uses a wheelchair.*

person with a hearing loss a deaf or partly deaf person. □ *My mother is a person with a hearing loss, so I have learned to speak loudly and clearly when I talk to her.* □ *Some people with a hearing loss can be helped by hearing aids.*

person with AIDS AND **PWA** a person who has the disease known as Acquired Immune Deficiency Syndrome. □ *The clinic serves people with AIDS and also provides low-cost AIDS testing.* □ *Laura works as a companion to a PWA, who sometimes needs help taking care of himself.*

person with diabetes a person who has the blood-sugar disease known as diabetes. (Replaces *diabetic.*) □ *People with diabetes must be very careful about their sugar intake.* □ *I am a person with diabetes. I need to take insulin injections regularly.*

person with paraplegia someone who cannot move his or her legs. (Replaces *paraplegic.*) □ *Persons with paraplegia will find the handrails easy to use.* □ *David uses a wheelchair because he is a person with paraplegia.*

person with something a person who has a disease or disability. □ *Some people with cancer are turning to alternative therapies.* □ *I work with people with Alzheimer's.*

perspiration sweat. □ *The perspiration was running down her face.* □ *Perspiration can leave such awful stains on shirts.*

perspire to sweat. □ *The hot sun really made me perspire.* □ *The aerobics instructor said, "It isn't exercise until you perspire, ladies."*

persuade someone to do something AND **convince someone to do something** to force someone to do something. □ *The Boss persuaded the store owner to pay protection money.* □ *If we mention that it would be a shame if anything happened to her children, we may be able to convince her to do what we want.*

persuasion choice of sexual partners. □ *I don't think Bill is interested in going out with girls. He is of a different persuasion.* □ *Mary tried to determine Jill's persuasion through subtle questions.*

pest an unwanted animal, especially an insect or rodent. □ *This spray kills seventy different garden pests.* □ *How can I control pests in the house without using poison?*

petite [of a woman] short. □ *She is petite and a bit heavyset.* □ *The store sells business wear for petite women.*

pet odor the smell of the urine and feces of pet animals. □ *This carpet cleaner wipes out pet odors.* □ *This new brand of cat litter reduces pet odor.*

pet with someone to kiss, hug, and caress someone. (See also **make out with someone**.) □ *They petted with each other in the back seat of the car.* □ *She had petted with guys before, but she had never gone all the way.*

phallus the penis. □ *The statues of this god show him with an enormous phallus.* □ *The stone carving is in the shape of a phallus.*

pharmaceuticals illegal drugs. □ *I can set you up with some pharmaceuticals, if you need any.* □ *Mark makes his money in pharmaceuticals.*

pharmacy a drugstore. □ *Our grocery store now contains a pharmacy that can fill any prescription.* □ *I went down to the pharmacy to get some aspirin.*

physician a doctor. □ *See your physician before starting any exercise program.* □ *Dr. Vogel is a respected physician.*

physician assisted suicide the practice of a doctor giving someone drugs or equipment for killing him- or herself. (See also **assisted dying, planned termination, self-termination**.) □ *Physician assisted suicide is illegal in this state.* □ *Her death was a physician assisted suicide.*

physique the breasts. □ *She had a rather eye-catching physique.* □ *Just look at the physique on her!*

pick-me-up an alcoholic drink taken in the middle of the day. □ *She needed a pick-me-up to get through an afternoon at the office.* □ *I think I'll have a little pick-me-up.*

pick someone up 1. to invite someone to have sex with you. □ *He tried to pick that girl up, but she wasn't interested.* □ *She picks men up in bars and goes home with them.* **2.** to arrest someone. □ *The officer picked him up on a burglary charge.* □ *The officers went to the suspect's house and picked her up.*

pilfer something to steal something. □ *The store owner suspected her employees of pilfering snacks and soft drinks.* □ *He had been pilfering money from his mother's purse.*

pill, the a pill that prevents pregnancy. (To *be on the pill* is to be in the habit of taking birth-control pills.) □ *We don't need to use a condom. I'm on the pill.* □ *I would like to get a prescription for the pill.*

pink slip a document that tells you that you are fired. □ *I got my pink slip at work today. So did ten other guys.* □ *She opened the envelope marked "Confidential." As she had feared, it contained a pink slip.*

piquant having to do with sex. □ *He told some rather piquant stories about his island vacation.* □ *The movie contained a number of piquant scenes.*

pit stop a stop in order to urinate or defecate. □ *Let me make a pit stop before we go.* □ *We'll be in need of a pit stop by the time we get to Taylor Falls.*

placement the putting of a person, usually a child, into an institution. □ *Johnny has been having some trouble in his current placement at the youth home.* □ *Foster care would be the best placement for this client.*

plainclothes officer a police officer who does not wear a uniform. (Replaces *plainclothesman*, which does not include women.) □ *A plainclothes officer has been patrolling the subway.* □ *The arrest was made by a plainclothes officer.*

planned termination AND **planned death** a suicide. (See also **assisted dying, physician assisted suicide, self-termination.**) □ *If my suffering gets to be too much, I will consider planned termination.* □ *"Surely a planned death is better than living on as a vegetable!" Mary said heatedly.*

plastic surgery surgery to improve one's looks. (See also **aesthetic surgery, cosmetic surgery, procedure.**) □ *After the car accident, I had to have plastic surgery.* □ *She wanted to have plastic surgery to make her stomach smaller.*

plausible deniability ignorance. □ *We did not inform the president about our activities. We were concerned to maintain plausible deniability on his part.* □ *The memo from the* *mayor clearly showed she was aware that her secretary was taking bribes. Once the memo appeared, she no longer had plausible deniability.*

playboy a man who has sexual relations with many women. (See also **Don Juan**.) □ *The rich playboy was famous for holding orgies in his mansion.* □ *He doesn't love you. He doesn't love any of the women he goes out with. He's just a playboy.*

play with oneself to masturbate. (Similarly: beat the bishop, choke the chicken, diddle, five against one, onanism, pull one's pudding, the secret vice.) □ *He felt ashamed of playing with himself, but he couldn't stop.* □ *She would read sexy stories and play with herself.*

pleasantly plump fat. (See also plump.) □ *She's not a skinny thing like most of your young girls these days. She's pleasantly plump.* □ *Honest, you're not fat. You're just pleasantly plump.*

pleasure someone to bring someone to orgasm. (To *pleasure oneself* is to masturbate.) □ *He knew many ways of pleasuring a woman.* □ *She was fond of using a vibrator to pleasure herself.*

pledge something to pawn something. □ *He pledged his father's gold watch to get money for drugs.* □ *I may have to pledge that fur coat of mine to cover the groceries this month.*

plumbing the stomach and intestines. (Slang.) □ *The doctor is going to take a look at my plumbing.* □ *All that rich food did something to my plumbing.*

plump fat. (See also pleasantly plump.) □ *He was a rather plump boy.* □ *I'm too plump to borrow your clothes, but thanks for offering.*

plus size a clothing size for fat women. (See also **extended size, queen-size(d), women's size.**) □ *These panties also come in plus sizes.* □ *Do you have this pair of jeans in a plus size?*

pocket something to steal something. □ *He pocketed the car keys that he saw on the table.* □ *The mayor had been pocketing most of the money that was set aside for a new city park.*

police action a war. □ *He had served in the police action in Korea.* □ *The president ordered troops to participate in a police action overseas.*

police officer a person who works for the police. (Replaces *policeman* and *policewoman*.) □ *Jane is studying to be a police officer.* □ *All police officers must pass a physical exam every year.*

politically correct politically liberal. □ *The candidate's views on women in the workforce were hardly politically correct. "The girls ought to stay home and raise babies," he said.* □ *It is not politically correct to speak of* non-whites. *The accepted term is* people of color.

polygraph a lie detector. □ *The suspect refused to submit to a polygraph.* □ *The polygraph showed that she was probably telling the truth about what she had done that night.*

polymer plastic. (See also **resin.**) □ *This fine collector's pen is made of high-impact polymer.* □ *This outdoor furniture is coated in water-resistant polymer.*

poop AND **poo** AND **pooey** feces. (Baby talk. To *go pooey* is to defecate. See also **do(-do), tooey.**) Other kinds of dung: ca-ca, cow flop, doody, fecal matter, hockey, **horse apple**, meadow muffin, ordure, **road apple**, turd.) □ *There's* *a big dog poop in our driveway.* □ *Do you need to go pooey?* □ *Is there poo in your diapers?*

poorly 1. very ill. □ *JIM: How's your dad doing? JILL: Poorly, I'm afraid.* □ *She is poorly, and the doctor says she should not have any visitors.* **2.** menstruating. □ *I don't care to go swimming when I'm poorly.* □ *She went on the hike even though she was poorly.*

poppycock nonsense. (A very mild replacement for *bullshit*.) □ *Oh, poppycock. You can't get cancer from talking on the phone.* □ *Stop talking poppycock. Of course you're going to pass the test.*

popular justice the punishment of criminals by civilians. □ *Jones was acquitted, but he did not escape popular justice. The townspeople broke into his jail cell, dragged him out, and hanged him.* □ *The sheriff had almost no authority in that little Western town. Popular justice reigned.*

population transfer the act of forcing people to move from one place to another. □ *A massive population transfer of minority citizens was taking place.* □ *The general ordered that passenger trains be used for population transfer.*

portly fat. (Usually used to describe men.) □ *He was a rather portly gentleman.* □ *Larry is the portly fellow over there, with the brown mustache.*

position a job. □ *I am seeking a position as a data entry clerk.* □ *We had sixty-three applicants for the position.*

positive HIV-positive; having the HIV virus, which is the precursor to AIDS. □ *Not all positive people develop full-blown AIDS.* □ *When he learned he was positive, he started to take better care of his health.*

posterior the buttocks. □ *He has a rather broad posterior.* □ *This hard chair is not kind to my posterior.*

post-traumatic stress syndrome AND **post-traumatic stress disorder** depression and fear caused by a stressful event, such as fighting in a war. (See also **battle fatigue**.) □ *When he returned from the war, his post-traumatic stress syndrome was so severe that he was barely able to function.* □ *Many crime victims show symptoms of post-traumatic stress disorder.*

potation an alcoholic drink. □ *Potations were freely available at the party.* □ *A cocktail called the "kamikaze" was his favorite potation.*

potty 1. a toilet. (Baby talk.) □ *Do you need to go to the potty?* □ *I have to sit on the potty for awhile.* **2.** mentally ill. (British slang.) □ *Don't listen to him. He's potty.* □ *She's potty about cats. She has twenty-six of them.*

potty mouth a habit of swearing. (*Potty* refers to a toilet.) □ *That friend of yours has kind of a potty mouth, doesn't he?* □ *I can't believe her parents let her get away with that potty mouth of hers.*

potty-trained See **toilet-trained**.

powder one's nose to defecate or urinate. (Usually used by or of women. Implies that one is going to the toilet to groom oneself.) □ *Where can I powder my nose?* □ *She left the table to go powder her nose.*

powder room a toilet for women or girls. □ *You'll find the powder room just down the hall.* □ *It's been almost twenty minutes since she went to the powder room. Do you suppose she's all right?*

pox, the syphilis. (Slang.) □ *He caught the pox from a lady of the evening.* □ *People used to die of the pox.*

PR See public relations.

prairie oysters the testicles of a bull, served as food. □ *He fried up a dish of prairie oysters.* □ *Ever tried prairie oysters?*

prearrangement See pre-planning.

precipitation rain or snow. □ *Expect about three quarters of an inch of precipitation.* □ *There is no precipitation in the forecast.*

predecease someone to die before someone. □ *If my wife should predecease me, I leave my property to my brother.* □ *Have you given any thought to what you would like to do in case, God forbid, your children predecease you?*

pre-driven [of a car or truck] used. □ *We sell high quality pre-driven vehicles.* □ *If the new models are out of your price range, perhaps you'd like to look at our pre-driven automobiles.*

pre-emptive strike See preventive strike.

pre-funding See pre-planning.

pregnancy interruption See therapeutic interruption of pregnancy.

preindustrial [of a place] not having factories. (See also industrial(ized), non-industrial(ized).) □ *The country has many natural resources, but is largely preindustrial.* □ *The majority of the population is engaged in agriculture. The country as a whole is preindustrial.*

preliterate not able to read or write. (Sometimes used as a replacement for *primitive*.) □ *The preliterate peoples in the area did not understand the importance that the European settlers attached to written agreements.* □ *The members of this tribe are preliterate hunter-gatherers.*

pre-need [of a funeral, coffin, or grave plot] paid for in advance. (Compare with **at-need**. See also **before need, pre-planning**.) □ *Perhaps you would like to consider pre-need arrangements for yourself and your husband.* □ *Our complete pre-need package includes floral tributes and perpetual care.*

pre-orgasmic never having experienced orgasm. (Replaces *frigid*.) □ *The sex therapist had frequently been able to help pre-orgasmic women.* □ *There may be a number of reasons why your wife is pre-orgasmic.*

pre-owned AND **previously owned** used. □ *All of the pre-owned cars and trucks we sell are in top condition.* □ *We sell previously owned furniture at discount prices.*

prepare someone to preserve someone's dead body. (Replaces *embalm someone*.) □ *For an open casket funeral, you will want to have us prepare your loved one.* □ *The mortician carefully prepared the old man.*

pre-planning AND **prearrangement** AND **pre-funding** the act of paying for a funeral in advance. (See also **before need, pre-need**.) □ *Pre-planning means your family won't have to worry about the arrangements.* □ *Many people find that prearrangement is more economical than at-need services.* □ *Pre-funding can give you great peace of mind.*

preposition someone or something to move soldiers or weapons in preparation for an attack. □ *The unit prepositioned the artillery.* □ *The commander prepositioned his soldiers early in the morning.*

presence a military occupation. □ *The protesters opposed the U.S. presence in Japan.* □ *The Soviet presence in Cuba caused great unease.*

present feces. (Cute.) □ *The baby left a present in her diapers.* □ *The puppy has given us a number of presents all over the kitchen floor.*

prevaricate to lie. (Formal.) □ *Do you accuse me of prevaricating?* □ *He made a poor attempt to prevaricate.*

preventive detention imprisonment without bail. □ *The suspect was kept in preventive detention.* □ *Preventive detention is intended to discourage repeat offenders.*

preventive strike AND **pre-emptive strike** an attack. (See also **anticipatory attack**.) □ *The enemy was escalating their preparations. It was decided to launch a preventive strike.* □ *Once we detect an enemy missile launch, will we have time for a pre-emptive strike?*

previously owned See pre-owned.

Prince of Darkness the Devil. □ *The satanists worshipped the Prince of Darkness.* □ *The Prince of Darkness was fighting for her soul.*

private function defecation or urination. (See also **bodily functions, natural functions**.) □ *She was fond of discussing private functions at the dinner table.* □ *He retired to perform a private function.*

(private) parts AND **privates** the genitals. □ *Make sure you wash everywhere, even your private parts.* □ *The magazine showed naked women with their parts on display.* □ *He has a medical condition which affects his privates.*

privileged rich and upper-class. (Compare with **under-privileged**.) □ *She came from a privileged background.* □ *He had a privileged upbringing.*

privy a toilet, especially an outdoor toilet. □ *The cabin has a privy out in back.* □ *She had to use the privy about twice an hour.*

problem an illness. (See also **trouble**.) □ *She has a stomach problem.* □ *I'm on medication for a skin problem.*

pro bono [of legal work] free. (See also **legal aid**.) □ *She is taking this case pro bono.* □ *The law firm encourages its attorneys to do pro bono work for underprivileged clients.*

procedure a surgery. □ *Dr. Gates will be performing the procedure.* □ *Your medical insurance will cover sixty percent of the cost of this procedure.*

process with someone to make someone agree with you. □ *I processed with Jane on the subject of appropriate workplace behavior, and she understands now that ethnic humor is out of place.* □ *The principal spent several hours processing with the students who had committed the vandalism. As a result, they agreed to clean up the mess they had made.*

pro-choice in favor of legal abortion. (Compare with **pro-life**.) □ *Is our state senator pro-choice or pro-life?* □ *The candidate appealed to pro-choice voters.*

procurer a person who finds customers for prostitutes. □ *Her procurer took most of the money she got from the johns.* □ *He is a procurer with six girls working for him.*

professional a person with a high-level office job. (Replaces *businessman* and *businesswoman*.) □ *The down-*

town restaurants are patronized mostly by professionals who work nearby. □ *Most airplane passengers are professionals traveling on business.*

professional car a car for carrying a dead body in a coffin. (Replaces *hearse.* See also **funeral coach.**) □ *The widow and children of the deceased will ride in the professional car.* □ *The bill for the arrangements will include a small fee for the use of the professional car.*

program a medical or psychological treatment for a disease. □ *When his alcohol problem became obvious, Jim was allowed to keep his job if he agreed to participate in an alcohol abuse program.* □ *The hospital's weight control program includes body image work in addition to diet and exercise.*

program someone to torture or brainwash someone. □ *The cult had programmed him to distrust everyone outside of it.* □ *The soldiers were trained to resist any attempt to program them.*

pro-life opposed to legal abortion. (Compare with **pro-choice.**) □ *The pro-life booklet described an abortion in great detail.* □ *The pro-life activists picketed the abortion clinic.*

prominent rich or important. □ *Several prominent professionals formed a committee for promoting ethical behavior in the workplace.* □ *He comes from one of the city's most prominent families.*

prophylactic a device for preventing pregnancy. (Often used to mean *condom.*) □ *He bought a box of prophylactics.* □ *In health class, we had to unroll prophylactics onto a banana.*

proposition someone to ask someone to have sex with you. □ *I stopped going to that bar. Every time I would go* *there, somebody would proposition me.* □ *Jane took a deep breath and propositioned the good-looking man.*

prosperous rich. □ *Jim is quite prosperous, I believe.* □ *Her grandparents were prosperous farmers.*

prosthesis AND **prosthetic device** an artificial body part. □ *Although Nancy is missing one leg, she does not wear a prosthesis. She uses crutches instead.* □ *Vincent is able to grasp large objects, such as door handles, with his prosthetic device.*

prostitute a person who has sex for money. □ *She became a prostitute when she was sixteen.* □ *The park is mostly a hangout for prostitutes both male and female.*

protected class a group of people whom the law protects from discrimination. □ *Older workers are a protected class.* □ *As a visually impaired Hispanic woman, Maria belongs to several protected classes.*

protection 1. a method for preventing pregnancy or sexually transmitted disease. □ *If you're going to have sex, you should use protection.* □ *"Have you got protection?" she whispered as they undressed.* **2.** a payment to keep criminals from harming someone or something. □ *All the business owners in town were paying protection to the Boss.* □ *I can't believe that thug wanted me to pay him protection!*

protective custody the practice of keeping someone in prison to prevent him or her from being harmed. □ *The state kept their star witness in protective custody.* □ *When Pretty Boy turned state's evidence, he asked to be put in protective custody.*

psychiatric hospital See mental hospital.

public aid welfare. □ *Public aid is available for indigent women with small children.* □ *After Dad lost his job, we went on public aid for awhile.*

public relations AND **PR** the practice of making someone or something look good to the public. □ *Jane does public relations for the mayor's office.* □ *After the accident at the power plant, the electric company needed a lot of help with PR.*

puddle a pool of urine. □ *The dog made a puddle on the floor.* □ *The baby left a puddle behind her.*

pudendum AND **pudenda** the sex organs. (Usually used to describe the female sex organs.) □ *The pornographic photographs in the magazine emphasized the female pudendum.* □ *He stole into his father's study, took down the medical book, and turned to the page that depicted the pudenda.*

puppy fat fat on a young person. □ *You could say she's chubby, but it's just puppy fat. She's going to be a knockout when she grows up.* □ *In seventh grade, he joined the track team, and lost the last of his puppy fat.*

pure having never had sex. □ *I'm keeping myself pure for marriage.* □ *The pastor encouraged young Christians to remain pure.*

put one's affairs in order to prepare for death by making a will. □ *The growth may very well be benign, but all the same, it would be best if you took some time to put your affairs in order.* □ *She put her affairs in order. All her wealth would go to her youngest nephew.*

put someone out of his or her misery to kill someone. □ *The suffering woman begged for someone to put her out of her misery.* □ *The soldier could not bear the screams* *of his dying comrade. So, with tears running down his face, he raised his pistol and put Jonesie out of his misery.*

put someone out of the way to kill someone. □ *His illness is such a terrible strain on the family, it would really be a mercy if someone would put him out of the way.* □ *The police suspected that she had put her uncle out of the way in order to inherit his property.*

put something away AND **put something down** AND **put something to sleep** to kill a pet animal. □ *Poor old Fluffy was suffering so much that we had the vet put him away.* □ *I hated to part with Fido, but he was old and sick, and it was time to put him down.* □ *If an animal at the pet shelter is not adopted, a trained veterinarian will put it to sleep in a humane manner.*

PWA See person with AIDS.

quantitatively challenged fat. (Usually jocular. See also challenged.) □ *The seats on this airplane are very uncomfortable for quantitatively challenged passengers.* □ *OK, so I weigh 350 pounds. Just say I'm quantitatively challenged.*

queen-size(d) a clothing size for fat women. (See also extended size, plus size, women's size.) □ *I bought four pairs of queen-sized pantyhose.* □ *This queen-size blouse is really comfortable.*

questionable dishonest or illegal. □ *Bob is involved in some questionable dealings.* □ *The records showed several questionable transactions involving a "Mr. Smith."*

quick entry law a law that allows police to enter any building without knocking first. (Replaces *no-knock law.*) □ *The quick entry law allowed the police to make raids on the drug houses in the neighborhood.* □ *Several officers had used the quick entry law as an excuse to break in and terrorize honest citizens.*

quiet cell a cell in which a prisoner is kept alone. (Replaces *solitary confinement.*) □ *After she yelled at the guard, she had to spend a week in the quiet cell.* □ *The guard threatened to send Pretty Boy to the quiet cell.*

R

racy See spicy.

raise one's hand to someone AND **lift one's hand to someone** to hit someone. □ *If you ever raise your hand to me, by God, you'll regret it.* □ *He lifted his hand to his children whenever they disobeyed him.*

rancher a person who raises cattle. (Replaces *cowman*, which does not include women.) □ *Mary invited other ranchers in the area to come to a meeting about grazing rights.* □ *The ranchers sent their cattle to market in the city.*

rationalize something to reduce something, especially a group of employees. □ *It has become necessary to rationalize the workforce.* □ *We are forced, most reluctantly, to rationalize the support staff.*

Rats! "I wish that had not happened!" (A mild replacement for *Damn!*) □ *Rats! I lost my keys again!* □ *Rats! The battery's dead!*

ravish someone to rape someone. (Literary.) □ *The soldier ravished the captive woman.* □ *He was accused of ravishing his host's wife.*

realtor a person who sells buildings and land. □ *The realtor showed us several homes in our price range.* □ *The realtor suggested that we make an offer on the store building.*

(rear) end AND **rear** the buttocks. □ *Behave, or I'll swat you on your rear end.* □ *She slipped and fell on her rear.* □ *These seats are too hard for my poor old end.*

reasonable cheap. □ *The car runs OK, and the price is reasonable.* □ *I like to go to this restaurant for lunch. The food is quite reasonable.*

receding hairline baldness at the front of the head. □ *Dan's receding hairline makes him look distinguished, don't you think?* □ *He tried to disguise his receding hairline by combing his hair down toward his forehead.*

receiver a person who buys and sells stolen things. (See also **buyer**.) □ *The woman who owns that antique shop is a well-known receiver who deals in jewelry and silver.* □ *The police were observing the receiver, hoping that the thief would sell him the goods.*

receiving blanket a blanket for covering a nursing baby and the mother's breast. □ *We gave Beth baby clothes and a supply of receiving blankets for her baby shower.* □ *She carefully placed the receiving blanket over her shoulder before unbuttoning her blouse.*

recession a time of poverty. (Replaces *depression*.) □ *Economists disagree as to what caused the recession of the early 1980s.* □ *We're in a recession, and jobs are hard to find.*

recidivism a return to crime or drug addiction. □ *We find that giving job training to prisoners can decrease recidivism.* □ *What is the recidivism rate for graduates of this alcohol abuse program?*

reconaissance the act of moving through a place, looking for and destroying something. □ *The unit was sent on a reconaissance into the nearest village.* □ *The bomber pilot was flying a reconaissance when he was shot down.*

recreational drug a drug. □ *Alcohol is the most popular recreational drug in the United States.* □ *When she was in college, she experimented with marijuana, cocaine, and other recreational drugs.*

recruit someone to force someone to work for you as a spy. □ *The agency recruited several former KGB operatives.* □ *Because of his Communist sympathies, the Soviets were eager to recruit him.*

redact something to censor something. □ *The company's lawyer redacted some of the material before releasing it to the press.* □ *The memo had rather obviously been redacted. Whole paragraphs had been blacked out.*

red-light district an area with many prostitutes and houses of prostitution. □ *Harbor Street was a famous red-light district at the turn of the century.* □ *He went looking for the city's red-light district.*

redline someone to refuse to loan money to someone because they live in a poor area. □ *When we tried to apply for a mortgage, the bank redlined us.* □ *The credit union was accused of redlining a number of black loan applicants.*

reduction in force AND **RIF** the firing of a large number of people. □ *Ever since the reduction in force, those of us who kept our jobs are feeling nervous and overworked.* □ *There were rumors that the managers were planning a RIF.*

reedlike thin. □ *The dancer's reedlike figure swayed in time to the music.* □ *He was a reedlike young man.*

re-educate someone to torture or brainwash someone. (Usually used to describe brainwashing done by Communist governments.) □ *The new regime re-educated intellectuals by sending them to labor camps.* □ *The guard was in charge of re-educating the prisoners.*

re-education camp a prison. (See also **re-educate someone**.) □ *The professor spent six years in a re-education camp, hoeing beets.* □ *The scientist's colleagues learned that she had been sent to a re-education camp.*

reengineer something to fire a lot of people from something. (See also **downsize, reduction in force, reorganize, streamline**.) □ *The vice president announced that the company plans to reengineer our division.* □ *The consultant suggested reengineering the Chicago plant.*

reform school AND **reformatory** a prison for young people. (Somewhat old-fashioned.) □ *If he keeps stealing stuff, he's going to wind up in reform school.* □ *After she ran away from home for the sixth time, she was sent to a reformatory.*

refreshment an alcoholic drink. □ *Would you care for some refreshment?* □ *Refreshments are available at the cash bar.*

refresh someone's memory to question someone under torture. □ *If you won't tell me where you were on the night of the murder, maybe I need to refresh your memory.* □ *The questioner lifted the club. "Maybe this will refresh your memory," he said.*

refuse garbage. (Pronounced with the accent on the first syllable.) □ *Deposit refuse in the appropriate container.* □ *The sanitation engineer will collect refuse once a week.*

regular 1. [of a product] small. □ *What size soft drink do you want? Regular, large, or jumbo?* □ *The cereal comes in regular, large, or economy sized boxes.* **2.** [of a person] defecating at regular times. □ *I drink prune juice to keep myself regular.* □ *You haven't been regular for weeks. I wonder what the problem is?*

relationship a sexual relationship. □ *James and Maria were in a relationship last year, but now they're just friends.* □ *I'm sorry. I'm just not ready for a relationship right now.*

release someone to fire someone. □ *The company released twenty managers at the end of the fiscal year.* □ *Our department alone had to release ten people.*

relief welfare. (Old-fashioned. See also **assistance**.) □ *Their family had to go on relief in the Great Depression.* □ *In the old days, we didn't go asking for relief. We took care of ourselves.*

relieve oneself to urinate or defecate. □ *He stopped by the side of the road to relieve himself.* □ *She needed badly to relieve herself, but there was no bathroom in sight.*

relieve someone of his or her duties to fire someone. (Often used in the passive voice.) □ *I am afraid I must relieve you of your duties.* □ *After the scandal, she was relieved of her duties at the embassy.*

relieve someone of something to take something from someone. □ *A pickpocket relieved him of his wallet.* □ *The kids I hired to paint my house broke in and relieved me of my TV.*

religious a person who has taken religious vows, such as a monk, nun, or priest. (The plural is **religious**.) □ *Brother*

Anthony is a religious. □ *Many religious work as teachers or nurses.*

religious affiliation religion. □ *Employers are not allowed to discriminate on the basis of religious affiliation.* □ *The form asked me to list my religious affiliation.*

religious orientation religion. □ *Our scripture study group welcomes people of all religious orientations.* □ *Our neighborhood has faith communities from a variety of religious orientations.*

relocate someone AND **resettle someone** to force someone to move from one place to another. □ *The invading army relocated all the villagers.* □ *The government ordered troops to resettle the Indians in lands farther west.*

relocation center a prison camp. □ *The detainees were sent to a nearby relocation center.* □ *The journalist took pictures of starving people in the relocation center.*

remains a dead body. □ *The ambulance removed the remains from the scene of the crime.* □ *The remains of three people were found buried in the backyard.*

remedial having to do with educating people who have not learned as much as they should. □ *Janie is taking a remedial reading class this year.* □ *The college offered remedial programs in English and math.*

remove someone to kill someone. □ *One by one, the dictator removed his political opponents.* □ *The Boss thinks Pretty Boy may be an informer. If he is, we'll have to remove him.*

remuneration payment. (Formal.) □ *The doctor treated people who had been hurt in the fire, and she would not* *accept remuneration.* □ *JILL: Do you like your new job? BILL: The remuneration is certainly generous.*

render someone ineffective to kill someone. □ *The sniper rendered a number of soldiers ineffective.* □ *The gunner was ordered to render the sniper ineffective.*

render someone inoperative to injure someone severely. □ *The sniper was not killed, but we did render him inoperative.* □ *The gun battle rendered two officers inoperative.*

reorganization the firing of a large number of people. □ *The reorganization left only a skeleton crew on the night shift.* □ *If productivity does not improve, we may have to consider reorganization.*

reorganize to fire a large number of people. (See also **downsize, reengineer something, streamline**.) □ *The company reorganized last fall, and we still haven't sorted out everyone's new job title.* □ *We had to face a tough choice— reorganize, or shut our doors.*

repairer a person who repairs things. (Replaces *repairman*, which does not include women.) □ *I took my poor old VCR to the TV repairer.* □ *Jane and Bob are expert bicycle repairers.*

replacement worker a non-union worker who has been hired to take the place of a striking union worker. □ *The replacement workers were driven across the picket line every morning in an armored vehicle.* □ *When the union went on strike, the management immediately hired replacement workers.*

repose death. □ *She lies in such beautiful repose.* □ *He drew one last breath, and then fell back into his last repose.*

representative 1. a salesperson. □ *One of our sales representatives will be with you shortly.* □ *A customer service representative will be happy to take your order.* **2.** a member of Congress. (Replaces *congressman* and *congresswoman*.) □ *If you oppose this bill, write your representative and say so!* □ *Jane Williams is the representative from South Dakota.*

reproductive freedom the ability to prevent pregnancy and obtain legal abortion. □ *I believe that every child should be a wanted child. I believe in reproductive freedom.* □ *The new law eliminating public funding for abortions is a serious blow to the reproductive freedom of poor women.*

reproductive health the practice of preventing sexually transmitted disease and unplanned pregnancy. □ *The booklet gave basic information about reproductive health, recommending the use of condoms and explaining how sexually transmitted diseases are passed from person to person.* □ *The high-school health class included several lessons on reproductive health.*

reproductive responsibility the prevention of unwanted pregnancy. □ *"The sex education program should include information about reproductive responsibility," one school board member argued.* □ *Because Jim had fathered five children and was not willing to support any of them, his social worker felt that he needed education on the issue of reproductive responsibility.*

resale shop a place that sells used things. □ *I get some great dresses at the resale shop.* □ *They bought old furniture at a resale shop and fixed it up.*

resettle someone See relocate someone.

residence a house or apartment. □ *Have you visited Bob in his new residence?* □ *1917 Oak Avenue is the residence of Arthur Martinez.*

residential treatment center a hospital where addicts live while they are being treated for their addiction. □ *After losing her job because of her drinking, Maria checked into a residential treatment center.* □ *After a six-month stay in a residential treatment center, Jim felt he had finally kicked the drug habit.*

resign to quit before someone fires you. (See also **invite someone to resign.**) □ *Jane felt pressure to resign.* □ *In order to cut short this painful scandal, I have decided to resign.*

resin plastic. (See also **polymer.**) □ *This reproduction of a famous statue is crafted of durable cast resin.* □ *The surface of the table is an attractive high-tech resin that resists stains.*

resources money. □ *I'd like to start my own business, but I don't have the resources.* □ *Maintaining that big house is a strain on Paula's resources.*

response form a form that allows you to write down what you think about something. (Replaces *complaint form.*) □ *If you were pleased with our service, tell others. If you weren't, please fill out a response form and let us know why.* □ *After the way that bus driver treated me, I'm going to fill out a response form and send it to the bus company.*

rest house AND **rest home** a mental hospital. □ *Perhaps you might benefit from some time in a rest house.* □ *When Sarah began to show signs of strain, we found her the best rest home in the state.*

rest in Abraham's bosom See **be in Abraham's bosom.**

resting unemployed. (Most often used to describe actors.) □ *No, I'm not working on a show right now. I'm resting.* □ *She has been resting ever since the movie wrapped up six months ago.*

restorative an alcoholic drink. □ *Would you care for a restorative, old man?* □ *I felt I deserved a restorative after such a rotten day at work.*

restroom a toilet. □ *Which way to the restroom?* □ *I stopped at a gas station to use the restroom.*

restructure to fire a large number of people. □ *The management restructured two departments, but thank goodness, they left ours alone.* □ *Larry was let go when the company restructured.*

retire 1. to go to the toilet. □ *She excused herself and briefly retired.* □ *May I retire for a moment?* **2.** to retreat. □ *B Company was forced to retire.* □ *The commander ordered the troops to retire.*

retiree a person who has retired from his or her job. (Implies that the person is old.) □ *Many retirees move to warmer climates.* □ *The cruise was full of retirees.*

retirement community a place designed for old people to live. □ *Grandma sold her house and moved to a retirement community.* □ *The retirement community provides its residents with two meals a day and free transportation to the grocery store.*

retroactive exemption a rule that makes an exception for people or things that existed at the time the rule was made. (Replaces *grandfather clause*, which does not include women and may be offensive to old people.) □ *All newly hired librarians must have a master's degree, but, due to a* *retroactive exemption, our current librarians do not need to have one.* □ *A retroactive exemption in the building code allowed existing houses to get by without certain safety features.*

returning student a college student over the age of twenty-two. (See also **non-traditional student**.) □ *Most returning students do not live on campus.* □ *I enjoy the returning students that attend my classes. They are able to bring a more mature point of view to class discussions.*

revenue gap a lack of money. □ *We must increase taxes if we are to close the revenue gap.* □ *The audit shows a revenue gap of a quarter of a million dollars.*

reverse discrimination a bias against white people or men. □ *The plaintiff claimed that, in hiring a woman who was less qualified, the company had practiced reverse discrimination.* □ *The school district defended itself against charges of reverse discrimination by showing that it had dismissed as many teachers of color as white teachers.*

reverse engineering the illegal copying of a design. □ *Through reverse engineering, the manufacturer was able to duplicate its competitor's product.* □ *The company considered reverse engineering as part of the normal process of research and development.*

revisionist biased. □ *The author's revisionist retelling of the labor movement of the 1920s ignores the dirty tactics used by management to suppress the unions.* □ *The revisionist history text left out many significant facts about the European settlers of the American continent.*

RIF See reduction in force.

rightsizing the firing of a large number of people. □ *The consultant's report suggested a strategy for rightsizing.* □ *With the threat of rightsizing hanging over their heads, the employees worked desperately hard, hoping not to be fired when the time came.*

right-to-work anti-labor union. □ *The company instituted a right-to-work policy that disallowed union organizers from talking to workers during work hours.* □ *The plant owners wanted the legislature to pass a right-to-work bill.*

rinse a hair dye. □ *My stylist recommended a light blonde rinse.* □ *We'll just give you a rinse to color-correct the gray, shall we?*

risk factor something that is likely to cause disease. □ *Being overweight is a risk factor for heart disease.* □ *I quit smoking once I realized that it was a risk factor.*

risque having to do with sex or nudity. □ *She told a number of risque jokes.* □ *The movie was rather risque.*

road apple See horse apple.

rob the cradle to have sex with a much younger person. □ *Have you met Jim's new girlfriend? She can't be a day over eighteen. He's really robbing the cradle.* □ *When Jane's friends found out that her husband was seven years younger than she was, they teased her, saying she was robbing the cradle.*

rock lobster a crayfish. (The crayfish is a common, cheap shellfish, while lobster is rare and expensive.) □ *We serve rock lobster sauteed in butter and herbs.* □ *Freshly caught rock lobster is grilled and served on a bed of polenta.*

romance sexual activity. □ *Prepare for a night of romance.* □ *She was involved in a romance with an older man.*

Romani having to do with a group of people of northwest Indian descent. (Replaces *Gypsy*.) □ *A group of Romani travelers came through our town every spring.* □ *I learned to play the guitar from a Romani musician.*

roommate a sexual partner with whom you are living. (See also **cohabit, live in sin, live together**.) □ *I'd like you to meet my roommate, Fred. We've been together for a year and a half.* □ *Jane broke up with her roommate, so she's going to need a new place to live.*

rotund fat. □ *The rotund young woman huffed and puffed as she climbed the stairs.* □ *He gained weight until he was quite rotund.*

round-file something to throw something away. (Slang. Refers to putting something in the "round file," the garbage can.) □ *I get a lot of junk mail. I don't read it. I just round-file it.* □ SECRETARY: *You have a letter here from Ms. Branson.* BOSS: *Round-file it.*

round out to develop breasts. (See also **fill out, develop**.) □ *She began to round out when she was twelve.* □ *I haven't seen her since she was a skinny kid. She has really rounded out!*

routine nursing care only the practice of not using machines to keep someone alive. □ *His living will says he wants routine nursing care only should he become terminally ill.* □ *Her family has requested routine nursing care only, and so the doctor will take her off the respirator.*

rubber goods condoms. (Slang.) □ *I'll need a supply of rubber goods for the weekend.* □ *Will you pick up some rubber goods at the drugstore?*

rubbish nonsense. □ *JILL: I heard that cats can give you malaria. BILL: That's rubbish.* □ *Oh, rubbish. You don't really believe that.*

Rubensesque [of a woman] fat and big-breasted. □ *The dress looked lovely on her Rubensesque figure.* □ *The singer, a Rubensesque woman with striking black hair, had tremendous stage presence.*

rump the buttocks. □ *He flicked at the horse's rump with his whip.* □ *The doctor stuck the needle right in my rump.*

runs, the diarrhea. (Slang.) □ *Something I ate last night gave me the runs.* □ *He got sick and had the runs for three days.*

safe sex sexual activity using a condom or other barrier to disease. □ *The sex education class included a chapter on safe sex.* □ *"In the age of AIDS, it is important to practice safe sex," said the nurse.*

sales clerk a person who sells things in a store. (Replaces *salesman* and *saleswoman*.) □ *The sales clerks in that department store are so helpful.* □ *The sales clerk went to see if they had any other dress shoes in my size.*

sales event a sale. □ *Buy your car now, during our annual sales event!* □ *This kind of home electronics sales event doesn't happen every day!*

Salisbury steak ground beef; hamburger. □ *We serve a Salisbury steak sandwich with the accompaniments of your choice.* □ *How would you like that Salisbury steak? Rare, medium, or well-done?*

saliva spit. □ *Saliva dribbled from his mouth.* □ *There was dried saliva on her face.*

salty having to do with sex. □ *He knew a large number of salty stories.* □ *She told a few salty jokes.*

same gender oriented AND **SGO** homosexual. □ *The center provides resources for same gender oriented men and women.* □ *I think Jill is SGO. At any rate, she doesn't seem to be interested in men.*

sanatorium 1. a tuberculosis hospital. □ *He went to a sanatorium in New Mexico, hoping that the dry air would clear his lungs.* □ *Her relatives were afraid to visit her in the sanatorium. They didn't want to catch TB.* **2.** a mental hospital. □ *She spent several years locked up in a sanatorium.* □ *His psychiatrist recommended a stay in a private sanatorium.*

sand box See litter box.

sanitary product AND **sanitary napkin** a pad for absorbing menstrual blood. □ CUSTOMER: *Where can I find tampons?* SALES CLERK: *Sanitary products are in aisle 7.* □ *My period is due to start today, so I'll put a sanitary napkin or two in my purse.*

sanitation engineer AND **sanitation worker** a garbage collector. □ *The sanitation engineers make their pickup every Friday morning.* □ *The city sanitation workers went on strike, and garbage piled up in the streets.*

sanitize something to remove unpleasant or unfavorable things from something, such as a story or a document. □ *The author had sanitized stories from the Bible, taking out all references to sex and death.* □ *The mayor's staff sanitized the financial records before turning them over to the press.*

sapphic lesbian. (Literary. From Sappho, a Greek poet.) □ *The poems praised sapphic love.* □ *She first recognized her sapphic tendencies when she was a young girl at school.*

sartorially challenged badly dressed. (Jocular. *Sartorial* means *having to do with clothes*.) □ *That job applicant* *was sartorially challenged, wouldn't you say?* □ *She's a smart woman, but she's rather sartorially challenged.*

saturation bombing bombing that causes complete destruction. □ *The saturation bombing of the city was beginning to demoralize the citizens.* □ *The general selected several key sites for saturation bombing.*

sauna a house of prostitution. (**Sauna** does not always have this meaning. Judge from the context.) □ *The neighbors wanted to close down the three saunas on Calhoun Street.* □ *His wife found out that he was visiting a sauna twice a week.*

save oneself (for marriage) to remain a virgin until marriage. □ *No, I can't. I love you, but I'm saving myself for marriage.* □ *His buddies teased him, asking if he was saving himself.*

scarlet woman a prostitute. (Old-fashioned.) □ *He fell in love with a scarlet woman and wanted to make her his wife.* □ *The preacher worked among the drunks and the scarlet women in the worst parts of the city.*

scenario a secret plot. □ *The Boss came up with a scenario for taking care of Big Ray.* □ *"We'll need some kind of scenario if we're going to pull this off," said the mayor.*

score adjustment the practice of giving unfairly high test scores to women or people of color. □ *Jane was furious when she found out that her high marks on the civil service exam were the result of score adjustment.* □ *"Some score adjustment is necessary if the college is to admit the required number of women and minorities," the administrator said.*

Scot a person from Scotland. (Replaces *Scotsman* and *Scotswoman*.) □ *Scots turned out in large numbers to vote on* *the referendum that might lead to the end of English rule.* □ *Moira is a Scot, and so is Donald.*

scout a Boy Scout or Girl Scout. □ *Buses filled with scouts arrived at camp on the first day.* □ *Scouts will find this pocket knife handy and easy to use.*

scout leader a person who leads a troop of Boy Scouts or Girl Scouts. (Replaces *den mother* for women and *scoutmaster* for men.) □ *Scout leaders met to discuss fund-raising.* □ *Rick enjoys being a scout leader, and so does Cindy.*

seasonal employee AND **seasonal worker** foreign workers who come to harvest crops. (See also **migrant**.) □ *Owners of fruit farms rely on seasonal employees.* □ *When winter comes, most seasonal workers return home.*

seasoned old and experienced. □ *Spangler is a seasoned politician.* □ *She is a seasoned reporter whose opinions are always interesting.*

seat the buttocks. □ *Get your seat back down in that chair, young man.* □ *That skirt barely covered her seat.*

sea vegetable seaweed. □ *The vegetarian plate comes with a salad of sea vegetable and sesame seeds.* □ *The rice is wrapped in a sheet of toasted sea vegetable.*

seclusion a prison cell or hospital room where a person is locked up alone. (Replaces *solitary confinement*.) □ *He swore at the guard, so he had to do a day in seclusion.* □ *The patient was out of control and had to be put in seclusion.*

secure facility a prison. □ *The state is building a new secure facility in Harristown.* □ *He was held in a secure facility until his trial.*

seek professional help to get psychiatric treatment. □ *If you are seriously thinking of suicide, now is the time to seek professional help.* □ *His friends suggested that he seek professional help.*

see someone 1. to have sex with someone. □ *Are you seeing anyone these days?* □ *Who's that new woman James is seeing?* **2.** to receive psychiatric treatment from someone. □ *If your depression gets worse, I think you ought to see somebody.* □ *I'm seeing a wonderful therapist. She has helped me so much.*

segregation the separation of people of different races. (Compare with **integration**.) □ *The law was meant to eliminate segregation in public schools.* □ *Segregation is still a fact of life in many cities and towns.*

segregation unit a group of cells where prisoners are locked up alone. (Replaces *solitary confinement*.) □ *The segregation unit in this facility can handle up to twenty inmates.* □ *He spent two weeks in the segregation unit.*

selective untruthful. □ *His account of his activities on the night in question was quite selective.* □ *The company's lawyer gave a selective history of its involvement with the defective product.*

selective ordnance thickened gasoline used as a weapon; napalm. □ *Selective ordnance was a factor in the maneuver.* □ *It is unfortunate that selective ordnance did cause some collateral damage.*

selective service the practice of drafting people into the military. □ *All young men must register for selective service when they reach the age of eighteen.* □ *His name came up in the selective service, and he had to go to war.*

selectperson a person elected to serve in the government of a city or town. (Replaces *selectman* and *selectwoman*.) □ *I called my selectperson to complain about the garbage service.* □ *Jane is a candidate for selectperson.*

self-abuse masturbation. (Somewhat old-fashioned. Implies that masturbation is harmful.) □ *Young man, do you practice self-abuse?* □ *When I was young, the doctors taught that self-abuse could make you sterile.*

self-deliverance suicide. □ *The pain became worse and worse. She began planning her self-deliverance.* □ *He chose self-deliverance rather than living on in disgrace.*

self-termination suicide. (See also **assisted dying, physician assisted suicide, planned termination**.) □ *The book described several effective methods of self-termination.* □ *He chose self-termination rather than facing another round of operations.*

seller a person who sells things. (Replaces *salesman, saleswoman*.) □ *The encyclopedia seller comes through our neighborhood every fall.* □ *The car seller of the month is Diane. She sold twelve cars in April!*

sell oneself to have sex for money. □ *She sold herself to support her kids.* □ *Several of the homeless kids I met were selling themselves to get money for drugs.*

senior (citizen) an old person. □ *Many senior citizens in this district are active in party politics.* □ *We have special discounts for seniors.*

sensitive secret and dangerous. □ *The scientist's report was highly sensitive.* □ *The spy was able to transmit a number of sensitive documents before she was caught.*

separate but equal having blacks and whites separate, with worse conditions for blacks. (This phrase was used in the U.S. court case *Plessy v. Ferguson* to justify racial separation.) □ *The school district claimed that the primary schools were separate but equal.* □ *The apartment manager felt that the units he rented to black occupants were separate but equal, when in fact they were small, noisy, and poorly maintained.*

separate development the practice of keeping black and white people separate; apartheid. □ *The government's policy of separate development was less and less acceptable to the country's trading partners.* □ *"We feel that separate development allows both races to pursue their own interests without the discomfort of having to deal with one another," said the separatist.*

separation the firing of an employee. □ *Bill's time with us unfortunately ended in a separation.* □ *We have decided that a separation would be best for everyone at this point, and so we must regretfully let you go.*

servant a slave. (**Servant** was often used to mean *slave* in the United States in the 18th and 19th centuries.) □ *The plantation owner had ten house servants and over a hundred field hands.* □ *He brought his favorite servants with him when he traveled abroad.*

server a waiter or waitress. □ *My name is Kevin, and I'll be your server this evening.* □ *Please give this tip to our server.*

service an army, navy, or air force. □ *He went into the service after he graduated from high school.* □ *JANE: You were in the service? What branch? BOB: The navy.*

service member a soldier or sailor. (Replaces *serviceman* and *servicewoman*.) □ *The president praised all the brave service members who had risked everything for their country.* □ *Many service members were lonely during their service overseas.*

service someone or something to have sex with a female animal in order to make her pregnant. □ *We had two bulls to service the whole herd of cows.* □ *That's a prize stallion. You'll have to pay a stud fee to have him service your mare.*

sewer a person who sews. (Replaces *seamstress*, which does not include men.) □ *Jim's a good sewer. Have him fix your shirt.* □ *Twenty sewers worked in the clothing factory.*

sewer hole AND **utility access hole** a hole that leads to a sewer. (Replaces *manhole*. Compare with **personhole**.) □ *The sanitation worker went down through the sewer hole.* □ *I shone my flashlight down the utility access hole.*

(sexual) act sexual intercourse. (See also **act of love, catch someone in the act**.) □ *The newspaper report claimed that the politician had performed the sexual act with several women other than his wife.* □ *They had done some heavy petting, but had not yet engaged in the act.*

(sexual) congress sexual intercourse. (Somewhat formal. Usually in the phrase *to have (sexual) congress with someone*.) □ *The trial hinged on whether or not the defendant had had sexual congress with her previous boyfriends.* □ *Have you had congress with that woman?*

(sexually) explicit showing or describing sexual intercourse. □ *The book was sexually explicit.* □ *That movie is very explicit. It is not suitable for young people.*

sexually transmitted disease AND **STD** a disease that is passed on through sexual relations. (Replaces *venereal disease*. See also **social disease**.) □ *Using a condom can help prevent the spread of sexually transmitted diseases such as AIDS.* □ *He was taking an antibiotic for an STD.*

sexual orientation AND **sexual preference** the choice of same-sex or different-sex sexual partners. □ *We do not discriminate according to race, creed, color, gender, or sexual orientation.* □ *Do you happen to know Jim's sexual preference? Is he gay?*

sexual variety sexual relations with a large number of partners. □ *He felt that marriage was too limiting. He needed more sexual variety.* □ *People who prefer sexual variety have a greater need to practice safe sex.*

SGO See **same gender oriented**.

shapely having big breasts, a small waist, and big hips. □ *The swimsuit looked great on her shapely figure.* □ *Who is that shapely girl over there talking to Frank?*

share something to confess something. □ *I'm glad that you felt you could share that. Thank you for telling me.* □ *If you have an issue with this plan, I wish you would share it.*

sharpshooter a person who shoots accurately. (Replaces *marksman*, which does not include women.) □ *When I was in the service, I trained as a sharpshooter.* □ *Linda is quite a sharpshooter. You should watch her at target practice sometime.*

sharpshooting the ability to shoot accurately. (Replaces *marksmanship*, which does not include women.) □ *Annie Oakley's sharpshooting was famous.* □ *The cadet got a high score for sharpshooting.*

sheath a condom. (Similarly: armor, diving suit, dreadnought, French safe, latex, overcoat, prophylactic, raincoat, rubber, safe.) □ *He put on a sheath before they had intercourse.* □ *We always use a sheath when we make love.*

shoeshiner a person who polishes shoes. (Replaces *shoeshine boy* and *shoeshine girl*.) □ *I stopped at the shoeshiner's booth to get my shoes shined before work.* □ *The shoeshiner did a good job on my dress shoes, didn't she?*

shoot! AND **shucks!** "I wish that had not happened!" (Mild replacements for *shit!*) □ *Oh, shoot, did you have to take a picture while I had food in my mouth?* □ *Shucks! I lost again!*

shoplifter a thief who steals from a store. □ *The plainclothes officer caught two shoplifters that afternoon.* □ *The store guard was on the lookout for shoplifters.*

shoppe AND **shop** a store. □ *Visit our exclusive dress shoppe.* □ *The main street was lined with the cutest shops.*

shortfall a lack of money. □ *The bank statement shows a considerable shortfall.* □ *Owing to a shortfall, I am unable to pay my rent this month.*

show to be obviously pregnant □ *Is she pregnant? I wouldn't have known. She isn't showing yet.* □ *She's four months gone and definitely starting to show.*

showcraft the ability to entertain an audience. (Replaces *showmanship*, which does not include women.) □ *The magician's expert showcraft kept us all spellbound.* □ *The company president's speech displayed a good deal of showcraft. She kept us in suspense about the new product until she unveiled it at the very end.*

shrinkage a loss from theft. (See also **inventory leakage.**) □ *The grocery store experienced a shrinkage of about ten percent.* □ *The manager planned to reduce shrinkage by using hidden cameras in the store.*

shucks! See **shoot!**

SIDS AND **sudden infant death syndrome** the unexplained death of a baby. (Replaces *crib death* and *cot death*.) □ *He was two months old when he died of SIDS.* □ *The doctor listed the baby's cause of death as sudden infant death syndrome.*

sight-deprived blind. □ *She has been sight-deprived from birth.* □ *The accident left him sight-deprived.*

silver [of hair] gray. □ *Some silver showed at her temples.* □ *His silver hair was neatly trimmed.*

single parent a person who is raising a child alone. (Replaces *single mother, single father*.) □ *Affordable day care is very important for single parents who work outside the home.* □ *The welfare law was designed to help single parents who want to return to school.*

siphon off something to steal something, especially money. □ *He had siphoned off the money for the new road into his private bank account.* □ *She siphoned off most of the company's income, while her employees went without paychecks.*

sister of mercy AND **sister of charity** a prostitute. (Jocular and possibly offensive. *Sisters of Mercy* and *Sisters of Charity* are orders of nuns.) □ *I was approached by a sister of mercy with an interesting offer.* □ *He sought a sister of charity to help him relieve his feelings.*

sit-down job an act of defecation. □ *I'll be on the toilet awhile. It's a sit-down job.* □ *Do you need to do a sit-down job?*

sit pretzel-style to sit with one's legs folded together. (Replaces *sit Indian style*, which may be offensive to American Indians.) □ *Let's all sit pretzel-style in a circle.* □ *He sat pretzel-style on the floor while I sat on the chair.*

situation a serious problem. □ *There appears to be a situation in the control room of the power plant.* □ *The police were called in to deal with the hostage situation.*

sit-upon the buttocks. □ *He fell on his sit-upon.* □ *Do as I say, or I'll spank you on your sit-upon.*

skim from something AND **skim a little off the top** to steal something, especially money. □ *The sales staff were skimming from the cash payments that came in.* □ *When an investigation found money missing from the new bridge fund, the mayor was accused of skimming a little off the top.*

slack fill the practice of filling a container only part of the way. □ *The bags of potato chips had about one quarter slack fill, which was puffed up with air before they were delivered to the store.* □ *It looks like a big box of cereal, but you have to allow for slack fill.*

sleep aid a drug that makes you sleepy. (Replaces *sleeping pill*.) □ *This sleep aid is for occasional use only.* □ *From time to time, I take a sleep aid, if I am restless at night.*

sleep around to have sex with many people. □ *I wouldn't go out with Harry for anything. I heard he sleeps around.* □ *He was sure that his wife was sleeping around.*

sleeper a spy who is waiting to be used. □ *He was a sleeper, deep undercover.* □ *The other side had a sleeper in the high levels of the weapons facility.*

sleep together to have sex. (See also sleep with someone.) □ *Do you think Bill and Maria are sleeping together?* □ *My boyfriend wants us to sleep together.*

sleep with someone to have sex with someone. (See also sleep together.) □ *I slept with William once. It was nothing special.* □ *I want to sleep with you, honey. Can't you come over?*

slow not intelligent. □ *Jill is a little bit slow. You have to explain things to her a few times.* □ *The teacher did his best to help the slow learners in the class.*

slowdown a reduction in work that nearly amounts to a strike. (See also work-to-rule.) □ *The union threatened a slowdown if management did not agree to their demands.* □ *The workers who did not participate in the slowdown were shunned.*

slumber room a room in which dead bodies are prepared for burial. □ *We will prepare your loved one in the slumber room.* □ *The slumber room, as you will see, is quiet, sanitary, and respectful.*

slum owner a person who owns houses or apartments in bad condition and rents them to others. (Replaces *slumlord*.) □ *The tenants withheld their rent from the slum owner until she agreed to have the roof repaired.* □ *He is a slum owner who never goes near the property he owns.*

smallest room, the AND **little room, the** a room with a toilet. □ *He can't come to the phone right now. He's using the smallest room.* □ *Excuse me. I must find the little room.*

smartaleck a disrespectful person. (Replaces *smartass.*) □ *Don't be such a smartaleck.* □ *When Bobby was a kid, he was a real smartaleck, always talking back to his teachers.*

snow figure a human figure built out of snow. (Replaces *snowman,* which does not include women.) □ *Snow fell all night. In the morning, we raced out to build snow figures.* □ *Look at the snow figures on the Smith's front yard!*

so-and-so a worthless person. (Replaces a number of swear words.) □ *I'm tired of taking orders from that old so-and-so.* □ *The angry waiter called the customer a so-and-so and walked out of the restaurant.*

S.O.B. son of a bitch. (See also **G.D., son of a gun.**) □ *Stay away from him. He's a real S.O.B.* □ *Can you believe it? That S.O.B. wouldn't give me my money back!*

social disease a disease that is passed on through sexual intercourse. (See also **sexually transmitted disease.**) □ *He caught a social disease from one of his many brief affairs.* □ *Don't be silly. You can't get a social disease from a toilet seat.*

social killing death as a punishment for crime. □ *Seventy percent of the people surveyed are in favor of social killing.* □ *Social killing once again became legal in this state in 1973.*

social lie a lie intended to make someone feel better. (Replaces **white lie,** which may be offensive to black people.) □ *I told Jim that his cooking was wonderful, but that was a social lie.* □ *There's no harm in telling a social lie.*

social security welfare. (Note: **social security** does not always have this meaning. Judge from the context.) □ *Many seniors depend on social security to pay their rent.* □ *"Social security was never intended to be a primary source of income for retirees," argued the member of Congress.*

soft commission a bribe. □ *The budget needs to allow for a few soft commissions for the customs folks.* □ *For a modest soft commission, the factory inspector was willing to overlook a few safety violations.*

soil something to defecate or urinate on something. □ *My little boy is almost potty trained, but from time to time he does still soil his pants.* □ *She has grown incontinent in her old age, and it is so sad. She feels terribly ashamed when she soils herself.*

soldier a person in the army. (Replaces *enlisted man* and *enlisted woman*. See also **enlistee**.) □ *The soldiers wondered when they would be sent overseas.* □ *Every soldier was in top physical condition.*

soldier of fortune a soldier who works for any country that will pay. (Replaces *mercenary*.) □ *The government hired a company of soldiers of fortune to help fight the rebels.* □ *After he was discharged from the army, he became a soldier of fortune.*

solicit someone [for a prostitute] to invite someone to copulate. □ *The prostitute stood on the corner, soliciting those who passed by.* □ *She worked in the hotel bar, soliciting lonely business travelers.*

solid waste feces. □ *This plant removes harmful bacteria from solid waste.* □ *Once the solid waste has been treated, it is released into the river.*

solitary sex masturbation. □ *Solitary sex is an option for those without a partner or those who are separated from their partners.* □ *His only sexual experience had been solitary sex.*

someone or something has seen better days someone or something is in bad condition. □ *My old car has seen* *better days, but at least it's still running.* □ *She's seen better days, it's true, but she's still lots of fun.*

someone's race is run someone is dead. □ *Poor James. His race is run.* □ *She fought the good fight, and now her race is run.*

someone's time has come someone is about to die. □ *The poor old dog's time has come.* □ *My time has come. I'm ready to go.*

someone uses a wheelchair someone uses a wheelchair because he or she cannot walk. □ *Bill is a person with paraplegia, and so he uses a wheelchair.* □ *Several of our customers use wheelchairs. These new grocery carts are at a more convenient height for them.*

something disagrees with someone something makes someone sick. □ *I'll skip the dessert, thanks. Ice cream always disagrees with me.* □ *Something I had at dinner disagreed with me. I spent the whole night throwing up.*

something-free without something. (Replaces *something-less*.) □ *Try our new sugar-free, fat-free ice cream.* □ *The airline featured ticket-free travel.*

something oriented interested mainly in something. □ *He is very work oriented and often stays at the office until ten o'clock at night.* □ *All my male oriented friends really enjoy looking at the handsome men in the T-shirt ads.*

son of a gun AND **son of a bachelor** a worthless person. (Replacements for *son of a bitch*. See also **S.O.B.**) □ *That tight-fisted son of a gun.* □ *He can be a real son of a bachelor when he's in a bad mood.*

sortie a bombing flight. □ *They were flying a sortie every hour during the course of the offensive.* □ *The target for this sortie was a munitions factory about fifty miles out of the city.*

source a person or device that passes secret information along. □ *The reporter would not reveal his source for the story about the secret negotiations with Iran.* □ *The agency has a source in the household of every major player, and those sources are monitored twenty-four hours a day.*

souvenir 1. something stolen. □ *The soldier collected souvenirs from the enemy dead.* □ *The poet's house was being slowly destroyed by tourists collecting souvenirs.* **2.** feces. (Jocular.) □ *Some kind of animal is leaving souvenirs all over my basement.* □ *Is there a souvenir in baby's diaper?*

sow one's wild oats to have sex with many people. □ *You should sow your wild oats while you're young.* □ *He sowed his wild oats, and then he settled down and got married.*

space a grave. □ *I have a space right next to Daddy where I'll go when I pass on.* □ *The family plot has spaces for both my parents and all their kids.*

spare tire a fat belly and sides. □ *As a young man, he was very trim, but when he hit middle age, he started to get a spare tire.* □ *I'm going to start going to the gym so I can work off this spare tire.*

special lacking the ability to do something. (Replaces *disabled* and *(mentally) retarded*. See also **exceptional**.) □ *The elementary school has separate classes for special students.* □ *It is difficult to find adoptive homes for special children.*

special guest an act that opens a show for the main performer. □ *Come to the Deth-Hed concert, with special guest*

Cockroach. □ *Please give a warm welcome to tonight's special guest.*

special treatment torture or killing. (This phrase is associated with Nazi treatment of Jews in World War II.) □ *Jews, Gypsies, and homosexuals were set aside for special treatment.* □ *The prisoners were subjected to special treatment.*

specimen a sample of urine or feces. □ *The doctor will need a specimen. You'll find the plastic cups in the bathroom.* □ *The nurses took a stool specimen twice a day.*

spend a penny to urinate. (British. At one time, public toilets in England cost a penny.) □ *Excuse me, chaps. I need to spend a penny.* □ *Anywhere I can spend a penny?*

spend the night with someone to have sex with someone. □ *Spend the night with me. Please.* □ *They went to his apartment and spent the night together.*

spicy AND **racy** having to do with sex. □ *There were some very spicy pictures in that magazine.* □ *He told a racy story of his adventures in New Orleans.*

spit a worthless person or thing. (Replaces *shit.*) □ *Did you hear what that little spit said to me?* □ *I don't give a spit for her opinion.*

spit up to vomit. (Usually used to describe babies and young children.) □ *The baby spit up again.* □ *Something in the formula made her spit up.*

spokesperson a person who speaks on behalf of a group. (Replaces *spokesman* and *spokeswoman.*) □ *Ms. Donat is the spokesperson for the committee.* □ *The department elected a spokesperson.*

sponsor an advertiser. □ *Glue-Zit is a proud sponsor of the 1996 Car Race Extravaganza.* □ *And now, a message from our sponsor.*

sporting house a house of prostitution. (Old-fashioned.) □ *His wife knew he could be found at the sporting house.* □ *What were you doing in that sporting house?*

spousal maintenance a payment made to a person you have divorced. (Replaces *alimony.*) □ *Her ex-husband asked for spousal maintenance.* □ *She will receive four hundred dollars spousal maintenance every month. Maintenance will cease if she marries again.*

spouse a husband or wife. □ *Spouses are invited to the party.* □ *If you wish your spouse to be your primary beneficiary, please check here.*

staff something to have employees work on something. (Replaces *man something*, which does not include women.) □ *The computer hotline is staffed twenty-four hours a day.* □ *Who will staff the cash register when you go on break?*

starter home a small, cheap house. □ *They looked into buying a starter home when they first got married.* □ *I had saved enough for a down payment on a starter home.*

state farm a state prison. □ *I spent six years at the state farm.* □ *The judge sent him to the state farm.*

state hospital a public mental hospital. □ *His family could not afford to send him to a private clinic, so he was placed in the state hospital.* □ *The study said that patients at the state hospital received too many tranquilizers.*

state of nature nakedness. □ *The beach was covered with men and women in a state of nature.* □ *The young people went swimming in a state of nature.*

station manager a person who runs a train station. (Replaces *station master*.) □ *The station manager announced that the Chicago train would be two hours late.* □ *The engineer called ahead to the next station manager.*

statuesque [of a woman] tall and fat. □ *Her statuesque figure drew all eyes.* □ *She was statuesque and queenly, with a beautiful face.*

status offender a young person who did something that is against the law for children but not for adults. □ *"Runaways are status offenders and should not be tried or punished as adults," said the social worker.* □ *This facility was designed for status offenders who need a minimum of supervision.*

statutory rape sexual intercourse with a child. □ *Because his girlfriend was only sixteen, Bill was charged with statutory rape.* □ *He was arrested for statutory rape and contributing to the delinquency of a minor.*

STD See sexually transmitted disease.

sticky-fingered See light-fingered.

stimulant an alcoholic drink. □ *May I offer you some stimulants?* □ *She felt she needed a stimulant to face her angry husband.*

stipend a payment. □ *The theater company offers its actors a modest stipend.* □ *The fellowship includes a tuition waiver and a fairly generous stipend.*

stocky fat; large. □ *She has a rather stocky build.* □ *Everyone in my family is short and stocky.*

stonewall to conceal the truth. □ *The mayor instructed her staff to stonewall if reporters asked them any questions.* □ *We tried to get an honest answer out of the manager, but he just kept stonewalling.*

stool feces. (A medical term.) □ *Have your stools been unusually loose?* □ *We will need a sample of the animal's stools.*

story a lie. □ *Don't tell me a story. I want to know what really happened.* □ *She gave me some story about missing her bus, but I don't believe her for a minute.*

stout fat. □ *He is tall and stout.* □ *She grew stout as she got older.*

strapped (for money) AND **strapped for cash** lacking money. □ *What with no job, two kids and another one on the way, Bill and Molly are strapped for money right now.* □ *I wish I could help you out, but I'm pretty strapped myself.* □ *I asked Jim for a loan, but house repairs have left him strapped for cash.*

strategic capability the possession of nuclear bombs. □ *How many nations in the Western Hemisphere have strategic capability?* □ *The administration viewed with alarm the reports of developing strategic capability in the Middle East.*

strategic exchange a nuclear war. □ *Would these missile silos be able to survive a strategic exchange?* □ *It is clear that a strategic exchange would not be survivable for those living in the major East Coast cities.*

(strategic) withdrawal AND **tactical withdrawal** a retreat. □ *The commander ordered a strategic withdrawal.* □ *The unit made a tactical withdrawal to its earlier position.* □ *The withdrawal of our forces leaves the enemy in complete possession of the disputed territory.*

stray to have sex with someone other than one's spouse. □ *He strayed once, and only once. The guilt was too much for him.* □ *How can you think I would ever stray? You don't trust me!*

streamline to fire a large number of people. (See also **downsize, reengineer, reorganize**.) □ *Ever since the company streamlined, profitability has gone way up.* □ *In order to maintain our historically high rate of return, we will need to streamline.*

street walker a prostitute. □ *Street walkers sauntered up and down Central Avenue.* □ *The officer arrested a street walker.*

stretch one's legs to urinate or defecate, especially after a long trip in a vehicle. □ *Do you guys need to stop and stretch your legs, or should we keep driving?* □ *Let's pull over at that rest stop. I need to stretch my legs.*

stretch the truth to lie. □ *When he claimed to have a Ph.D., he was stretching the truth.* □ *Sally tends to stretch the truth when telling tales about her wild teenage years.*

strong language swearing. □ *The movie contains strong language and may not be appropriate for younger viewers.* □ *My boss is certainly not afraid to use strong language when she feels it is called for.*

structured environment an institution with very strict rules. □ *We felt that Bobby would benefit from a more struc-*

tured environment, and so we sent him to the military academy. □ *We found that many prisoners responded well to a structured environment with a set of mandatory daily tasks.*

studio (apartment) a one-room apartment. (See also efficiency.) □ *Studio apartments start at just $500 a month.* □ *Jim is living in a studio over near the university.*

sub rosa in secret. □ *He was, sub rosa, an active spy for the other side.* □ *She told it to me sub rosa. I don't feel I can tell anyone else.*

subsidy publishing See vanity publishing.

substance abuse drug addiction. □ *Substance abuse is definitely an issue in her family. Her father drank, and her mother took tranquilizers.* □ *The doctor tried to help Jane overcome her substance abuse.*

substandard housing houses or apartments in bad condition. □ *He rented substandard housing at market rates.* □ *The neighborhood is full of substandard housing. That is why it would be a good candidate for urban renewal.*

substantial 1. rich. □ *Several substantial businesspeople made contributions to the symphony.* □ *Her father is a substantial banker, and she plans to take over the bank when he retires.* **2.** fat. □ *He was tall and substantial.* □ *She had a solid, substantial figure.*

succumb to something to die of something. □ *After battling lung cancer for almost a year, Mike finally succumbed to it.* □ *In the end, she succumbed to pneumonia.*

sucker a worthless person or thing. (A mild replacement for *fucker*.) □ *I can't get this sucker to fit in the trunk.* □ *Can you believe what that sucker did to me?*

sudden infant death syndrome See SIDS.

sugar daddy a man who supports someone in exchange for sex. (Slang.) □ *She wished she could find a sugar daddy to take care of every little thing.* □ *Live with me, baby. I'll be your sugar daddy.*

suggestive having to do with sex. □ *He made a suggestive remark.* □ *She gave him a suggestive smile.*

supervisor a person in charge; a boss. (Replaces *foreman*, which does not include women.) □ *The factory floor supervisor told me I could go on break.* □ *Check with the supervisor when you arrive in the morning.*

support money. □ *This program is made possible by the generous support of the Engstrand Foundation.* □ *The work we do would not be possible without your support.*

support someone or something to give money to someone or something. □ *JOHN: How come Jane can afford to sit around painting pictures all day? JILL: Her parents support her.* □ *Support public television today.*

support staff assistants, such as secretaries and clerks. □ *The firm has two hundred attorneys and approximately one hundred and fifty support staff.* □ *The support staff receive a holiday bonus every December.*

supreme penalty, the death as a punishment for crime. □ *The murderer paid the supreme penalty.* □ *He was convicted, and faced the supreme penalty.*

supreme sacrifice See ultimate sacrifice, the.

surgical strike a bomb attack. (See also **preventive strike**.) □ *The surgical strike was intended to take out a major muni-*

tions plant. □ *This missile is designed for surgical strikes against precise targets.*

surrender to someone to have sex with someone. (Usually used to describe women having sex with men, who are assumed to be the pursuers.) □ *She surrendered to him there on the beach, under the full moon.* □ *"I will never surrender to you, never!" she cried, her bosom heaving.*

surrogate mother a woman who carries and gives birth to a baby for someone else to raise. (See also **gestational mother**.) □ *As a surrogate mother, you must waive your parental rights to the child.* □ *We are so grateful to the surrogate mother who brought our daughter into this world.*

surveillance secret watching; spying. □ *They continued their surveillance of the president's compound.* □ *Warning. This store is under surveillance. Shoplifters will be prosecuted.*

survivability the ability to survive a nuclear war. □ *Survivability would be nil for everything within a hundred-mile radius of the city.* □ *What's our survivability for an all-out nuclear attack?*

surviving spouse a person who outlives his or her wife or husband. (Replaces *widow* and *widower*.) □ *The policy benefits will go to the surviving spouse.* □ *The support group helps surviving spouses face the loss of their life partner.*

sweetheart unfairly favorable. (Slang.) □ *The law firm got a sweetheart deal on all their Pleasant Airways plane travel, because Pleasant Airways was a client of theirs.* □ *They offered me a sweetheart contract to get me to leave my current employer.*

s-word, the "shit." (See also f-word, the.) □ *That car is a real piece of, well, I don't like to use the s-word.* □ *I heard* *him yell the s-word, and then I saw smoke coming out of his room.*

syndicate a criminal organization. (See also **organization, the.**) □ *A percentage of every deal goes to the syndicate, understand?* □ *The syndicate had quite a few police officers on their payroll.*

syndrome a disease. (See also **Down's syndrome, SIDS.**) □ *A number of different therapies have been tried with this syndrome.* □ *This is a congenital syndrome. A birth defect, in other words.*

T

tactical withdrawal See (strategic) withdrawal.

take advantage of someone to have sex with someone, especially someone who does not want or intend to have sex with you. □ *The villain tried to take advantage of her, but she fought him off.* □ *He took advantage of me when I was drunk.*

take (an) early retirement to retire in order to avoid being fired. □ *The firm encouraged its senior employees to take early retirement.* □ *After twenty-three years with the company, Mary had to take an early retirement.*

take care of someone to kill someone. □ *Don't worry, Boss. I'll take care of that little stool pigeon.* □ *"Want me to take care of that reporter?" Big Jim asked.*

take French leave to leave without permission or without saying goodbye. (Possibly offensive to French people. Use with caution.) □ *He took French leave from the navy and has been in hiding ever since.* □ *We took French leave from the party, I'm afraid.*

take legal action to sue. □ *If you will not return the purchase price in full, I will be forced to take legal action.* □ *She* *threatened to take legal action against the company that had fired her.*

take liberties with someone to kiss, hug, or caress someone against his or her will. (Old-fashioned.) □ *My sister tells me you have tried to take liberties with her.* □ *He came in drunk and took liberties with the upstairs maid.*

take precautions to use something that prevents pregnancy. □ *Are you sexually active? Are you taking precautions?* □ *We forgot to take precautions, and now I'm pregnant.*

take someone to have sex with someone. (Usually the man is described as *taking* the woman.) □ *"Take me," she sighed and leaned back upon the grass.* □ *He carried her upstairs, laid her on the bed, and took her.*

take someone's life to kill someone. (To **take one's own life** is to kill oneself.) □ *He hunted down his rival and took his life.* □ *In despair, she took her own life.*

take something under advisement to think about something. (Often used to imply *to ignore something.*) □ *My boss says he'll take my suggestion under advisement. Well, I know what that means.* □ *Thanks for the information. I'll take it under advisement.*

take the coward's way out to kill oneself. (See also **take the easy way out.**) □ *When faced with financial disaster, Sarah took the coward's way out.* □ *I can't believe that Bill would take the coward's way out. His death must have been an accident.*

take the easy way out to kill oneself. (See also **take the coward's way out.**) □ *When life got rough, he took the easy way out.* □ *Her family said she died of a sudden illness, but her friends thought she had taken the easy way out.*

take up with someone to start a sexual relationship with someone. (Folksy.) □ *She hadn't been married six months before she took up with another man.* □ *Jim took up with the boss' daughter.*

tall clock See floor clock.

tamper with someone to kiss, fondle, or have sex with a child. □ *He was sent to prison for tampering with a number of young girls.* □ *She accused her stepfather of tampering with her.*

tamper with something to damage something. □ *Someone had tampered with the brake lines on the car.* □ *He was accused of tampering with important computer files.*

T.B. tuberculosis, a lung disease. □ *Cases of T.B. are on the increase again.* □ *She died of T.B. when she was only forty.*

technical adjustment a stock market crash. □ *The technical adjustment of 1987 contributed to a substantial downturn.* □ *Some market forecasters fear we are due for another technical adjustment.*

technician a worker. □ *One of our file technicians can help you locate those records.* □ *The data entry technician is responsible for inputting all the orders into the computer.*

temperance the practice of refusing to drink alcohol. (Old-fashioned.) □ *Carry Nation was a famous crusader for temperance.* □ *Temperance is the only answer for the widespread drunkenness we see all about us.*

temporarily abled able-bodied. (See also **nondisabled**.) □ *Temporarily abled voters may someday be grateful that public money was spent on making public facilities accessible* *to the disabled.* □ *I am temporarily abled, and my sister uses a wheelchair.*

temporary setback a disaster. □ *The candidate claimed that the scandal was just a temporary setback.* □ *The explosion in the factory is a temporary setback for the company, it is true.*

tendencies homosexuality. □ *I am aware of Mike's tendencies, but that doesn't change my opinion of him one way or the other.* □ *As a teacher, I don't dare make my tendencies public.*

terminal care care of the dying. □ *The nurses at the hospice are trained in terminal care.* □ *Terminal care often includes pain management.*

terminate a pregnancy to get an abortion. □ *She asked the doctor how to go about terminating her pregnancy.* □ *She decided to terminate the pregnancy.*

terminate someone 1. to fire someone. □ *The manager terminated the troublesome employee.* □ *If your work habits do not improve, we may be forced to terminate you.* **2.** to kill someone. □ *The agent received an order to terminate Jones.* □ *If anyone should see you, terminate him at once.*

terminate someone with extreme prejudice to kill someone. (Often used in the passive voice.) □ *Locate the enemy agent and terminate him with extreme prejudice.* □ *The spy had been terminated with extreme prejudice.*

terminological inexactitude a lie. □ *I grant you that my speech may have contained one or two terminological inexactitudes.* □ *The statement that there would be no layoffs was a terminological inexactitude.*

thanatologist a person who studies death and dying. □ *The thanatologist asked the terminally ill patients to talk about what they were experiencing.* □ *Thanatologists have contributed to our understanding of the dying process.*

that time (of the month) a menstrual period. □ *You're in a crabby mood today. Is it that time of the month?* □ *Boy, do I feel bloated. It's that time, you know.*

that way inclined homosexual. (Possibly offensive to homosexual people. Use with caution.) □ *"I had no idea that Dan was that way inclined until he asked me out," said Bill.* □ *Jane has three sons, and two of them are that way inclined.*

therapeutic interruption of pregnancy AND **pregnancy interruption** an abortion. □ *Her doctor advised a therapeutic interruption of pregnancy, as the fetus was not viable.* □ *The doctor agreed to perform a pregnancy interruption.*

they he or she. □ *Everyone should bring their own lunch.* □ *What's a person supposed to do if they don't have enough money?*

thing the penis or vagina. (Slang.) □ *He rubbed his thing against her leg.* □ *She let him touch her thing.*

thinning hair baldness. □ *She wore a wig to cover her thinning hair.* □ *His thinning hair made him look older than he was.*

thin on top bald, or going bald. □ *Bill has been a bit thin on top ever since he was thirty.* □ *He noticed that he was going thin on top.*

third party payment a bribe. □ *My bank will arrange whatever third party payments are necessary.* □ *The mayor has requested a third party payment.*

Third World poor countries without industry. (See also First World, industrial(ized).) □ *I have traveled all over the Third World, and I can tell you that child labor is common in many places.* □ *The agency provides funding to decrease infant mortality in the Third World.*

three sheets to the wind very drunk. □ *Can you believe it? He came to the meeting three sheets to the wind!* □ *She was three sheets to the wind. She could hardly walk.*

thrifty unwilling to spend money. □ *Clara is a thrifty soul. She uses coffee grounds three times.* □ *He could afford a new car if he wanted one, but he's thrifty, so he prefers to drive his rusty old one.*

throat the neck. □ *Apply the moisturizing lotion to the face and throat.* □ *He clasped the diamond necklace about her throat.*

throw up to vomit. (Similarly: be sick, blow chunks, bring up something, drive the porcelain bus, lose one's lunch, purge, regurgitate, toss one's cookies, upchuck, urp, woof one's cookies, yodel groceries.) □ *I could hear him in the bathroom throwing up.* □ *Something in that lunch made me throw up.*

tinkle to urinate. (Cute.) □ *Mommy, I have to tinkle.* □ *Excuse me, but I really have to tinkle.*

tint hair dye. □ *"We could use some tint to correct that gray,"* the hair stylist suggested. □ *Just brush this all-natural tint through your mustache and beard. The gray is gone!*

tipple 1. to drink alcohol. □ *He tipples rather a lot.* □ *I do not tipple often.* **2.** an alcoholic drink. □ *Gin was her favorite tipple.* □ *White wine was the usual tipple at those dinner meetings.*

tipsy drunk. □ *I'd better not drive. I'm tipsy!* □ *He felt a little tipsy after that second martini, but he ordered a third one anyway.*

to bed someone to have sex with someone. □ *He had bedded several young women.* □ *Do you think Jane has really bedded Bob?*

to leave in order to pursue other interests to be fired. □ *Jean has left in order to pursue other interests. We wish her well in the future.* □ *Mark is no longer with us. He left in order to pursue other interests.*

toilet tissue See bathroom tissue.

toilet-trained AND **potty-trained** able to hold one's urine and feces. □ *My older boy was toilet-trained by the time he was two.* □ *She's not potty-trained, so she still wears diapers.*

token included only because of one's race or gender. □ *The show has one token black character.* □ *Maria is the token woman on the board of directors.*

tooey feces. (Baby talk. See also **poop**.) □ *Did you make a tooey in the toilet?* □ *Baby did a tooey in his diaper.*

topless 1. [of clothing] leaving the breasts naked. □ *She wore a topless bathing suit.* □ *The dress was so low-cut it was almost topless.* **2.** having to do with bare-breasted women. □ *The club features topless dancers.* □ *He liked the topless act.*

torso the breasts. □ *She has a big torso.* □ *The dress showed off her well-developed torso.*

touch oneself to masturbate. □ *When I touch myself, I think of you.* □ *In the darkness of her room, she touched herself.*

touch someone to touch someone sexually. □ *Touch me. Kiss me. Hold me.* □ *He had never touched a woman before.*

touch something up to dye gray hair. □ *I see a little gray peeking out at your temples. Would you like me to touch that up?* □ *Uh-oh. We've got some gray hairs in back. Let's just touch them up.*

toupee a man's wig. □ *His toupee matched his hair almost exactly.* □ *Everyone could tell that Bill was wearing a toupee.*

town house a small house sharing a wall with the houses on either side. □ *She bought a town house out in the suburbs.* □ *A two-bedroom town house starts at just $100,000.*

trade, the prostitution. (See also **life, the.**) □ *She had been in the trade for five years.* □ *Her drug pusher got her started in the trade.*

transit center a bus or train station. □ *At the transit center, change to a number 7 bus.* □ *The train will arrive in the Aurora transit center at 6:07.*

transitional See **in transition.**

travelers' tummy diarrhea from foreign food or water. □ *I had a bout of travelers' tummy my first few days in Cairo, but after that, I was fine.* □ *I forgot to boil my drinking water, and wound up with a case of travelers' tummy.*

triage the practice of deciding which people to help and which to ignore. □ *The doctors did triage on the incoming wounded.* □ *The test was a form of triage. Those who passed it would get attention from the teachers. Those who did not had to do the best they could on their own.*

tribute band a band that imitates famous musicians. □ *The tribute band looked and sounded like the real thing. It was just like seeing Deth-Hed live.* □ *The tribute band sang all of the Beatles' greatest hits.*

trots, the diarrhea. (Slang.) □ *I caught some kind of bug that gave me the trots for two days.* □ *Whenever I get really nervous, I get the trots.*

trouble an illness. (See also **problem**.) □ *She has some kind of trouble with her kidneys. She has to go for treatment every week.* □ *He had some stomach trouble that kept him in bed for a week.*

troubled 1. mentally ill. (See also **disturbed (in one's mind)**.) □ *This medication can help many troubled people.* □ *She was so troubled that her friends advised her to seek professional help.* **2.** troublesome. □ *The counselors work with troubled youth.* □ *He is a very troubled young man, who may well turn to violence if no one is able to earn his trust.*

troubles, the the fighting between Protestants and Catholics in Northern Ireland. □ *He was killed in the troubles in 1916.* □ *The troubles pitted neighbor against neighbor.*

tubby fat. □ *She's kind of a tubby kid, isn't she?* □ *He may be a little tubby, but I think he's just the right size.*

tummy AND **tum-tum** the belly. (Baby talk.) □ *My tummy hurts.* □ *I'm going to tickle your tum-tum!*

tummy ache menstrual cramps. □ *Got an aspirin? I've got a little tummy ache. It's that time.* □ *I always get a tummy ache at that time of the month.*

tummy tuck an operation to remove fat from the belly. □ *I went in for a tummy tuck. Let me tell you, I feel so much better in a bathing suit now.* □ *The cosmetic surgeon does face lifts, tummy tucks, you name it.*

tum-tum See tummy.

twilight home AND **eventide home** an institution for old people. □ *Our twilight home offers round-the-clock nursing care.* □ *Mother is in an eventide home just outside of the city.*

ultimate reality, the AND **ultimate truth, the** death. ☐ *He has gone beyond us to the ultimate reality.* ☐ *She faced the ultimate truth with courage.*

ultimate sacrifice, the AND **supreme sacrifice, the** dying for a cause. ☐ *So many soldiers made the ultimate sacrifice.* ☐ *He made the supreme sacrifice to save his family.*

ultimate truth, the See ultimate reality, the.

unavailable AND **not available right now** not willing to talk to you. (See also **in a meeting**.) ☐ CALLER: *May I speak with Ms. Ronder?* SECRETARY: *Ms. Ronder is unavailable. Can someone else help?* ☐ *I'm sorry. Bill is not available right now. Would you like to leave a message?*

unbalanced mentally ill. ☐ *His lawyer claimed that he was unbalanced and should be institutionalized rather than sent to prison.* ☐ *Only an unbalanced person could have done such a thing.*

uncertain definitely bad. ☐ *The quality of the food there is uncertain.* ☐ *He has a rather uncertain track record when it comes to working well in groups.*

unconventional extremely strange. □ *Her unconventional behavior made her family consider having her committed.* □ *His unconventional approach to writing history makes him an untrustworthy source.*

underachiever a student who does not work. □ *Jill was an underachiever in school.* □ *Our study program helps underachievers realize their potential.*

underarm the armpit. □ *Try our new underarm deodorant.* □ *Do you shave your underarms?*

underdeveloped [of a country] poor; without industries. (See also **developing, emerging**.) □ *The aid worker went to underdeveloped countries to teach ways of improving agriculture.* □ *It is an underdeveloped nation that is eager to partner with the United States in business ventures.*

undergarment AND **underthings** AND **undies** underpants. □ *She preferred plain cotton undergarments.* □ *I need to do some laundry. I'm almost out of undies.* □ *He bought her some sexy underthings.*

underprivileged poor. (Compare with **privileged**.) □ *I work in an after-school program for underprivileged children.* □ *The fund provides money for heating and electricity for underprivileged families.*

under the counter bought or sold illegally. □ *I know where you can get antibiotics under the counter.* □ *He traded in foreign videos under the counter.*

under the influence drunk. (Short for *under the influence of alcohol*.) □ *The suspect was clearly under the influence when the officers picked him up.* □ *She was arrested for driving under the influence.*

under the table extremely drunk. (Implies that the person described is so drunk as to fall off the chair.) □ *After four cocktails, he was under the table.* □ *She was tipsy, but hardly under the table.*

under the weather ill. □ *I'm feeling a little under the weather, so I won't be in today.* □ *I was sorry to hear you're under the weather.*

underthings See undergarment.

underutilization unemployment. □ *The economic survey showed an underutilization rate of about seventeen percent.* □ *The factory closed, and underutilization in the region hit an all-time high.*

undesirable poor, lower-class, or criminal. □ *Some of Billy's new friends seem rather undesirable.* □ *I'm glad to see the cops walking a beat in the neighborhood. Maybe they can keep the undesirable elements from hanging out on the street corners like they used to.*

undies See undergarment.

undocumented person AND **undocumented resident** AND **undocumented worker** a person who is in the country illegally. (Replaces *illegal alien.* Compare with documented worker.) □ *The Immigration Service is looking for any undocumented persons who may be living in the area.* □ *The state government will not pay for medical care for undocumented residents or their children.* □ *The orchard owner denied employing undocumented workers.*

undraped naked. (Often used to describe figures in works of art.) □ *The paintings showed undraped women dancing in green meadows.* □ *The statue of an undraped man was considered unsuitable for a public park.*

unenlightened having an opinion that differs from the speaker's. □ *Joe's views on race relations strike me as rather unenlightened.* □ *Nancy's opinions about women in the workplace seem unenlightened to me.*

uneven bad. □ *This artist's work is uneven at best.* □ *The quality of the cars manufactured here is quite uneven.*

unfaithful having sex with someone other than one's spouse. (See also **infidelity**.) □ *He was crushed when he learned that his wife was unfaithful.* □ *Her husband was unfaithful and did not bother to hide it from her.*

unfinished business bad feelings. □ *Paula and I have some unfinished business that I suppose we'll have to take care of someday.* □ *I have some unfinished business with my parents. It makes going home for the holidays kind of a growth experience.*

unfortunate disastrous. □ *This scandal is unfortunate, but I am sure that we are all ready to put the past behind us.* □ *It is unfortunate that this investment did not perform as well as we had hoped.*

unilateral agreement a decision by one person or group. □ *We propose a unilateral agreement to restrict further nuclear research.* □ *The airline announced a unilateral agreement to lower prices.*

uninhibited eager to have sex. □ *He says his new girlfriend is delightfully uninhibited.* □ *He is quite uninhibited. He will make love anywhere, anytime.*

unmarried homosexual. (**Unmarried** is not often used to imply *homosexual*. Use with caution, and judge from the context.) □ *He is forty, unmarried, and lives at home with* *his mother.* □ *My older son is unmarried. He lives with his friend Mr. Harrison.*

unmentionables underwear. (Old-fashioned.) □ *The drawer was full of the lady's unmentionables.* □ *He caught a glimpse of her unmentionables.*

unnatural homosexual. (Old-fashioned. Offensive to homosexual people. Use with caution.) □ *The two young men had committed an unnatural act.* □ *The townsfolk would not allow an unnatural woman to teach their children.*

unorthodox very unusual or controversial. □ *He has some very unorthodox ideas about the practice of medicine. For one thing, he tends to prescribe music for his patients.* □ *She has some unorthodox habits. Few other people buy expensive cars for their dogs to live in.*

unprepossessing ugly. □ *His appearance is unprepossessing, but if you talk to him, you will soon see that he is charming and intelligent.* □ *Her unprepossessing features softened into a smile.*

unrest violence. □ *Unrest followed the announcement of the unpopular verdict.* □ *We have received reports of unrest in the capital following these latest rebel attacks.*

unsightly ugly. □ *That run-down house is very unsightly.* □ *He had a number of unsightly blemishes.*

unsteady on one's feet drunk. □ *He left the bar, quite unsteady on his feet.* □ *Are you OK? You look a bit unsteady on your feet.*

untruth a lie. □ *The reporter caught the mayor in an untruth.* □ *I believe that what Jane told you was an untruth.*

unwaged working for no money. □ *The economist argued that housewives and other unwaged workers should be included in calculations of the country's gross national product.* □ *Women have traditionally done unwaged labor such as housekeeping, cooking, and child care.*

upperclass student a student in the third or fourth year of high school or college. (Replaces *upperclassman*, which does not include women.) □ *When I was a fresher, I felt a little afraid of the upperclass students.* □ *There were several upperclass students in my biology class.*

urban renewal the destruction or rebuilding of old city buildings in order to attract rich people to live and work in a place. □ *The south central neighborhood was scheduled for urban renewal.* □ *As a result of urban renewal, we now have an attractive downtown mall.*

us See we.

use to use drugs. (Slang.) □ *I'm not using anymore, man. I quit.* □ *All my friends used, so I started using, too.*

use foul language to swear. □ *There's no need to use foul language.* □ *When she gets angry, she tends to use foul language.*

use the bathroom AND **use the toilet** to urinate or defecate. □ *May I be excused to use the bathroom?* □ *I have to use the toilet.*

use the toilet See use the bathroom.

utility access hole See sewer hole.

vague not able to remember easily. (Replaces *senile*.) □ *Grandpa got vague in his old age.* □ *She was old and vague, but she could remember the dress she was wearing the night she first met her husband.*

vanity publishing AND **vanity press** AND **subsidy publishing** the business of getting authors to pay for publishing their own books. □ *True, he has published six books, but they were all printed by a vanity publishing outfit.* □ *Don't be too impressed by the fact that she got her novel published. It was done by a vanity press.* □ *You know you've got a best-seller, but you can't get the big publishing houses to sit up and take notice. Subsidy publishing may be the answer for you.*

variety meats organ meats, such as kidneys, intestines, and brains. □ *Mom cooked with variety meats a lot, because they were cheap.* □ *The meat counter is having a special on variety meats.*

vendor a seller. □ *The vendor gave me a really good price.* □ *Call some vendors and ask them to bid on the project.*

venison deer meat. □ *Bill brought back a deer, so his family will be having lots of venison this winter.* □ KATHY: *What's the meat in this casserole?* BILL: *It's venison.*

vertically challenged short. (Jocular.) □ *Who's that vertically challenged guy with the yellow shirt?* □ *My date was vertically challenged and quantitatively enhanced. I'm not going out with him again.*

viable profitable. □ *The board decided that the electronics division was no longer viable and should be reorganized.* □ *Are these small downtown stores really viable?*

vibrator a battery-operated, vibrating massager designed to stimulate sexually. (See also **(cordless) massager.**) □ *She used a vibrator to pleasure herself.* □ *The catalog of marital aids had several different kinds of vibrators.*

Vienna roll a round bread roll. (Replaces *kaiser roll*, which may be offensive to Germans.) □ *I'll have a ham sandwich on a Vienna roll.* □ *I bought a dozen whole-wheat Vienna rolls.*

viewing room a room in which a dead body is viewed. □ *The mourners filed through the viewing room and went to sit down in the funeral chapel.* □ *The reviewal will take place in the viewing room at seven o'clock.*

violate someone to rape someone. □ *The murderer had violated his victim before killing her.* □ *The soldiers violated the captured women.*

visitation a gathering of mourners to view a dead body. □ *The visitation will be Tuesday night. The funeral is Wednesday morning.* □ *At the visitation, the dead man's friends told stories about what a fine person he had been.*

visit from the stork a birth. (According to legend, babies are brought to their parents by a stork.) □ *I hear that Maria is expecting a visit from the stork.* □ *The young couple had a visit from the stork.*

visiting card See calling card.

visitor a menstrual period. □ *My visitor came a day early.* □ *I'm feeling a little under the weather today. I have a visitor.*

visually impaired blind or partly blind. (See also **partially sighted**.) □ *I am visually impaired, but I like TV just as much as the next person.* □ *The disease left him visually impaired.*

vitals the stomach and intestines. □ *I felt a terrible pain in my vitals.* □ *She was stabbed in her vitals.*

vital statistics the measurements of a woman's breasts, waist, and hips. (Possibly offensive to women. Use with caution.) □ *She's got some nice vital statistics, eh?* □ *The beauty contestants had to list their vital statistics.*

vocation a job. □ *What do you do, Ms. Wilson? What is your vocation?* □ *School should help students prepare for a vocation.*

vocational(/technical) school a school that teaches mechanical skills. (Replaces *trade school*.) □ *He got his auto repair certificate from a vocational/technical school.* □ *After just six months in vocational school, Rita was able to find work as a computer repair technician.*

volatile unpredictable and dangerous. □ *The stock market has been quite volatile lately.* □ *She has a volatile temper.*

voluntary death suicide. □ *Her life ended in voluntary death.* □ *He sought voluntary death as a way to end his emotional suffering.*

voluntary euthanasia See auto-euthanasia.

voluptuous having big breasts and hips. □ *The voluptuous woman walked proudly across the room.* □ *Steve likes voluptuous women.*

vulnerable adult an adult who cannot take care of him- or herself. □ *Six vulnerable adults live in this group home.* □ *Pam is a caretaker for a vulnerable adult. She washes, dresses, and feeds him, and makes sure he gets enough exercise.*

wage freeze the practice of not increasing wages. (See also **freeze, hiring freeze**.) □ *The company instituted a wage freeze for all support staff.* □ *Kathy got a promotion, but due to the wage freeze, she didn't get a raise.*

waitron AND **waitperson** a waitress or waiter. □ *The waitrons were very busy that Friday night.* □ *Could you ask our waitperson to bring us the check?*

waitstaff the people who wait on tables in a restaurant; waiters and waitresses. □ *One of our waitstaff will be with you shortly.* □ *The restaurant has a very professional waitstaff.*

wander to have sex with someone other than one's spouse. □ *She was sure that her husband had wandered during her absence.* □ *She promised never to wander again.*

wardrobe supervisor a person who takes care of the costumes for a play or movie. (Replaces *wardrobe mistress*, which does not include men.) □ *The wardrobe supervisor for this film was Nancy Hopkins.* □ *James was wardrobe supervisor for the big musical.*

wash one's hands to urinate or defecate. (Implies that one is going to the bathroom to wash.) □ *There's the* *bathroom, if you'd like to wash your hands.* □ *After I got off the plane, I stopped in the ladies' room to wash my hands.*

washroom a toilet. □ *Where's the washroom?* □ *The washroom in that gas station was just filthy.*

waste feces and urine. □ *Human waste is collected for treatment in these concrete tanks.* □ *When the sewers overflowed, waste went running into the streets.*

waste management the process of taking care of garbage. □ *The city hired a contractor to take care of waste management.* □ *Recycling is an important part of waste management.*

watch one's pennies to be unwilling to spend money. □ *She watched her pennies and saved as much as she could.* □ *JIM: Bill is really cheap. BETH: He does watch his pennies, it's true.*

watch one's weight to eat less in order to lose weight. □ *No dessert for me. I'm watching my weight.* □ *She's a heart patient, so she has to watch her weight.*

water closet AND **W.C.** a toilet. (British. Compare with earth closet.) □ *Where's the water closet?* □ *I used the W.C. in the library.*

water landing a crash landing in water. □ *In case of a water landing, use your seat cushion as a personal flotation device.* □ *In the unlikely event of a water landing, your flight crew will issue instructions.*

W.C. See water closet.

we AND **us** you. □ *Why don't we get into this hospital gown for the doctor?* □ *"We should get those letters ready to mail this morning," Linda said to her secretary.*

wee See go wee(-wee).

welfare government payments to the poor. □ *After I lost my job, I was on welfare for two years.* □ *The new law would cut spending on welfare.*

well-endowed 1. [of a woman] having large breasts. □ *She has a pretty face, and she's well-endowed.* □ *Jim prefers well-endowed women.* **2.** [of a man] having a large penis. □ *He bragged that he was unusually well-endowed.* □ *That man's swimsuit is so tight that you can tell he's well-endowed.*

well-off AND **well-to-do** very rich. □ *I believe Lisa is quite well-off.* □ *His family is well-to-do.*

well-preserved appearing to be younger than you are. □ *She was a well-preserved woman in her fifties.* □ *He is seventy years old, but quite well-preserved.*

well-to-do See well-off.

well-upholstered fat. □ *Bill is kind of chunky, and his wife is also well-upholstered.* □ *He was tall and well-upholstered.*

wet something to urinate on something. □ *The little girl wet her bed.* □ *Did you wet your pants?*

What the Sam Hill? "What?" (A replacement for "*What the Hell?*") □ *What the Sam Hill are you doing with that knife?* □ *What the Sam Hill? I can't understand a thing you just said.*

wherewithal 1. money. □ *If I had the wherewithal, I'd like to start my own business.* □ *His father gave him the where-*

withal to buy his first house. **2.** intelligence. □ *She's willing to learn, but she hasn't got the wherewithal to be a first-class scholar.* □ *He just doesn't have the wherewithal to solve technical problems, I'm afraid.*

whipping person a person whom it is safe to abuse. (Replaces *whipping boy,* which does not include females.) □ *I'm tired of being the whipping person for the entire office. I quit.* □ *Jane is the usual whipping person whenever Fred gets upset.*

white lie a lie told to make someone feel better. (See also social lie.) □ *I told her a little white lie. I said I thought she had a talent for drawing.* □ *What do you really think of this dress? Don't tell me any white lies.*

white meat the breast meat of a bird. (Compare with dark meat.) □ *Would you like white meat or dark meat?* □ *Just cut some of that white meat for me.*

white slavery prostitution. (Possibly offensive to black people. Use with caution.) □ *White slavery did a thriving business in the growing town.* □ *White slavery was the only life she had ever known.*

whitewash something to lie about something. □ *Charles tried to whitewash his involvement with the fraudulent scheme.* □ *The mayor's public relations representative whitewashed the episode with the bridge fund.*

widdle to urinate. (British.) □ *The dog widdled on the floor.* □ *I need to find a place to widdle.*

willie See willy.

willowy [of a woman] thin. □ *She was tall and willowy.* □ *She bent her willowy waist.*

willy AND **willie** the penis. (Slang.) ☐ *He needed to pee, so he just took out his willy and did it right there in the schoolyard.* ☐ *Billy kicked Tommy right in the willie.*

with child pregnant. (Literary.) ☐ *His wife is with child.* ☐ *She was soon with child again.*

with Jesus dead. (Folksy.) ☐ *Daddy is with Jesus now.* ☐ *All my brothers and sisters are with Jesus.*

with us 1. alive. ☐ *Is old Mr. Podmore still with us?* ☐ *Poor old Fido isn't with us anymore.* **2.** employed by us. (Usually in the phrase *no longer with us.*) ☐ SMITH: *Does Jones still work here?* JEFFERSON: *Jones is no longer with us.* ☐ *I'm afraid Michael is no longer with us. Can someone else help you?*

woman Friday See gal Friday.

woman of easy virtue See easy woman.

woman of ill repute a prostitute. ☐ *His favorite companion was a woman of ill repute.* ☐ *If you can't be faithful to your husband, you're no better than a woman of ill repute.*

women's size a clothing size for fat women. (See also **plus size, extended size, queen size(d).**) ☐ *Do you have this dress in women's sizes?* ☐ *Have you tried the women's size department?*

wommon a woman. (By spelling *woman* in a way that does not include the word *man, wommon* implies that women are or should be separate from men. The plural is *womyn* or *wimmin.*) ☐ *This journal is dedicated to art from a wommon's perspective.* ☐ *The wimmin's health fair celebrates the wonderful diversity of the female body.* ☐ *All womyn are welcome at the MoonStruck Coffee Shoppe.*

workforce adjustment the firing of a large number of people. ☐ *About thirty percent of middle managers were let go in the workforce adjustment.* ☐ *A workforce adjustment will require the remaining employees to seek ways to improve productivity.*

working class AND **working people** lower-class people. ☐ *The working class cannot afford luxury vacations.* ☐ *Most houses in that neighborhood are beyond the means of working people.*

working girl a prostitute. ☐ *At night, the downtown was full of working girls.* ☐ *Mike went outside the office for a smoke and was propositioned by a working girl.*

working people See working class.

work release program the practice of allowing prisoners to leave jail in order to work. ☐ *He spent twenty hours a week in the work release program, working on a construction job.* ☐ *The work release program provides valuable job training.*

work stoppage a strike. ☐ *The union voted for a work stoppage, effective immediately.* ☐ *The work stoppage lasted for six weeks.*

work-to-rule a reduction of work as a way of bargaining for better conditions. (British. See also **slowdown**.) ☐ *Productivity dropped drastically during the work-to-rule.* ☐ *Union leaders threatened a work-to-rule if management would not agree to their demands.*

world non-European. ☐ *I like the exciting rhythms of world music.* ☐ *The video store has many world titles from Africa, Asia, and Latin America.*

world to come, the death. (See also **next world, the.**) □ *We shall meet again in the world to come.* □ *I hope to see my long-lost darling in the world to come.*

worse for drink, the drunk. □ *He was rather the worse for drink when he came back from lunch.* □ *She left the party somewhat the worse for drink.*

wrong side of the tracks See **other side of the tracks.**

XYZ (PDQ) your pants zipper is open. (Cute. The letters stand for *eXamine Your Zipper (Pretty Darn Quick).*) □ *Hey, Jim! XYZ!* □ *Wait. Before you go into that meeting, XYZ PDQ.*

yard worker a person who takes care of plants in a yard. (Replaces *yardman*, which does not include women.) □ *I don't mow my own grass. I've got a yard worker who comes in twice a week.* □ *Maria is a good yard worker.*

you-know-what an embarrassing or secret thing. □ *Did you talk to Greg about the you-know-what for Dad's birthday?* □ *Her dress was so low, you could see almost all of her you-know-whats.*

youth a teenager. □ *The Sunday School camping trip for youth was a great success this year.* □ *The offender was a youth and could not be punished as an adult.*

youth center a prison for children. □ *He was sentenced to six months in the county youth center.* □ *His counselor at the youth center said he should think about finishing high school when he got out.*

Thematic Index of Euphemisms

ADVERTISING

appetite suppressant
attorney
(authentic)
   reproduction
bonded bronze
bonded stone
boudoir photo
breath freshener
cash advance
commode
community
compact (car)
complimentary
courtesy
creamery butter
deluxe
direct mail
eat-in kitchen
economy
efficiency
emporium
encore presentation
facial tissue
faux
festival seating
filler
fixer-upper
food product
for your convenience
free gift
general seating
handyman's special
historic
home
homemade
institute

large
merchandize
   something
message
mobile home
non-dairy
package store
pharmacy
polymer
PR
pre-driven
pre-owned
previously owned
public relations
realtor
regular
resale shop
resin
rock lobster
sales event
Salisbury steak
shoppe
slack fill
something-free
sponsor
starter home
studio (apartment)
subsidy publishing
town house
vanity publishing
variety meats

AGE

active
advanced in years
ageism
aging

character line
chronologically
   advantaged
confused
distinguished
elder statesman
elderly
evening of life
eventide home
getting on (in years)
golden ager
golden years
home
in one's mid-years
longer-lived, the
mature
middle age
middle-aged spread
midlife
no longer young
no spring chicken
not a kid anymore
not as young as one
   used to be
nursing home
of a certain age
of mature years
older
one's sunset years
retiree
retirement
   community
rob the cradle
seasoned
senior (citizen)
silver
status offender

twilight home
well-preserved
youth

ALCOHOL

afloat (See intoxicated.)
awash (See intoxicated.)
bacchanal(ia)
bent out of shape (See
  intoxicated.)
blind (See intoxicated.)
blitzed (See intoxicated.)
blotto (See intoxicated.)
bombed (See intoxicated.)
bon vivant
bottle, the
comfortable (See
  intoxicated.)
confused
dead to the world (See
  intoxicated.)
decks awash (See
  intoxicated.)
drink
drown one's sorrows
dry
Dutch courage
elevated (See intoxicated.)
fall off the wagon
far gone
feeling no pain
hammered (See
  intoxicated.)
happy
happy hour
have a drinking
  problem
have a few too many
have an alcohol
  problem
have one too many
high
hospitality
imbibe
in liquor (See intoxicated.)
in one's cups (See
  intoxicated.)
in recovery
indulge
inebriated
intoxicated
John Barleycorn
loaded (See intoxicated.)
lounge
mellow

morning after, the
nightcap
on the town
on the wagon
overcome
over-tired
package store
pick-me-up
plastered (See
  intoxicated.)
potation
refreshment
restorative
seeing double (See
  intoxicated.)
stimulant
temperance
three sheets to the
  wind
tight (See intoxicated.)
tight as a tick (See
  intoxicated.)
tipple
tipsy
toasted (See intoxicated.)
under the influence
under the table
unsteady on one's feet
wasted (See intoxicated.)
worse for drink, the

BIRTH

accident
belly full (See expecting.)
big (See expecting.)
broken-legged (See
  expecting.)
carry
condition
eating for two
enceinte
expectant mother
expecting
father-to-be
fragrant
full of heir (See
  expecting.)
gestational mother
gone
happy event
have a baby on the
  way
have a belly full (See
  expecting.)
have a bun in the oven

have an accident
have to get married
illegitimate
in a delicate condition
in a fix (See expecting.)
in an interesting
  condition
in the family way
in the pudding club
  (See expecting.)
in trouble
knocked up (See
  expecting.)
little stranger
love child
maternity
miscarriage
mother-to-be
on the way (See
  expecting.)
overdue
perinatal mortality
preggers (See expecting.)
show
surrogate mother
visit from the stork
well along (See
  expecting.)
with child

BODY PARTS

abdomen
abdominal protector
alter
anatomically correct
anatomy (See backside.)
appliance
appurtenances (See
  bosom.)
(athletic) supporter
au naturel
back way (See backside.)
backdoor (See backside.)
backside
balcony (See backside.)
bazooms (See bosom.)
behind
bikini
birthday suit
bobbles (See glands.)
bone (See member.)
boobs (See bosom.)
booty (See backside.)
bosom
bottom

boulders (See bosom.)
bum (See backside.)
buns (See backside.)
bust
buxom
caboose
cache-sexe
can (See backside.)
Cape of Good Hope
    (See particular.)
charms
chassis
cheeks (See backside.)
chest
cleavage
cleft (See particular.)
clock-weights (See
    glands.)
clothing optional
conundrum (See
    particular.)
cow-brute
crotch
crumpet (See particular.)
cup
curvaceous
dark meat
decent
decollete
dentures
derriere
develop
ding-dong (See member.)
dingle (See member.)
dingus (See member.)
disrobe
doodad (See member.)
down there
drumstick
duff
dugs (See bosom.)
duster (See backside.)
emasculate someone
equipment
everything
exhibitionist
expose oneself
extremity
factotum (See particular.)
(family) jewels
fanny (See particular.)
feminine
figure
fill out
five-o'clock shadow

fix something
free beach
front
fundament
gadget (See member.)
gazongas (See bosom.)
glands
globes (See bosom.)
gluteus maximus
gonads (See glands.)
groin
happy valley (See
    particular.)
he-cow
healthy
heinie (See backside.)
hind end
hindquarters
hinterland (See backside.)
hirsute
Holy of Holies (See
    particular.)
honey-pot (See
    particular.)
hooters (See bosom.)
in one's altogether
in the altogether
indecency
insides
jock (See member.)
John Thomas (See
    member.)
jugs (See bosom.)
keester (See backside.)
knockers (See bosom.)
lady dog
loins
love chamber (See
    particular.)
Low Countries (See
    particular.)
male member (See
    member.)
mammary glands
manhood
marbles (See glands.)
melons (See bosom.)
member
membrum virile (See
    member.)
middle
midriff
midsection
muff (See particular.)
nads (See glands.)

naturist
nether parts
nick someone or
    something
nonesuch (See particular.)
nuts (See glands.)
one's all
one's person
pair (See bosom.)
part (See member.)
particular
phallus
physique
pizzle (See member.)
plumbing
posterior
(private) parts
privates
privy member (See
    member.)
pudendum
(rear) end
round out
rump
rumpus (See backside.)
seat
secret parts (See
    particular.)
shapely
sit-upon
state of nature
tail (See backside.)
temple of Venus (See
    particular.)
testimonials (See
    glands.)
thing
thingamabob (See
    member.)
third leg (See member.)
throat
tochus (See backside.)
topless
torso
tummy
underarm
undraped
vital statistics
vitals (See glands.)
well-endowed
whatsis (See member.)
white meat
wick (See member.)
willy
woccus (See member.)

BODY PROCESSES

accident
accouchement
adjourn
adjust one's dress
altar room (See
    bathroom.)
anticipating
antiperspirant
back talk (See pass
    gas.)
backfire
barf (See throw up.)
bathroom
bathroom tissue
be sick (See throw up.)
bedpan
biffy (See bathroom.)
blemish
blessed event
bloody Mary (See curse,
    the.)
blow chunks (See throw
    up.)
B.M.
B.O.
bodily functions
break wind
breath freshener
bring up something
    (See throw up.)
burp
ca-ca (See poop.)
call of nature
calling card
chamber pot
change (of life)
cloakroom
comfort station
commode
convenience
cow flop (See poop.)
cow pie
curse of Eve (See curse,
    the.)
curse, the
defecate
deodorant
do a job (See evacuate
    one's bowels.)
do(-do)
do one's business
do one's duty
dog dirt
doody (See poop.)

drain one's radiator
    (See make water.)
drive the porcelain bus
    (See throw up.)
drop one's load (See
    evacuate one's bowels.)
droppings
dung
earth closet
ease oneself
eating for two
eliminate
evacuate one's bladder
    (See make water.)
evacuate one's bowels
excuse-me (See
    bathroom.)
expectorate
facilities, the
family planning
fecal matter (See poop.)
feeling poorly (See curse,
    the.)
fertilizer
fill one's pants (See
    evacuate one's bowels.)
flatulence (See pass gas.)
flatus (See pass gas.)
flowers (See curse, the.)
foul something
freshen up
friend
gents' (room)
glow
go
go pee(-pee)
go upstairs
go wee(-wee)
hair loss
halitosis
have an accident
having a friend to stay
    (See curse, the.)
having a little visitor
    (See curse, the.)
head (See bathroom.)
hockey (See poop.)
holy week (See curse,
    the.)
hormones
horse apple
house-trained
housebroken
incontinence
incontinence pad

incontinent
indigestion
indisposed
indulge
irregularity
jane (See bathroom.)
job
john (See bathroom.)
kill a tree (See make
    water.)
ladies' (room)
late developer
latrine
lavatory
library (See bathroom.)
litter box
little boys' room
little girls' room
little room, the
loo
loose bowels
lose one's lunch (See
    throw up.)
lounge
make a deposit (See
    evacuate one's bowels.)
make a raspberry (See
    pass gas.)
make a rude noise (See
    pass gas.)
make water
manure
May I be excused?
meadow muffin (See
    poop.)
menstruate
mess
micturate
monthlies (See curse,
    the.)
natural functions
necessary, the
needs of nature
night soil
nuisance
number one
number two
nurse
nurse someone
observing holy week
    (See curse, the.)
old soldier's home, the
on the rag (See curse,
    the.)
ordure (See poop.)

outhouse
pass gas
pass water
pass wind (See pass gas.)
pay a visit
pee
pellets
period
perspiration
perspire
pet odor
piddle (See make water.)
pit stop
poop
poorly
post a letter (See
    evacuate one's bowels.)
potty
potty-trained
powder one's nose
powder room
present
private function
private office (See
    bathroom.)
privy
puddle
puff (See pass gas.)
purge (See throw up.)
raspberry (See pass gas.)
receiving blanket
red flag is up (See curse,
    the.)
regular
regurgitate (See throw
    up.)
relieve oneself
restroom
retire
riding the cotton
    bicycle (See curse,
    the.)
road apple
roses (See curse, the.)
saliva
sand box
sanitary product
siphon the python (See
    make water.)
sit-down job
smallest room, the
soil something
solid waste
souvenir
specimen

spend a penny
spit up
step on a frog (See pass
    gas.)
stool
stretch one's legs
take a dump (See
    evacuate one's bowels.)
take a leak (See make
    water.)
take a squat (See
    evacuate one's bowels.)
take a whiz (See make
    water.)
that time (of the
    month)
throw up
tinkle
toilet tissue
toilet-trained
tooey
toss one's cookies (See
    throw up.)
tummy ache
turd (See poop.)
upchuck (See throw up.)
urp (See throw up.)
use the bathroom
visitor
void (See make water.)
wash one's hands
washroom
waste
water closet
W.C.
wee
wet something
widdle
woof one's cookies (See
    throw up.)
yodel groceries (See
    throw up.)

BUSINESS
adjustment
administrative assistant
ask someone to step
    down
assertive
associate
at liberty
attorney
between jobs
brave attempt, a
budget

budget constraint
business class
businessperson
capacity
cash flow problem
client
close its doors
commission
competency
concern
consultant
contingent worker
counsel
counterproductive
customer service
    representative
develop something
developer
differential
difficult
discharge someone
dispense with
    someone's
    assistance
diversify
downsize
effect change
empower someone
engineer
facilitate something
free enterprise
freeze
furlough someone
gal Friday
ghost (writer)
give (one's) notice
glass ceiling
go under
golden handshake
golden parachute
guest worker
guy Friday
harass someone
hiring freeze
house-cleaning
human resources
I hear you
in (a) conference
in a meeting
inappropriate
incentive
independent contractor
industrial relations
interment industry,
    the

invite someone to
resign
issue
job turning
keep banker's hours
labor organizer
landscape architect
lay someone off
leave of absence
let someone go
loss reserve
make someone
redundant
male-intensive
occupation
man Friday
marketing
migrant
network
news management
not available right now
open shop
organize someplace
outplacement
outsource something
parallel pricing
patron
paying guest
personnel
pink slip
position
professional
rationalize something
realtor
reduction in force
reengineer something
release someone
relieve someone of his
or her duties
reorganization
reorganize
replacement worker
representative
resign
response form
restructure
reverse engineering
RIF
right-to-work
rightsizing
seasonal employee
seasoned
separation
shrinkage
slack fill

slowdown
streamline
supervisor
support staff
sweetheart
take (an) early
retirement
take something under
advisement
technician
terminate someone
to dialogue with
someone
to leave in order to
pursue other
interests
unavailable
under the counter
underutilization
unilateral agreement
vendor
viable
wage freeze
with us
woman Friday
work stoppage
work-to-rule
workforce adjustment

CLASS
blue collar
cleaning lady
(culturally) deprived
culturally
disadvantaged
epicure
inner city
other side of the tracks
privileged
prominent
slum owner
undesirable
working class
wrong side of the
tracks

CRIME
blood money
buyer
confiscate something
connections
controlled substance
convince someone to
do something
creative

deal with someone
delinquent
divert something into
someplace
do (one's) time
doctor something
domestic violence
douceur
enhance something
expropriate something
extortion
extralegal
fix something
flexible
foul play
graft
have one's finger in the
till
have one's hand in the
till
help oneself to
something
highway robber
hit
imaginative
inoperative
intruder detector
intrusion detector
inventory adjustment
inventory leakage
irregularities
kickback
kleptomaniac
launder money
liberate something
light-fingered
liquidate someone
make away with
someone
make away with
something
make it worth
someone's while
malefactor
misappropriate
something
miscreant
misdeed
offender
offense
on the up and up
organization, the
parallel pricing
peculation
penetrate someplace

perpetrator
persuade someone to
    do something
pharmaceuticals
pilfer something
pocket something
polygraph
popular justice
protection
questionable
ravish someone
receiver
relieve someone of
    something
remove someone
scenario
shoplifter
siphon off something
skim a little off the top
skim from something
soft commission
souvenir
status offender
statutory rape
sticky-fingered
sucker
syndicate
tamper with something
third party payment
under the counter
undesirable
violate someone

DEATH
active euthanasia
afterlife
afterworld
alternative container
answer the call
answer the final
    summons (See pass
    (away).)
asleep (in Jesus)
asleep in the Lord
assisted dying
at-need
at peace
at rest
auto-euthanasia
be gathered to one's
    fathers
be in Abraham's bosom
be taken home
before need
bereavement counselor

body
breathe one's last
burial vault
buy the farm (See pass
    (away).)
call, the
capital
cash in one's chips (See
    pass (away).)
casket
casualty
cemetery
churchyard
cinerarium
claim the lives of some
    number of people
claim
clinical death
cold (See asleep (in
    Jesus).)
columbarium
committal
cosmetic preparation
cremains
crematorium
cross over
cull something
curl up one's toes (See
    pass (away).)
Davy Jones' locker
deal with someone
death benefit
deceased, the
decedent
demise
depart (this life)
departed
destroy something
die after a brief illness
die after a long illness
die by one's own hand
disinter someone
dispatch someone
dispose of someone
dissolution
do away with someone
do oneself harm
do someone in
done for (See asleep (in
    Jesus).)
drop off the hooks (See
    pass (away).)
eliminate someone
end it (all)
end, the

estate
eternal life
eternal rest
euthanasia
everlasting life
expire
fade (See pass (away).)
fall asleep
final curtain, the
(final) disposition
final process of life, the
finish someone off
floral tribute
foul play
funeral chapel
funeral coach
funeral director
funeral facilitator
funeral home
funeral service
    practitioner
garden niche
garden of honor
give up the ghost
go
go home
go the way of all flesh
go to a better place
go to join someone
go to meet one's
    Maker
go to one's (last)
    reward
go West
gone
gone before
gone the way of all
    flesh (See asleep (in
    Jesus).)
gone to glory (See asleep
    (in Jesus).)
gone to Kingdom
    Come (See asleep (in
    Jesus).)
gone to the last muster
    (See asleep (in Jesus).)
gone to the last sleep
    (See asleep (in Jesus).)
great certainty, the
great leveller, the
Grim Reaper, the
hand in one's dinner
    pail (See pass (away).)
happy release
harm oneself

harvest something
have one's name
  inscribed in the
  book of life
heavenly rest
hereafter, the
hit
immediate burial
immolate oneself
in extremis
in the sweet by and by
  (See asleep (in Jesus).)
in heaven
inoperative
inter someone
interment industry, the
inurnment
it is all up with
  someone
join the great majority
  (See pass (away).)
kick the bucket (See
  pass (away).)
land of no return
last mile, the
last muster (See asleep
  (in Jesus).)
last sleep (See asleep (in
  Jesus).)
late
lay down one's life for
  something
lay someone to rest
leave-taking
lie in state
life everlasting, the
life insurance
lights out (See asleep (in
  Jesus).)
liquidate someone
living
living will
lose someone
loss of life
loved one
make it
make the arrangements
marker
mausoleum
medical examiner
memorial
memorial park
memorial service
memory image
mercy killing

miscarriage
monument
moribund
(mortal) remains
mortality
mortician
mortuary
next world, the
not doing well
obituary
obsequies
one's last resting
  place
other side, the
pass (away)
passive euthanasia
pay one's last respects
  (to someone)
perinatal mortality
perish (See pass (away).)
perpetual care
physician assisted
  suicide
planned termination
predecease someone
pre-need
prepare someone
pre-planning
professional car
pushing up daisies (See
  asleep (in Jesus).)
put one's affairs in
  order
put someone out of his
  or her misery
put someone out of
  the way
put something away
quietus (See asleep (in
  Jesus).)
ran the good race (See
  asleep (in Jesus).)
remains
remove someone
repose
rest in Abraham's
  bosom
self-deliverance
self-termination
SIDS
slip one's cable (See
  pass (away).)
slumber room
social killing
someone's race is run

someone's time has
  come
space
succumb to something
sudden infant death
  syndrome
supreme penalty, the
supreme sacrifice, the
surviving spouse
take care of someone
take someone's life
take the coward's way
  out
take the easy way out
terminal care
terminate someone
thanatologist
ultimate reality, the
ultimate sacrifice, the
ultimate truth, the
viewing room
visitation
voluntary death
voluntary euthanasia
with Jesus
world to come, the

DISABILITY
ableism
adultism
aesthetically
  advantaged
challenged
classism
deficit
developmentally
  challenged
functional limitation
handicappism
hygienically challenged
impaired
Jellinek's disease
mobility impaired
nondisabled
otherly abled
partially sighted
person with a disability
person with a hearing
  loss
person with AIDS
person with diabetes
person with paraplegia
prosthesis
protected class
PWA

sartorially challenged
sight-deprived
someone uses a
    wheelchair
special
temporarily abled
visually impaired

DRUGS (See also ALCOHOL)
bibulous
convivial
detox
high
in recovery
permissive
pharmaceuticals
pharmacy
recreational drug
sleep aid
substance abuse
use

EDUCATION
communication arts
developmentally
    challenged
difficult
educator
enrichment program
exceptional
extension class
fair
hold someone back
independent school
language arts
learning disorder
(learning) resource
    center
mainstream someone
maladjusted
negative reinforcement
non-traditional student
open enrollment
remedial
returning student
structured environment
underachiever
upperclass student
vocational(/technical)
    school

FAT
adipose
ample

bay window
big-boned
body shaper
broad-beamed
burly
buxom
cellulite
chubby
chunky
corpulent
cuddly
eating disorder
embonpoint
extended size
flatter someone's figure
fluffy
foundation (garment)
frontage
full-figured
generously
    proportioned
grande dame
have a weight problem
healthy
heavy(-set)
Junoesque
larger
less active
like one's food
love handles
mature figure
middle-aged spread
of classic proportions
overweight
pleasantly plump
plump
plus size
portly
puppy fat
quantitatively
    challenged
queen-size(d)
reedlike
rotund
Rubensesque
spare tire
statuesque
stocky
stout
substantial
tubby
watch one's weight
well-upholstered
willowy
women's size

GENDER
actor
angler
artisan
attendant
aviator
ball attendant
bar assistant
base player
bat attendant
best woman
birth name
Britisher
businessperson
busperson
busser
career politician
caregiver
chair(person)
char
checker
chess piece
choir director
coat room attendant
concert leader
council member
court attendant
cowhand
crewed space flight
deliveryperson
differently (blank)-ed
director
disability
disabled
display figure
dock worker
drafter
employee hour
enlistee
equestrian skills
executive
face in the moon
farm hand
female identified
female-intensive
    occupation
firefighter
first-year student
flight attendant
flower carrier
foreperson (of the jury)
Founders, the
freshperson
gamestership
gender

gender-free language
generalist
gingerbread cookie
grant-writing skills
Greek society
gunner
harass someone
harbor chief
head
head brewer
heir
hero
herstory
high scorer
highway robber
hoist operator
Hollander
homemaker
host
houseparent
human-made
humankind
ice-cream vendor
journey worker
keelboater
layperson
letter carrier
lineworker
logger
longshore worker
lookism
male-identified
male-intensive
    occupation
member of Congress
member of the clergy
member of the laity
meter reader
middleperson
military diver
moderator
muscle-powered
(news)paper carrier
no-pops
nonidentical twins
nurse's aide
ombuds
one-upping
page-style hairdo
parental leave
parentalism
-person
personhole
personhood
police officer

professional
protected class
rancher
repairer
representative
reverse discrimination
sales clerk
score adjustment
scout
scout leader
selectperson
seller
server
service member
sewer
sharpshooter
sharpshooting
shoeshiner
showcraft
single parent
snow figure
soldier
spokesperson
spouse
staff something
surviving spouse
they
token
upperclass student
waitron
waitstaff
wardrobe supervisor
whipping person
wommon
yard worker

HEDGE WORD
basically
challenge
complication
compromising
episode
event
fragrant
growth experience
happen to be
heavy going
inconvenience
learning experience
less active
less attractive
less fortunate
less than (blank)
misadventure
miscommunication

mixed
modest
monkey business
negative
negative growth
negative patient care
    outcome
no scholar
no spring chicken
not as (blank) as one
    might wish
not going to win any
    beauty contests
not what we had
    hoped
on the (blank) side
one
situation
something oriented
technical adjustment
temporary setback
uncertain
unconventional
uneven
unfortunate
unorthodox
us
volatile
we
you-know-what

INTELLIGENT
backward
gifted
limited intelligence
mental impairment
slow
wherewithal

LYING
categorical inaccuracy
contain something
doctor something
embroider something
fib
fiction
inflated
inoperative
massage something
misleading
misrepresentation
misspeak
misstatement
not (quite) right
on the up and up

polygraph
prevaricate
questionable
sanitize something
scenario
selective
social lie
stonewall
story
stretch the truth
terminological
    inexactitude
untruth
white lie
whitewash something

MEDICINE
active euthanasia
aesthetic procedure
Alzheimer's (disease)
big C, the
blood disease
cardiac arrest
chemical health
    services
clinical death
coitus
condition
coronary
cosmetic surgery
critical care facility
D&C
dependency
detox
detumescence
dilation and curettage
disorder
Down's syndrome
eating disorder
eliminate
euthanasia
face-lift
female trouble
genitals
growth
Hansen's disease
health care
hemorrhage
in extremis
incontinence
incontinence pad
incontinent
indiscretion
indisposed
inoperable

irregularity
Jellinek's disease
jock itch
living will
loose bowels
lump
male itch(ing)
medical center
medication
negative patient care
    outcome
neoplasm
nocturnal emission
nurse's aide
nursing home
old man's friend
pain management
person with AIDS
physician
pill, the
plastic surgery
poorly
positive
post-traumatic stress
    syndrome
pox, the
pregnancy interruption
problem
procedure
program
PWA
reproductive health
residential treatment
    center
risk factor
routine nursing care
    only
runs, the
safe sex
sanatorium
sexually transmitted
    disease
social disease
something disagrees
    with someone
stool
syndrome
T.B.
therapeutic interruption
    of pregnancy
travelers' tummy
trots, the
trouble
under the weather

MENTAL ILLNESS
a few bricks short of a
    load (See not quite
    right.)
a few cards short of a
    full deck (See not
    quite right.)
a few enchiladas short
    of a combination
    plate (See not quite
    right.)
all there
asylum
behavior disorder
certifiable
commit someone
confused
dementia
disturbed (in one's
    mind)
eccentric
go through some hard
    times
have bats in the belfry
    (See not quite right.)
home
institution
institutionalize
    someone
loony (See not quite right.)
loopy (See not quite right.)
low
mental (See not quite right.)
mental fatigue
mental hospital
(nervous) breakdown
non compos (mentis)
not quite right
not (quite) right
nuts (See not quite right.)
nutty (See not quite right.)
off one's rocker (See not
    quite right.)
potty
psychiatric hospital
rest house
round the bend (See not
    quite right.)
sanatorium
seclusion
see someone
seek professional help
state hospital
troubled
unbalanced

307

MILITARY

acceptable damage
account for someone
action
adviser
agent
air support
anticipatory attack
antipersonnel
appeasement
area bombing
armed reconnaissance
battle fatigue
blip
Bomb, the
camp follower
casualty
cease fire
civilian impacting
claim responsibility for
    something
clandestine
clean bomb
collaborator
collateral damage
combat fatigue
combat ineffective
concentration camp
conflict
confrontation
contain something
conventional
counterinsurgency
counterintelligence
covert action
defense
defense community,
    the
delivery
detente
deterrent
device
discharge something
dispatch someone
effective casualty
    radius
electronic
    countermeasures
emergency
encounter
enemy action
engage with someone
engagement
entrenching tool
-era

escalate something
ethnic cleansing
exchange
executive action
expendable
fall
fatality
first strike
fragmentation device
fraternize with
    someone
freedom fighter
friendly fire
gold star mother
gunner
hardware
incursion
international crisis
internment camp
intervention
irregular, an
late unpleasantness,
    the
latrine
liberate something
listening device
materiel
MIA
military adviser
military diver
missing in action
neutralize someone
nuclear capability
offensive
operative
ordnance
ordnance success
other than honorable
    discharge
pacify someone or
    something
paramilitary
patriot
peace-keeper
peace-keeping mission
personnel
police action
population transfer
pre-emptive strike
preposition someone
    or something
presence
preventive strike
program someone
reconaissance

relocate someone
relocation center
render someone
    ineffective
render someone
    inoperative
resettle someone
retire
saturation bombing
selective ordnance
selective service
service
service member
sleeper
soldier
soldier of fortune
sortie
strategic capability
strategic exchange
(strategic) withdrawal
surgical strike
survivability
tactical withdrawal
terminate someone
    with extreme
    prejudice
troubles, the

MOCK SWEARING

almighty
applesauce
balderdash
baloney
basket
beggar
blankety-blank
blarney
blasted
blazes
bleep
blessed
blighter
blinkered
blinking
blooming
borscht!
bovine excrescence
B.S.
bull
bullpeep
bunk(um)
bushwa
by George!
by Jove
claptrap

confounded
cripes!
crumbs!
CYA
dang
darn
deuce
dickens, the
do(-do)
doggone(d)
drat
effing
egad!
fink
foot!
foul something up
frigging
fudge!
gadzooks
G.D.
gee
gee whiz
golly (Moses)
good grief
gosh
goshdarn
gracious (me)!
Great Scott!
guff
Halifax
hogwash
Holy cow!
horsefeathers
I'll be hanged
jeepers (creepers)
jeez (Louise)
Jiminy Cricket(s)
Judas Priest!
Laws!
Mercy!
Merde!
muck something
  up
My foot!
My word!
perdition
poppycock
Rats!
rubbish
shoot!
smartaleck
so-and-so
S.O.B.
son of a gun
spit

sucker
What the Sam Hill?

MONEY
acquire something
acquisitiveness
adjustment
affordable
aid
assistance
backward
borrow something
bread (See means.)
buckage (See means.)
business class
capital (See means.)
careful (with one's
  money)
cash advance
cash flow problem
close with one's money
collection agency
commission
compensation
consideration
culturally advantaged
(culturally) deprived
culturally
  disadvantaged
currency adjustment
delinquent
differential
divert something into
  someplace
divest
donate something to
  someone or
  something
donation
douceur
dough (See means.)
down-turn
economic insufficiency
economical
economically
  disadvantaged
economically inactive
economy
embarrassed
emerging
emolument
ex gratia payment
finances
financial aid
financial services

fiscal
fiscal health
fixed income
funding
gaming
get something
go Dutch
go through some hard
  times
golden handshake
golden parachute
gratuity
have one's hand in the
  till
home equity loan
honorarium
(housing) project
improvident
in the black
in the red
in transition
income bracket
income level
income maintenance
independent means
indigent
inner city
insolvent
job turning
kickback
less affluent
less fortunate
leveraged
life insurance
liquidity crisis
low-income
market value
marketing
means
member
misappropriate
  something
moolah (See means.)
needy
negative saver
nominal
non-performing asset
other side of the tracks
pennies (See means.)
pledge something
privileged
pro bono
prominent
prosperous
public aid

reasonable
recession
redline someone
relief
remuneration
resources
revenue gap
shortfall
social security
soft commission
spousal maintenance
stipend
strapped (for money)
substantial
sugar daddy
support
support someone or
    something
technical adjustment
third party payment
thrifty
transitional
underprivileged
unwaged
wage freeze
watch one's pennies
welfare
well-off
well-to-do
wherewithal
working class
working people
wrong side of the
    tracks

POLITICAL CORRECTNESS

Alzheimer's (disease)
appropriate
Before the Common
    Era
biological father
biological mother
Britisher
categorically needy,
    the
chemical health
    services
challenged
chronologically
    advantaged
codependent
companion animal
culturally advantaged
(culturally) deprived

culturally
    disadvantaged
disadvantaged
diversity
documented worker
domestic partner
domestic science
domestic violence
domestic worker
drinking driver
dying process, the
economically
    disadvantaged
enslaved person
experientially enhanced
farrier
Hansen's disease
in the Common Era
-ly advantaged
marginalized
non-traditional student
nonhuman animal
person of color
person with a disability
person with a hearing
    loss
person with AIDS
person with diabetes
person with paraplegia
person with something
personhole
personhood
preliterate
PWA
quantitatively
    challenged
religious
retroactive exemption
Scot
sit pretzel-style
station manager

POLICE

apprehend someone
bracelets
bring someone to
    justice
children's ranch
client
community treatment
    center
cooperate with
    someone
correctional institution
corrections

detain someone
detainee
detention
drinking driver
electronic
    countermeasures
excessive force
fatality
felony augmentation
homicide
house of correction
in
in custody
informant
inmate
inside
intake room
intern
intern someone
internment camp
interrogate someone
juvenile
law enforcement
law-enforcement
    officer
medical examiner
Morals Division
nightstick
noncustodial
    punishment
offender
offense
pay one's debt to
    society
peace officer
penitentiary
perpetrator
pick someone up
plainclothes officer
preventive detention
protective custody
quick entry law
quiet cell
re-educate someone
re-education camp
recidivism
reform school
refresh someone's
    memory
seclusion
secure facility
segregation unit
social killing
state farm
supreme penalty, the

bad place, the
belief system
faith community
father of lies, the
fundamentalist
Higher Power
holiday
little people, the
lord of the flies
member of the clergy
member of the laity
moment of silence
old Harry, (the)
Old Nick
other place, the
perdition
Prince of Darkness
religious affiliation
religious orientation

SEX
aberration
abstinence
AC/DC
accost someone
act of love
act of shame (See act of love.)
active
adult
(adult) novelty
affair
afterthought
ambidextrous
ambivalent
amour
armor (See sheath.)
arouse someone
assignation
association
attachment
attentions
autoeroticism
avail oneself of someone
available
bachelor's wife
bathhouse
bawdy house
be intimate with someone
be with someone
beat the bishop (See play with oneself.)
bedroom

bestiality
betray someone
B-girl
bi
birds and the bees, the
birth control
bit of fun (See act of love.)
blood disease
blue movie
body worker
bold
bordello
born on the wrong side of the blanket
bother someone
boudoir photo
brothel
bump uglies with someone (See make love.)
call girl
camp follower
carry on with someone
catch someone in the act
chamber of commerce
cheat on someone
choke the chicken (See play with oneself.)
closet
cohabit
coition (See act of love.)
coitus
commerce
(commercial) sex worker
commit to someone
companion
condom (See sheath.)
confirmed bachelor
conjugal relations
conjugal rites (See act of love.)
connubial pleasures
consenting adult
console someone
consort with someone
consummate a relationship
conversation (See act of love.)
copulate
(cordless) massager

couple with someone (See make love.)
courtesan
crime against nature
customer
deceive one's spouse
demimondaine
detumescence
diddle (See play with oneself.)
disorderly house
disport oneself
diving suit (See sheath.)
do it
do the nasty with someone (See make love.)
Don Juan
dreadnought (See sheath.)
easy woman
effeminate
embraces
entanglement
erotica
err
errant
escort service
experienced
extracurricular
extramarital
facetiae
facts of life, the
fallen woman
family
family planning
fancy house
fancy woman
favors
female identified
fille de joie
five against one (See play with oneself.)
flamboyant
fornicate
frank
free love
French kiss
French letter
French safe (See sheath.)
friend
fun
fun and games (See act of love.)
gay

genitals
gentleman cow
gentleman friend
get physical
girl
glamour photograph
go all the way
go steady with
    someone
go to bed with
    someone
go with someone
graphic
gratification
gratify someone's
    desires
hanky-panky
harass someone
harlot
have a reputation
have a roving eye
have carnal knowledge
    of someone
have intimate relations
    with someone
have one's way with
    someone
have relations with
    someone
have to get married
hooker
horizontal exercise (See
    act of love.)
horizontally
hostess
house of ill repute
illegitimate
illicit
improper
impropriety
in flagrante (delicto)
inamorata
indecency
indiscretion
infidelity
intercourse
interfere with someone
intrigue
involved with someone
involvement
Jezebel
just good friends
kept woman
know someone
    biblically

lady friend
lady of the evening
latex (See sheath.)
lavender
lay (See act of love.)
liaison
life, the
lifestyle (choice)
light woman
like that
live as man and wife
live in sin
live together
live with someone
loose woman
love
love life
love that dare not
    speak its name
madam
magdalene
make an honest
    woman of someone
make love
make out with
    someone
male identified
marital aid
marital relations
massage parlor
matinee
men's magazine
ménage à trois
model
molest someone
morning after, the
morning-after pill
Mrs. Warren's
    profession
naughty
nocturnal emission
nooky (See act of love.)
oldest profession, the
on one's back
on the side
onanism
one of those
open marriage
other woman, the
outcall service
outside sexual contact
overcoat (See sheath.)
painted woman
paramour
partner

perform
permissive
persuasion
pet with someone
pick someone up
pill, the
piquant
play doctor with
    someone (See make
    love.)
play with oneself
playboy
pleasure someone
pox, the
pre-orgasmic
procurer
prophylactic (See
    sheath.)
proposition someone
prostitute
protection
pull one's pudding (See
    play with oneself.)
pure
racy
raincoat (See sheath.)
red-light district
relationship
reproductive health
risque
rob the cradle
roll in the hay (See act
    of love.)
romance
roommate
rubber (See sheath.)
rubber goods
safe (See sheath.)
safe sex
same gender oriented
sapphic
sauna
save oneself (for
    marriage)
scarlet woman
score (See make love.)
secret vice, the (See play
    with oneself.)
self-abuse
sell oneself
service someone or
    something
(sexual) act
(sexual) congress
sexual orientation

313

sexual preference
sexual variety
(sexually) explicit
SGO
sheath
sister of mercy
sleep around
sleep together
sleep with someone
social disease
solicit someone
solitary sex
sow one's wild oats
spend the night with
    someone
spicy
sporting house
stray
street walker
sugar daddy
suggestive
surrender to someone
take advantage of
    someone
take liberties with
    someone
take precautions

take someone
take up with someone
tamper with someone
tendencies
that way inclined
to bed someone
touch oneself
touch someone
trade, the
tumble (See make love.)
unfaithful
uninhibited
unmarried
unnatural
vibrator
wander
white slavery
woman of easy
    virtue
woman of ill repute
working girl

SWEARING
Anglo-Saxon
bad language
barnyard epithet
blue language

expletive
four-letter word
f-word, the
strong language
s-word, the

UNDERWEAR
body shaper
briefs
cache-sexe
chemise
cup
drawers
foundation (garment)
intimate apparel
lingerie
panties
undergarment
unmentionables

VIOLENCE
assault someone
colors
fun
graphic
heated
interrogate someone